FLETCHER CONFERENCE 2001

NATIONAL SECURITY FOR A NEW ERA: FOCUSING NATIONAL POWER

November 14–15, 2001
Ronald Reagan Building and International Trade Center
1300 Pennsylvania Avenue, N.W., Washington D.C., 20004

General Editors

Omar J. Jones IV, Captain, United States Army

Kelley Reese, Research Associate
Institute for Foreign Policy Analysis

Co-Sponsored by

The International Security Studies Program of
The Fletcher School of Law and Diplomacy, Tufts University

Institute for Foreign Policy Analysis, Inc.

Office of the Secretary of Defense for Net Assessment
The United States Army

The material presented is based upon work supported by the U.S. Army War College under contract no. DABT43-00-P-1111. Any opinions, findings, conclusions, or recommendations expressed are those of the authors and do not necessarily reflect the views of the U.S. Army War College.

Photographs by Guy Nolfsinger

CMH Pub 70-80-1

The 2001 *Fletcher Conference* was held November 14 and 15, 2001 in Washington, DC and was sponsored by the Fletcher School of Law and Diplomacy, Tufts University; the Institute for Foreign Policy Analysis; Office of the Secretary of Defense – Net Assessment, and the United States Army. This conference was a landmark event that provided a timely forum for debate and candid discussion of how to best focus our national power on the challenges of the 21st century. This compendium provides a historical record of the conference and contributes to future policy discussions and the on-going national security dialogue.

The theme of the conference was *National Security for a New Era – Focusing National Power*. In light of the terrorist attacks on the United States and the President's decision to create an Office of Homeland Security, we believe this year's conference contributed substantially to the global war on terrorism, to ensuring the enduring security of our homeland, and to the effort to fully focus and synchronize all instruments of national power – diplomatic, information, military, and economic.

In honor of the 34th President of the United States, we have renamed this conference the *Dwight D. Eisenhower National Security Conference*. The Army and our conference partners will continue this important forum for dialogue on broad issues of national and international security. This conference will be the culmination of the annual *Dwight D. Eisenhower National Security Series*, a group of diverse events that maintain this important dialogue throughout the year. For further information, please visit our website at www.eisenhowerconference.com.

The 2002 conference will held September 26-27, 2002 at the Ronald Reagan Building and International Trade Center, 1300 Pennsylvania Avenue, Washington, DC. We value the open and frank exchange of ideas with the national security community and see this conference as a positive way to continue that discussion

Sincerely,

Eric K. Shinseki
General, United States Army

CONTENTS

INTRODUCTION

The Fletcher School of Law and Diplomacy, the Institute for Foreign Policy Analysis, the Office of the Secretary of Defense for Net Assessment, and the United States Army cosponsored the thirty-first annual Fletcher Conference on November 14 and 15, 2001, in Washington, D.C. The conference examined and advanced ways to more effectively focus our instruments of national power on the full range of security challenges confronting America. Speakers included current and former national security policy makers, senior military officials, congressional leaders, internationally recognized security specialists, corporate and industry leaders, and representatives from the national news media. The Conference provided a high-level forum for the more than 450 participants to discuss national security visions, with a specific focus on the more effective use of the diplomatic, economic, and military instruments of national power.

The conference consisted of five panels and five addresses. Addresses were delivered by Governor Tom Ridge, Director, Office of Homeland Security; Dr. Paul Wolfowitz, Deputy Secretary of Defense; General Richard Myers, Chairman, Joint Chiefs of Staff; Mr. Sean O'Keefe, Deputy Director, Office of Management and Budget; and General William Kernan, Commander-in-Chief, U.S. Joint Forces Command.

The first panel contemplated security visions and priorities from interagency and congressional perspectives and featured The Honorable Avis Bohlen, Assistant Secretary of State for the Bureau of Arms Control; The Honorable Douglas Feith, Under Secretary of Defense for Policy; Senator James Inhofe (R-OK), Senate Armed Services Committee; and Ambassador Paul Bremer III, Chairman, National Commission on Terrorism. The second panel dealt specifically with the role of military power in complex environments and featured Congressman Curt Weldon (R-PA), Chairman, Procurement Subcommittee, House Armed Services Committee; General (Retired) Wesley Clark, former Supreme Allied Commander, Europe; Rear Admiral Kathleen Paige, Technical Director, Ballistic Missile Defense Organization; Lieutenant General Edward Anderson, Deputy Commander-in-Chief, United States Space Command; and General (Retired) Barry McCaffrey, former Commander-in-Chief, U.S. Southern Command, and former Director, Office of National Drug Control Policy. The third panel addressed the requirements for homeland security and counterterrorism. Panelists included The Honorable Gary Hart, Co-Chair of the U.S. Commission on National

Security/21st Century; Ms. Michelle Van Cleave, President, National Security Concepts, Inc.; Admiral James Loy, Commandant, U.S. Coast Guard; and Major General John Parker, Commanding General, U.S. Army Medical Research and Materiel Command.

On day two, the fourth panel examined ways to focus the multiple instruments of national power—diplomatic, information, military, and economic—within our current interagency structure. Panelists included The Honorable Frank Carlucci, former National Security Advisor and Secretary of Defense; General (Retired) Anthony Zinni, former Commander-in-Chief, U.S. Central Command; and Dr. Gordon Adams, George Washington University. The fifth and final panel discussed the United States' relationship with allies and coalitions. Panelists included Admiral (Retired) Joseph Prueher, former Ambassador to the People's Republic of China; Dr. Keith Payne, President, National Institute for Public Policy; General Montgomery Meigs, Commanding General, U.S. Army Europe; and Air Vice-Marshal John Thompson, Defence Attache, British Embassy.

SUMMARY

Key Outcomes

Throughout the conference two themes remained constant: the need for greater intergovernmental cooperation and the requirement for military transformation. Participants unanimously agreed that interagency cooperation and information sharing must be improved at all levels of government. However, the scarcity of specific proposals to improve cooperation illustrates the difficulty of accomplishing this objective. Conference participants also reaffirmed the necessity to properly resource military transformation to enhance each Service's agility, flexibility, and jointness. The resourcing, shape, and speed of that transformation remain subjects open to debate.

The Emerging Security Environment

In today's evolving security environment, the United States is now exposed to a wide range of global threats, while U.S. territory and American citizens are the direct targets of our adversaries. In this new era, many of our adversaries are difficult to identify, challenging to isolate, difficult to defeat as this new enemy uses the liberties and freedoms of free societies to blend into civilian populations and freely move across borders. Senator Hart noted that the U.S. Commission on National Security/21st Century identified the outlines of this new era, but few of the Commission's recommendations have been implemented. Several participants noted that the September 11th terrorist attacks served as a "wake-up call" to demonstrate unequivocally that the U.S. homeland is now exposed to a wide range of threats that emanate from multiple sources, such as terrorism, ballistic missiles, weapons of mass destruction or effects (WMD/E) and cyber attack.

The current geopolitical dominance of the United States forces our state and nonstate adversaries to confront us by using the cover of democratic liberties to attack the nation with asymmetric means in order to avoid force on force, conventional warfare. This method allows our adversaries to choose the time and place to inflict maximum harm and impose disproportionate costs while forcing other democracies and the U.S. to take wide-ranging and expensive precautions. Unlike terrorism in the 1960s and 1970s, in which terrorists sought to achieve narrow political objectives, today's terrorists do not seek political negotiation but instead inflict mass casualties in direct attacks to force the U.S. and other democratic nations into self-imposed isolation. In the past, terrorism was countered most effectively within a legal context by treating terrorists as criminals. Combatting this new form of terrorism requires the synchronization of all instruments of national power across global networks and a shift from threat-based to capabilities-based planning.

"New" terrorism takes many forms, from the attacks of September 11th to the spread of biological agents and the employment of weapons of mass destruction. While the need to confront the threat posed by catastrophic acts of terrorism is clear, there was some disagreement among panelists regarding the prioritization of this threat within national security policy. Ambassador Bremer suggested that terrorism poses the single greatest danger to American national security, while Dr. Adams held that terrorism is only one "vector" among many U.S. national security concerns. There was general consensus that while the United States government and the American people must adapt their security thinking to deny and deter terrorism, the U.S. military must retain a strong, balanced, conventional capability to address both existing and unforeseen threats to U.S. security and interests. Additionally, the terrorist attacks highlighted the necessity of maintaining current capabilities, enforcing nonproliferation regimes, and developing and fielding a missile defense system for the United States and its allies.

According to Deputy Secretary of Defense Wolfowitz, the lack of American preparedness demonstrated in the September 11th attacks had its origins in "a poverty of expectations." Throughout the Cold War the United States based its national security strategy on countering a known threat. Today, the threats to U.S. national efforts are diffused and hidden, and through the use of asymmetric means, capable of inflicting catastrophic damage using surprise. It is now imperative that the U.S. government plan for and adapt to surprise. There are three categories of required measures to better meet the requirements of this new national security era: developing new capabilities, revitalizing neglected institutions, and reinvesting in human capital.

The conference discussions included a variety of recommendations to meet these requirements with new capabilities. The majority of the conference participants viewed missile defense as an essential capability to address existing and potential threats to the United States and its allies. Similarly, U.S. space capabilities remain a critical asymmetric advantage over potential adversaries. Homeland security is also vital both to prevent and to respond to attacks against U.S. territory. Finally, conference participants noted that the United States must develop transformed, rapidly deployable, full-spectrum, joint military forces that can deter, preempt, and respond to crises abroad.

Revitalizing the U.S. Government

The U.S. must revitalize traditional agencies and institutions to ensure they are more effective in influencing and shaping international events. For example, numerous speakers noted the inadequate funding of the State Department and the need to improve and expand the use of public diplomacy.

The effectiveness of our military and government agencies depends on the quality and skill of their personnel. Panelists noted the United States must reinvest in human capital and promote public service. The U.S. must restore the regional and language expertise neglected since the end of the Cold War. Our military leaders must be trained in the art of war, and in political science and other fields, to give them the necessary tools to lead and operate in a complex world.

General Zinni stated the United States must employ its diplomatic and economic powers proactively before crises develop. But due to a hesitancy to apply diplomatic and economic resources, there is a tendency to rely on the military's size, speed, and effectiveness to reestablish stability. Military intervention often comes too late to achieve political objectives, thus a long-term military presence evolves. However, once the military is involved, tremendous leverage may be applied by synchronizing the military, diplomatic, and legal tools toward the political aim. According to General Clark, we do not have to be militarily decisive to be strategically decisive if we effectively employ the other instruments of national power.

Information Operations

The participants debated the proper role of information in this new security environment. Although information operations efforts rarely affect hardened adversaries, an effective communications campaign dampens the support upon which terrorists rely and the U.S. requires to help maintain the coalition against terrorism. It was noted that in the current war against terrorism the United States allowed the adversary to seize the initiative in the war of ideas. Lieutenant General Anderson highlighted how technological advances increase the potential of information operations and the evolving importance of information management in our military doctrine. General Clark stated that in "modern warfare" it was essential that America project a positive image of its values and society. However, the impact of information operations remains limited against this new brand of terrorism. Ambassador Bremer stated that we are unable to influence "new" terrorists through information operations; they already understand American values and hate us for those values. However, he and others acknowledged the potential to influence the moderate populations in Muslim states.

Homeland Security

Homeland security remains a significant organizational challenge, since the forty or fifty agencies involved have little overarching coordination.

Participants widely agreed that any Director of Homeland Security must have budgetary authority over these agencies to encourage cooperation. In a special address, Governor Ridge noted that the Office of Homeland Security, working through the Office of Management and Budget, is sufficiently involved in the budget process to synchronize these efforts. There was disagreement, however, as to whether the Director should be a cabinet-level position, accountable to both the President and Congress.

Governor Ridge also noted that the terrorist attacks of September 11th created a shared sense of urgency and common purpose within America, fueling an immediate and comprehensive national response. Yet, as crucial as the current efforts are, Governor Ridge remarked that neither the country nor the Office of Homeland Security could focus exclusively on present responses. He further pointed out that we must strengthen our domestic security for the long term through greater interagency cooperation.

It is widely recognized that the first responders—police, firemen, and local medical practitioners—have the primary responsibility for consequence management. To adequately respond to attacks on the homeland, these organizations must be standardized—or at least interoperable—in training and equipping, and must have the latest technology. In the aftermath of this attack, experts note the military must continue to play a large, but supporting, role. General McCaffrey advocated the creation of a "national gendarmerie" to patrol U.S. borders and the modernization of the U.S. Coast Guard. He was one of several speakers to recommend the redirection of the mission of the National Guard to homeland defense.

Enhancing the Military's Capability to Address Terrorism

This new security era requires the development and enhancement of certain military capabilities to adequately provide for U.S. national security needs. Asymmetrical threats demand that U.S. military forces act quickly and decisively across the globe while synchronizing our efforts throughout the U.S. interagency and with the resources of alliance and coalition partners. Although alliances and coalitions ensure that forward basing remains a valuable strategic asset, U.S. military forces must be able to operate without bases. We must continue developing long-range, full-spectrum precision strike capabilities. Despite these new threats, the military must retain a strong conventional force with a broad range of capabilities to meet traditional threats.

The role of the military in the current war against terrorism will be varied. Under Secretary of Defense Feith asserted that the United States must eliminate terrorist bases to defeat the threat of international terrorism. Many panelists further suggested that the war on terrorism must expand to other countries and could involve significantly more forces over a protracted period of time.

Panel members emphasized that continuing to enhance military jointness is essential to sustain U.S. military power. According to General Myers, jointness begins with the acquisition process. Systems should be "born joint" to receive funding. Various other proposals were discussed, such as the creation of a standing Joint Task Force headquarters with interoperable communications and seamless information sharing.

Dr. Payne noted that a broad spectrum of coalition capabilities is needed to deter and defend against multiple threats across a wide variety of contingencies, a situation that is exacerbated by the increasing lethality of small groups. He remarked on the importance of thoroughly understanding the threats in the new security environment in order to construct effective deterrence policies.

The instruments of national power—diplomatic, information, military, and economic—reinforce each other. Each instrument has its limits, and national security strategy must apply all of these instruments in order to meet the current and future security needs of the United States. Interagency communication and cooperation at all levels of government focus these instruments of national power, and strategic leadership is essential to achieving an integrated national security strategy.

CONFERENCE CHARTER

NATIONAL SECURITY FOR A NEW ERA— FOCUSING NATIONAL POWER

The emerging security environment holds both promise and peril for the United States and its allies. The complexity of evolving threats, the limitations of finite resources, and, finally, increasing vulnerability to a diverse set of traditional and less traditional challenges make it necessary that decision makers develop a more integrated approach to national security. The challenges of this security setting—now and in the future—require a comprehensive strategy, focused on synchronizing all of the elements of national power simultaneously to achieve an unprecedented unity of effort. Because the boundaries between foreign and domestic security policy are increasingly blurred, a comprehensive approach to national security based on the fullest integration of the instruments of national power is the only viable course in planning for, responding to, and ultimately dominating the full-spectrum of future threats and challenges. The 2001 IFPA-Fletcher Conference, *National Security for a New Era—Focusing National Power*, will cut to the core of this issue. Representatives from a diverse spectrum of backgrounds and perspectives will be brought together for in-depth discussion of national security for the 21st century. The conference is intended to afford the new Administration an opportunity to showcase its vision for national security; to initiate an informed debate on a comprehensive approach to national security policy making; and to advance the concept of wholesale security transformation as a joint force, interagency, and multinational strategic imperative.

The recent terrorist attacks on the United States have made the demand for a comprehensive national security policy even more urgent. A broad and sustained campaign to eradicate global terrorism will require the synchronized employment of all instruments of national power. However, the United States must successfully prosecute this campaign while continuing to adapt to the emerging security environment of this new era.

The United States interacts and competes not only with other state actors but also with a diverse collection of transnational, international, and subnational entities and actors ranging from the legitimate—multinational corporations and nongovernmental organizations—to the illicit—organized crime syndicates, terrorists, and paramilitaries. The countervailing influences of globalization, integration, and fragmentation contend worldwide in many previously uncontested arenas for primacy with the sovereign rights of established states. In the transnational and subnational arenas, in particular, no one state—including the United States—can either exercise power with impunity or accurately predict the course of future events. Indeed, a new class of empowered actors of consequence—state and nonstate—has risen from the structural vacuum left in the wake of the tense but more predictable order of the previous era. Unlike the ritualistic unity governing alliances in the last half-century, a new global disorder has emerged with actors motivated by nascent and divergent conceptions of vital interests, including survival.

Within this environment, the United States remains alone—for the foreseeable future—at the pinnacle of comprehensive global power. Nevertheless, where necessary and possible, the United States seeks to mobilize allied and coalition efforts in support of shared interests and values. Its willingness to lead under the most difficult and perilous conditions; its commitment to its interests, responsibilities, and values; a global economy; and finally, its demonstrated capability and willingness to apply decisive military power have positioned the nation to exploit unique opportunities while at the same time managing—where possible—the effects of widespread disorder. As retention of position and influence remain critical to the United States entering the new century, the nation can ill-afford complacency in the face of increasingly diverse security challenges. The potential for war and for other forms of violent conflict is a persistent condition inevitably in the nation's future. Though homeland security and counterterrorism rightfully remain the current focus of our national security efforts, the emerging security setting presents challenges to our interests and values that will not allow the nation the luxury of ignoring any portion of the broad spectrum of threats.

Clearly, the instruments of state power, acting in unison, provide the greatest promise for exploiting opportunities, as well as overcoming and prevailing against a complex array of threats and challenges. IEPA-Fletcher 2004 focuses on the synergy required for defeating global terrorism and sustaining American preeminence and decisive influence. The conference will open with a focus on the *Opportunities and Challenges for American Power* from the perspective of the Bush Administration followed by two days of frank discussions and diverse presentations relevant to focusing and synchronizing domestic, national, and international efforts to effect broad and enduring resolution of the most compelling security issues facing the United States in the new century.

PANEL 1

SECURITY VISION AND PRIORITIES FOR A NEW ERA

Chair: Mr. John McWethy, Chief National Security and Pentagon Correspondent, Washington Bureau, ABC News

The Honorable Avis T. Bohlen, Assistant Secretary of State for the Bureau of Arms Control

The Honorable Douglas J. Feith, Under Secretary of Defense for Policy

The Honorable James Inhofe (Republican, Oklahoma), Senate Armed Services Committee

Ambassador L. Paul Bremer III, Chairman, National Commission on Terrorism

Panel Charter

The instruments of national power—diplomatic, military, economic, and cultural—possessed by the United States are without peer. How they are to be used is related to the security vision that shapes our national priorities. Our security vision and priorities encompass a broad range of threats, risks, and issues on which the instruments of national power must be focused. As the events of September 11th have amply demonstrated, the relative importance and utility of such instruments depend on the issue or interest at stake. There are enduring elements of our security vision—a world in which our values and interests are protected. The challenges to such values and interests at any one time translate into priorities that determine how, when, and where the instruments of national power will be employed.

This panel examined each of these instruments of national power. For example, the importance of diplomacy arises from the need to build coalitions of support within and beyond the alliances of which the United States is a member, and to communicate with adversaries. Although it may be preferable for the United States to act when possible in cooperation with allies or coalitions of nations, there are occasions when United States will find it necessary to take action alone. Among the topics for this panel was a discussion of security cooperation: what type and for what purposes. This includes political/mil-

itary trade-offs between coalitions and unilateral action as well as consideration of how coalition size may affect overall effectiveness.

In supporting values and interests shared by the United States and its allies
and in dealing with enemies, diplomacy must be backed by military means,
hence the synergism between the diplomatic and military instruments.
Inevitably, there are cases in which military forces must be used early, just as
there are times when the military is best employed only as a last resort. How
to calibrate the employment of force with the conduct of diplomacy as an
instrument of power is an enduring question. The timing of the use of military
power, no less than when, how, and where such capabilities will be employed,
is of utmost importance for sound national security planning.

The foundation for the economic instrument of power lies in sustained
economic growth. As recent events have clearly demonstrated, the ability to
provide for national security is the vital prerequisite for prosperity. The environment in which the economy can function to its maximum level is decisively shaped by the extent to which national security is safeguarded. How we
employ diplomatic and military resources has profound implications for our
economy. At the same time, a highly developed economy is essential if we are
to maintain other instruments of national security, including the advanced
technologies that are indispensable to our military forces.

Last but not least, as a society the United States is shaped by cultural infu-
sions from those who have come to its shores first from Europe and then from
other parts of the world. Its unity lies in its diversity. The United States derives
strengths from many sources, from the numerous groups who have become
Americans, bringing with them talents, energy, and values that have enriched
our national culture and who thus in themselves represent a powerful instrument in broadening the appeal of the United States to other societies around
the world.

Our national security vision and priorities will be shaped by events such
as those that we have just witnessed but also by the ability of the Congress and
the Administration to reach a consensus that has necessary public support. In
times of national crisis such agreement has been forthcoming. How well the
separate branches of government work together is of pivotal importance. No
less a requirement is the need to achieve synchronization within the executive
branch of government across the numerous departments and agencies having
a role in national security policy formulation and implementation. This
requires sustained public support.

In sum, as the United States conducts a broad and continuing effort to end
global terrorism and to support the broader security mission, we will have to
focus all instruments of national power—diplomatic, military, economic, and
cultural—in ways previously not envisaged. The paradigm in which domestic
tranquility stood in sharp contrast from conflicts across the expanse of oceans
has been obliterated by attacks against our centers of financial and military

Left to right: *The Honorable Avis T. Bohlen, Mr. John McWethy, The Honorable Douglas J. Feith, The Honorable James Inhofe, Dr. Robert L. Pfaltzgraff, Jr., and Ambassador L. Paul Bremer III*

power that were launched from within the United States itself. As we develop national security strategy for the twenty-first century, it becomes essential to think of security at home and abroad as inextricably linked in a seamless web that should be reflected as fully as possible in our interagency/congressional perspectives as well as our strategies and capabilities based on a vision that shapes priorities for the decades ahead.

Discussion Points

• What is the twenty-first-century conflict spectrum that should shape defense priorities?

• What are other security priorities in the new era aside from combating terrorism? How should they be addressed?

• How can the United States achieve essential synchronization among the instruments of power?

• How adequate are the existing arrangements for security cooperation? What should be done to strengthen them?

• What are the requirements for achieving bipartisan consensus for foreign policy and national security? How much is necessary? What is possible?

• How do the events of September 11th affect the emerging national security relations between the Congress and the Administration?

• The information age shapes our perspectives in security and its implications for security. What are the threats to critical infrastructure, including the potential for cyberwar?

Summary

The Honorable James Inhofe, United States Senator, Oklahoma

- *Cuts in defense spending during the 1990s have jeopardized U.S. national security and the readiness of our military forces. Congress must renew its efforts to make national security the number one priority by setting new spending priorities, making the necessary sacrifices for the common defense, and providing the resources needed to bolster our national security.*

- *Congress should reexamine the national security establishment and focus on how agencies and departments interact. More than ever before, today's threat demands a focused, integrated, and comprehensive approach to national security.*

    1. The new threats of today present challenges with which our current interagency structure does not adequately deal. There is no longer a clear distinction between foreign and domestic matters, between peace and war, or between law enforcement and national security.

    2. Congress should consider updating the National Security Act of 1947.

- *Congress must reexamine the intelligence community, focusing on the organization and the structure of our present system. Both the intelligence community and the cooperation between other national security organizations must be strengthened. This cannot be accomplished without a cultural change across the government.*

    1. The United States must recruit and train more linguists and analysts to reduce the current lack of language capability.

    2. The Federal Government should compel agencies to work together more effectively and efficiently and should ensure that their computer systems can communicate. Agencies should focus on establishing a common intelligence picture, rather than protecting parochial interests.

    3. Despite its culture of not sharing information adequately, the intelligence community also needs to reexamine who needs access to the intelligence and analysis and disseminate that information appropriately.

- *Congress must support transformation of the military, but must guard against sacrificing the current core competencies and systems for tomorrow's technology.*

    1. One of the key elements of transformation must be a further move toward jointness, not just in how we fight but in how the military is equipped.

    2. Missile defense must be a top transformation priority. The United States should not allow itself to be blackmailed by groups or states possessing ballistic missiles or weapons of mass destruction.

The Honorable Douglas Feith, Under Secretary of Defense for Policy

- *Just days before September 11th, the Defense Department completed a major reassessment of U.S. defense strategy, known as the Quadrennial Defense Review*

(QDR). In light of the campaign against global terrorism, this review has increased relevance.

    1. Planning should reflect that even with the best intelligence and the most careful analysis, surprises are unavoidable and we should plan and prepare to handle them.

    2. The military needs forces that can take action quickly anywhere in the world and that are agile, versatile, and lethal, even in relatively small-scale deployments. These forces need to be responsive, capable of being moved quickly and easily, and of operating in multiple locations simultaneously.

    3. The military must recognize that having access to bases abroad is an important strategic asset. However, the military must also plan for the likely circumstance that forces will have to operate without bases and must therefore maintain long-range precision strike capabilities.

    • *Homeland security is a long-term concern for the Department of Defense (DOD). The terrorist attacks on the United States have implications for organizing military forces, developing capabilities, and planning operations.*

    1. The government did not anticipate the scope of the territorial security challenge and the difficulty of defining the appropriate military role.

    2. The Department of Defense is learning innovative ways of exploiting our comparative advantages and working with local authorities and forces. This will shape our conception of security cooperation with our allies in peacetime and lay the basis for cooperation in war.

    • *The current campaign against global terrorism must focus on denying to terrorists state support and the territory from which to operate. The United States and its allies should have a territorial, not an organizational, approach.*

    1. There are simply too many terrorist organizations and cells to be targeted individually.

    2. State sponsorship of terrorism provides the nexus of terrorism and weapons of mass destruction. Many states that support terrorism are also pursuing nuclear, biological, and chemical weapons and the missiles needed to deliver them.

    3. Much of the hatred directed towards the United States cannot be appeased; we must simply defend ourselves against these organizations. However, some terrorists have a political agenda that is focused against their own regime and not the United States.

    4. We must engage in the battlefield of ideas to influence not only the enemy, but also the enemy's possible supporters. In this respect, we have a tremendous strategic and moral advantage.

    • *The Federal Government should encourage more thinking on how the different instruments of national power can reinforce one another to maximize their effectiveness while accepting that each instrument has its limits.*

1. National security policy must take all of the instruments into account to change the international environment and the way people define victory in the war on terrorism.

2. The use of military force can improve the conditions for diplomacy or intelligence collection. Likewise, intelligence is crucial to the effective application of military force, and diplomacy can aid in the achievement of military ends.

The Honorable Avis Bohlen, Assistant Secretary of State for Arms Control

• *September 11th did not really catapult the United States into a different world. The threat posed by sub-state actors has been apparent for the last decade, both in terms of their capabilities and their motivations.*

1. The Quadrennial Defense Review states that "while the United States cannot predict with confidence which adversaries will pose threats in the future, the types of military capabilities that will be used to challenge U.S. interests and U.S. military forces can be identified and understood."

2. We are no longer dealing with an easily identifiable foe with large, recognizable forces easily spotted by our intelligence.

3. Threats today are multiple and unpredictable. We do not know the "who" and the "when," but we can guess the means that they will use to attack.

4. Asymmetrical means will predominate, as future adversaries will seek to avoid U.S. strengths by using terrorism, information operations, and missile attacks.

• *Since we cannot calculate the probability of one threat against another, we need a full range of capabilities to defend ourselves from each of them. Consequently we need a better interagency process, greater flexibility, and a comprehensive strategy. Beyond the military forces and intelligence capability, we need a broad range of policy responses to the challenges with which we are dealing today. The fight against terrorism embraces the full panoply of instruments.*

1. We need an appropriate set of military capabilities. The proliferation of weapons of mass destruction and delivery methods makes missile defense an essential ingredient for effective homeland security.

2. Our leaders need innovative economic and diplomatic policy options to deal with the new threats.

3. Diplomatic tools need to be strengthened, and we need better integration between agencies. We need to revive U.S. public diplomacy programs which have been underfunded over the last ten years. We need a broad effort that addresses the cultural roots of other peoples. To strengthen diplomatic instruments, we need more linguists and more regional expertise.

4. The United States must think strategically about its partners and friends. We should, above all, not lose sight of long-term allies such as the

NATO countries, Japan, South Korea, and others. These allies are irreplaceable in endeavors such as counterproliferation and the cutting off of financial support to terrorists.

Ambassador L. Paul Bremer III, Chairman, National Commission on Terrorism

• *The terrorist attacks on September 11th represent the major threat to American national security for approximately the next decade. The trends in terrorism for the last decade led many to predict mass casualty terrorism.*

1. Terrorism is the ultimate asymmetrical warfare because it allows the weak to attack the strong. Terrorists benefit from two specific asymmetries. First of all, we have to defend across the entire range of our vulnerabilities, whereas the terrorists can choose a single spot to attack. Second, terrorists benefit from a gross asymmetry in costs.

2. Old style terrorists before the 1990s were motivated by narrow political objectives and relied on public support; therefore they had self-imposed limits on the number of casualties they would inflict. The United States developed an effective method of meeting their threat by not making concessions to terrorists, treating terrorists as criminals who should be brought to justice, and not allowing states to use terrorism as an instrument of national policy.

3. The new terrorists of the early 21st century—having evolved since the late 1980s—are motivated not by limited political goals but by hatred, sometimes revenge, and often ideological or religious extremism. They have planned fewer, but more deadly, attacks and often committed suicide. During the 1990s, the number of international terrorist incidents declined while the number of casualties increased. Additionally, fewer terrorist incidents were claimed by any specific group.

4. This new style of terrorism has rendered irrelevant two-thirds of the old antiterrorist strategy. These terrorists are not looking for concessions and typically cannot be brought to justice. Therefore, the United States must focus solely on eradicating state support for terrorism.

5. The end of the Cold War left the United States in a position of geopolitical dominance, which is without equal and without comparison at any time in recorded history. There are a lot of people who hate us for that dominance. Public diplomacy and presenting the best side of American life is not the only answer. These terrorists know and understand American values and hate America for those values.

• *The United States is now at a critical point in its foreign policy, very similar to that in 1946 and 1947, when the postwar leaders of the United States had to find an organizing principle to guide American foreign policy.*

1. The United States must employ the entire spectrum of American capabilities and be absolutely clear about its strategic objective: to deny terrorists state support and territory.

2. Destroying terrorist organizations with a global reach is not sufficient. The United States cannot sustain an international coalition against terrorists if we target only groups that kill Americans. Therefore, the focus must be to stop any state that supports terrorism.

Analysis

The first panel discussed the disparate security perspectives of the various executive departments and the Congress as each seeks to develop a comprehensive security vision for the United States in this new era. The panelists reached broad agreement that the United States faces a combination of unique factors, including decreased military readiness due to funding cuts, a burdensome interagency process, and a period of unprecedented geopolitical dominance on the part of the United States. This situation, together with the terrorist attacks and ensuing war on terror, requires new thinking on how to exploit our comparative advantages and maximize the effectiveness of the entire spectrum of U.S. capabilities to counter the predominance of asymmetric threats and ensure U.S. national security. The formation of a new organizing principle may entail updating the National Security Act of 1947.

There was broad agreement on Ambassador Bremer's assessment that suicidal mass terrorism is the primary threat to the United States for the next 10-15 years. The best way to counter this new enemy is to deny him a territorial base within state or nonstate entities that support terrorists and to reduce the ungoverned or undergoverned space associated with weak governments that terrorists exploit to plan and support major operations.

To counter such threats and integrate the various instruments of national power, the United States must undertake four main tasks.

First, the U.S. must integrate the actions of the national security establishment and strengthen communications between and among the various agencies and departments, especially with regard to the intelligence community.

Second, the United States must reinvest in national security, especially in the transformation of the military. Undersecretary of Defense Douglas Feith emphasized recent QDR conclusions that the United States must be prepared for surprises with military forces able to take action anywhere in the world, even without forward bases. Indeed, the focus of efforts must be to maintain and enhance agile, lethal, and survivable joint forces with long-range precision strike capabilities. In addition, missile defense must be a priority in order to deny terrorist groups or states the opportunity to blackmail the United States. The proliferation of weapons of mass destruction and delivery methods makes missile defense an essential ingredient for effective homeland security. Senator

Inhofe cautioned against taking unnecessary risk in the readiness levels of our core competencies during the transformation.

Third, the United States' diplomatic tools need to be strengthened, Assistant Secretary of State Avis Bohlen noted, by increased funding and enhancement of language and regional expertise. Enhancing diplomatic tools also includes reviving public diplomacy programs to dissuade nations from directly or indirectly supporting terrorists while assuring potential U.S. allies against these mutual adversaries. Ambassador Bremer advised that the terrorists hate American values and cannot be convinced otherwise, but that information operations can be effective against the less committed populace in order to inhibit terrorist attempts to recruit support for anti-American activities.

Fourth, the coordination of the instruments of power must keep in mind the requirement to build and maintain coalitions. The United States, as Ms. Bohlen remarked, must think strategically about its long-term allies, as they are irreplaceable in endeavors such as counterproliferation and ceasing financial support to terrorists.

Transcript

Note: The conference and each panel were preceded by a video introduction. While transcripts of these videos are not included in this document, the videos and their transcripts are available at the conference website: www.ifpafletcherconference.com.

INTRODUCTION: For 31 years the Fletcher Conference has convened the nation's most renowned thinkers and influential decision makers in a two-day discussion of national security issues. This year our participants will examine, debate, and advance better ways to focus our national power on the full range of security challenges confronting America in the new century. The more likely threats to our national interest will come from regional conflicts due to ethnic, religious, or cultural differences or from terrorists. Within today's security environment the United States stands as the world's sole superpower with critical instruments to alter the effects of widespread disorder: diplomatic, economic, and military power.

Panel one will explore the opportunities and limitations of each, followed by candid and diverse viewpoints about new ways to synchronize these instruments. The power of our military is the foundation of our national security. And in response to changing world conditions, our armed forces are currently undergoing the most significant transformation in over 100 years. Their goal is full-spectrum dominance in any mission from peacekeeping to war. But while few would argue that they are the best prepared of all government agencies for crisis response, many would debate when and how they should be best employed. Complexity will be the order of the day. As the diversity of the threats and nonstate actors increases, so will the complexity of military tasks.

Panel two will scrutinize this sensitive issue by exploring a host of related topics: the essential nature of decisive force, readiness, and modernization; countering a threat of ballistic missiles; and the future of military operations in space. The panel will contrast the use of military power, in an era where both challenges and opportunities range from high-intensity conflict to ballistic missiles and weapons of mass destruction to peacekeeping operations. And they'll examine how our overseas presence advances our global interests.

Panel three will be a discussion of today's most prominent security challenge, homeland security and counterterrorism. We'll examine the threat of terrorism in America, transnational threats, homeland security, and the role of the military to contribute to the ongoing campaign to end global terrorism. Still, the military alone can't guarantee favorable and enduring outcomes to the complex challenges of today's security environment. The once discrete instruments of power—diplomatic, military, economic, and cultural—must merge seamlessly to produce a comprehensive security strategy or to respond to a crisis. But how?

Panel four is a frank discussion of ways to harness the individual capabilities of our various federal agencies and leverage them to a far greater effect when needed. The United States with its allies, therefore, must make certain that it has the right forces, that it has the right combinations of allies and coalitions, and that it has the will to make certain that large-scale conflict does not break out in places of global significance. In virtually all contemplated scenarios, the United States will not or cannot act alone to mitigate a threat unilaterally.

Panel five will take synchronization to the next level—achieving a unity of effort between us, our allies, coalitions, and international organizations. How do we achieve a military unity of effort, for instance, when the national self-interests of our allies differ from ours? How will the current technology mismatch affect coalition operations? How can operational diplomacy among allies be used more effectively to achieve a common cause? And like the Cold War system, the globalization system has its own rules, logic, pressures, incentives, and moving parts that will and do affect everyone's company, country, community and armed forces. For two days a coalition of national leaders will examine and advance ways to better focus our national power on the full range of security challenges confronting America in the new century. The Fletcher Conference, November 14 and 15, 2001, Washington.

SPEAKER: Ladies and gentlemen, please welcome Dr. Robert L. Pfaltzgraff, Jr., President, Institute of Foreign Policy Analysis. (Applause).

DR. PFALTZGRAFF: Ladies and gentlemen, after that beautiful opening video, what is there to say? That was well done, and it gives a wonderful

overview of what we plan to do here
during the next two days. This confer-
ence is the latest in a long series that
the Institute for Foreign Policy
Analysis has organized with the
International Security Studies
Program of the Fletcher School of Law
and Diplomacy, Tufts University.
Each of these conferences, held in
Washington, D.C., or in Cambridge,
Massachusetts, has been organized
with one of the military services and
other official cosponsorship. Since
1995, we have had the support of the
United States Army and the Chief of
Staff for five of these conferences. And
in earlier years the Army was several
times our cosponsor.

Dr. Pfaltzgraff

So, we have a long history of
working with the United States Army
in these conferences. But we've also
worked with the other services—the
Navy, the Air Force, and the Marine Corps—to organize meetings of this kind.
This year again, we are delighted to be able to work with the United States
Army and its senior leadership and also to have the cosponsorship, as in previous years, of the Office of the Secretary of Defense for Net Assessment.
Incidentally, this year, 2001, is especially important to us at the Institute and
at the Fletcher School because it marks IFPA's 25th anniversary and the 30th
anniversary of the Fletcher School's International Security Studies Program.
The theme of this conference is National Security for a New Era—Focusing
National Power.

This theme was developed many months ago before the tragic events of
September 11th which, of course, have given new meaning to the focusing of
national power to provide national security in a new era. In fact, some of the
rooms in the Pentagon in which I met with our Army cosponsors in July and
August cannot yet again be used as a result of the terrorist attack. Although the
essential theme and most of the issues to be discussed here over the next two
days were developed before September 11, we have, of course, adapted our
agenda to reflect the implications of the terrorist attack in our discussions as
fully as possible. Although we originally framed this conference around the
synchronization of all of the elements of national power, the need to achieve
unprecedented unity of effort has become all too vividly apparent. At the same
time, in designing this conference, we sought originally to provide a timely

forum to discuss the new Quadrennial Defense Review, as well as the other recently completed or ongoing national security strategy reviews and studies. Therefore, we envisaged this conference as being especially appropriate in this setting at this time even without what came upon us on 9-11.

We have, therefore, structured the agenda to include first a discussion of the security vision and priorities for a new era—that is our opening panel this morning—followed by a consideration of the relationship between the political, the military, and the economic instruments of power. We provide an opportunity in this afternoon's sessions to survey the spectrum of military capabilities that will be required in this new security setting, followed by an examination of the principal facets of homeland security and counterterrorism. In tomorrow's sessions we will turn to an assessment of the key organizational issues that need to be addressed if we are to assure the most effective utilization of the instruments of national power. Last, but not least, there are important issues associated with the requirements for unity of effort in alliances, coalitions, and other forms of international cooperation. As in all of the other panels, the alliance/coalition dimension has been brought into sharper focus in recent weeks. Unity of effort means utilization of necessary national capabilities, but it also encompasses how the United States works with others and mobilizes support among countries sharing common interests with us.

For each of these panels we have set forth a list of issues, many of which we hope will be included in the presentations and discussions. We have assembled an outstanding group of speakers. In doing so, we have sought to bring together a mix from the present Administration and from previous administrations. We have attempted, to the extent possible, to bring together a distinguished group of civilian and military panel members and to include Congressional and international perspectives as well. This is the largest of the conferences we have ever held. All of us who have worked on this conference, and there have been many of us, have labored, of course, in the shadow of the unfolding events of recent weeks. That we are even able to be here at this time is in itself something for which we are grateful. So, therefore, at the outset, I would like to express my thanks to the senior leadership of the United States Army and, in particular, to General Shinseki, its Chief of Staff, for their enduring support and unwavering determination to press forward in the midst of all that has taken place over the past two months. As a result, we have a unique forum in which to discuss the most important national security issues of the early 21st century and, hopefully, to contribute to the development of strategies, capabilities, and organizational frameworks that will advance our interests and values.

From this conference we will be preparing and publishing a major report, together with other outputs, in order to give broader dissemination to its proceedings. We are also able to provide immediate video streaming of the conference as well as CD-ROMs, thus expanding greatly its outreach and, hopefully, its impact. Although time is limited, of course, and we have many presentations. I hope that as many of you as possible will be able to take part in our discussions. So, on behalf of the organizers and the cosponsors, I welcome you to what promises to be a period of two days of important, informed, and timely discussions.

So again, really a wonderful warm welcome to you. I have now a couple of administrative announcements that I need to make. One is that I would reiterate that we should make sure that our cell phones, our pagers, are turned off or on vibrate. Also, I've been asked to announce that there is coffee available outside. And, if you have any problems getting around this complex building, there are many staff people—you'll see the badges. They are prepared to assist you and make sure that you don't get lost in this wonderful but very complex building. And now, I have the opportunity to welcome the members of our first panel, which will be chaired by John McWethy, who is a familiar face and voice to many of you because, as you know, he is the Pentagon correspondent of ABC News. So, we now turn to the opening session of our conference. And again, welcome to everybody. (Applause)

MR. McWETHY: Good morning. I'm John McWethy. I'm going to introduce our panel members. I'd like them to come out now. Senator James Inhofe. Bring him on out. Thank you. Doug Feith. And, I'm going to introduce each of them in detail before they speak. Avis Bohlen from the State Department and Paul Bremer. We're going to talk about the institutions of national power today. Hopefully—go ahead and sit down, guys.

Hopefully, we will explore how these institutions should work together to better American security. Hopefully, we will also be willing to discuss how the institutions in the past have sometimes worked against the best interests of the country. Budget battles, turf fights, vested interests. Hopefully we will discuss how sometimes the military services' reluctance to give up some of their traditional ways of thinking need to change. Sometimes Congress' refusal to do things like shut down bases stands in the way of improving national security. And, how sometimes tensions between institutions like law enforcement and intelligence sometimes stand in the way, sometimes blind the government in its ability to fight things like terrorism. Are the institutions of government capable of out-of-the-box thinking? Hopefully, our panel members will address that.

Clearly September 11th is driving the nation in new directions, but the question we should ask every day is, "Are these the right directions?" What level of risk is the United States willing to take to protect our freedoms, and what freedoms are we willing to risk in order to better protect the nation? And finally, what are America's responsibilities in the world to lead; to intervene, when; to expend national treasure for purely humanitarian reasons; to nation build; and what are our responsibilities sometimes to say, "No," when all of

Mr. McWethy

these calls go out? What responsibilities do we all have in trying to answer the question that I have been asked so many times, and I'm sure you have, too: Why do they hate us so much and with such passion? What do we, as a nation, do about it, think about it, and reflect about it as part of our response to September 11th.

Our first presentation this morning is going to be from Senator James Inhofe, who was first elected to the Senate in 1994. He is a member of the Senate Arms Services Committee and the Intelligence Committee. On the Armed Services Committee he has been the Chairman and the Ranking—and is now the Ranking Member on the Subcommittee on Military Readiness. He believes that overseas military missions should serve vital national interests and is one of the Senate's primary advocates for a national missile defense system. He has had a long career of public service, dating all the way back to the Oklahoma State House. He was the mayor of Tulsa. He is the only member of the U.S. Congress to fly an airplane around the world when he re-created the Wiley Post trip around the globe. And despite the fact he is dressed in the uniform of the Senate, he is wearing cowboy boots this morning. Senator? (Applause)

SENATOR INHOFE: Thank you very much. I appreciate being invited here to the Fletcher Conference. And I believe the topic you have chosen this year is very, very appropriate in light of what happened on September 11th. And what I would like to do is share the Congressional perspective on this new era. I'm quick to say that my Congressional perspective isn't necessarily shared by all members of Congress. We'll cover four actions that I believe Congress must take, and they are on the chart in front of us at this time.

First, Congress must set new spending priorities and provide the resources needed to bolster our national security. Congress has got to be willing to make the sacrifices to provide for our common defense. It is difficult for any free people to focus on national security at a time of peace and prosperity, which was true in America before September 11th. In T.R. Fehrenbach's book, *This Kind of War*, he says, "But the abiding weakness of the free people

is that their governments cannot or
will not make them prepare or sacrifice before they are aroused." Well,
ladies and gentlemen, on September
11th, we were aroused. And we've
had administrations and currently
have members of Congress who hon-
estly believe in their hearts—they
won't tell you this—but they believe
if all nations will stand in the circle
and hold hands and unilaterally dis-
arm, that all the threats will go away.
I like it the way that Phil Graham says
it. He says, "We all lust for the day
when the lion and the lamb will lie
down together, but when that happens I want to be the lion."

As I said, the American people
are aroused. They are focused on the
subject of national defense and
they're asking the question, much as
they did after Pearl Harbor, of "Why

Senator Inhofe

weren't we better prepared?" And let me illustrate with some charts to show
our lack of commitment to the national security in the past. First of all, in this
chart it goes back to the percentage of GDP (Gross Domestic Product) we as a
nation have spent on defense over the last 60 years. You notice prior to World
War II that we were not even thinking about security—we thought we had
security. And notice what happened right after Pearl Harbor; again, pre-Korea
and post-Korea.

Finally, notice the trend in the GDP spending. During the Clinton
Administration it reached the lowest point since 1940. I think that I mentioned
that one quote. I want to mention another one of a famous Oklahoman. He
said, "If you want to know when a war is coming"—this is Will Rogers, one of
my great heroes in Oklahoma—"If you want to know when a war is coming,
just watch the United States and see when it starts cutting down on its defenses. It is the surest barometer in the world."

The next two charts I have a hard time making people believe this, but
watch it carefully and take these charts, because they are in your packet, and
study them because it's true, during the period of time since 1993 total defense
spending amounted to $476 billion below the rate of inflation. In other words,
go back to 1993, put the figure down there, take—just apply the cost of living
increase, and at the end of this period of time it is 476 billion below. During
that same period of time, using the same model, the total spending on labor,

HHS (Department of Health and Human Services), and education amounted to $286 billion above the rate of inflation. And I hope we get some questions about this during question-and-answer time. I've seen the results of this decreasing funding firsthand. I spent for five years, back when Republicans were important, I was the Chairman of the Senate Armed Services Committee on Readiness. I traveled around to virtually all the installations and I saw what was happening to our deteriorating ability to defend America. I can remember seeing the substandard military housing. I was at Fort Bragg during a rain storm when our troops were actually covering up their equipment to keep them dry. I've seen the substandard maintenance facilities they have to work in, the decreased training time. They are allocated in a simulated exercise that they use as a substitute for live-fire. And it shows that in every area except our troops' unwavering devotion to duty and country, it has deteriorated. And, thank God they haven't because now we're expecting them to defend us in a war.

So, the first thing we've got to do in Congress is to be willing to sacrifice a little and put the necessary resources into the defense of our country. And the question is, can we do it? The answer is a resounding yes. You know, what is proposed right now in defense spending increase by the Administration as they're making that adjustment after September 11th, is still about an 11 percent increase over the previous year. And this is a time when we have $153 billion in surplus. Now, let's go back 20 years and look during the Reagan Administration when we were faced with a similar situation. At that time we had $128 billion deficit, and yet the President was able to accomplish in fiscal year 1982 a 20 percent increase over the previous year.

Secondly, Congress must reexamine the national security establishment with a critical eye as to how agencies and departments interact. Today's threat, now more than ever, requires a focused, integrated, comprehensive approach to national security. On September 20th the President said, "We will direct every resource at our command, every means of diplomacy, every tool of intelligence, every instrument of law, every financial influence, every necessary weapon of war to the disruption and defeat of global terror networks." And this is exactly the right approach. Focus all of our resources. Congress should look seriously at the National Security Act of 1947 with an eye to updating it. This Act unified the defense establishment for the first time. This is when the NSC (National Security Council) and the CIA (Central Intelligence Agency) came along. The organizations established a framework for the interagency process that still works today. But that was 1947, after we had learned the lessons of not having an integrated system.

New threats of today present challenges that our interagency structure doesn't adequately deal with. There is no longer a clear distinction between foreign and domestic matters, between peace and war, between law enforcement and national security. The terrorists who recently attacked America operate around the world, both in and outside of the United States. The INS (Immigration and Naturalization Service), Border Patrol, CIA, FBI (Federal Bureau of Investigation), Coast Guard, National Guard, states and the cities and local governments must all work together to fight the future threat. So, this is a unified approach. We must establish a type of interagency structure that allows us to fight these groups as one United States of America, not 13 separate intelligence agencies, not four armed services, 14 departments in 50 states—a unified approach. And, it may be time for a National Security Act of 2002.

Third, Congress must reexamine the intelligence community in particular and help change the culture that does not share information adequately. Our intelligence community actually does a reasonable job, but still their budget is tied to the defense budget and so they have suffered proportionately with the military. We must carefully examine, as we did after Pearl Harbor, what we knew about September 11th, who knew it, who shared it and who did they share it with, and what actions were taken and not taken, and, most importantly, how do we fix it. We don't have to wait for an analysis to take some action today. We're talking about the intelligence now. First, we have known for some time that we are critically short of linguists and analysts that take this unconscionable amount of information and pour it into some type of actionable intelligence. And we can fix this now. Secondly, we need to force agencies to talk to each other. Isn't that absurd? You know, we now put language into the Defense Bill that forces them to do that. So we've already fixed that one. Third, we need to make sure that computer systems can talk to each other between agencies. Today they can't. Fourth, we must stop the turf battles and establish a common intelligence picture. Finally, we need to reexamine who needs to know and share the information with them. I know the Administration is working diligently to bring these 13 separate agencies together in this common effort, again a unified approach. And, I think they are meeting with some success. However, these administrative efforts alone cannot change the culture that exists within these organizations. Simple things like the spelling of Arabic terrorists names are different from agency to agency. How do you know who they're talking about? We have some of the best technology in the world, but what good is it if the people who need the information can't get it?

My fourth category, I believe, is the most significant, and that is that Congress must support transformation of the military, but guard against taking unnecessary risks in the present capability. As we transform our military to face the challenges of the new era, much of what has been said applies here also. One of the key elements of transformation must be a further move toward jointness, jointness not in just how we fight but in how we equip our forces. We must provide the CINCs with an array of tools. They must have ground forces, air forces, naval forces with different capabilities that can be applied to different nations. It reminds me of the quote by Abraham Mostel. He said, "When the only tool you have in your toolbox is a hammer, all of the problems start looking like nails." But, as you transform, keep a few things in mind. First, we are focused on terrorists today, but they may not be the threat of the future. As you transform don't lose sight of our core competencies that have served us so well. Just a year ago before our Committee we had testimony that the aircraft carrier was obsolete. And yet every time we had one of these conflicts, we seemed to find a new need for them. They're not only launching aircraft to attack the Taliban, but they are operating as a base for Special Ops today. Likewise, we have had them say, "We'll never fight a ground war again." Well, we are fighting a ground war right now. And, they say we should transfer our Army into a peacekeeping corps. And that's ridiculous. You know, we are needing our ground forces. I hate to think where we'll need them next, but we will.

So, my advice is simple. Make sure we don't sacrifice today's capabilities to become enamored with tomorrow's technology. Make sure you maintain your joint approach, do your requirements in warfighting and make sure you tell Congress what you need in spite of what the Administration might suggest that you tell them. There are those who will constantly raise the question of costs, but we can't afford to allow our soldiers, sailors, airmen, and marines to fight with inferior equipment as they are today. We've got to buy systems like the F-22 because the F-15 and the F-16 are no longer the very best out there. We've got to buy a system like the Crusader, because the Paladin that we're using today is not as good as four other nations are making and are on the battlefield today in terms of rapid fire and in terms of range. We have to have the very best and we have to get our uniformed men and women better and the more modern equipment than our potential adversaries because they don't have that today, and that will mean more money.

Finally, as we transform we must make missile defense the top priority. We must not give the future Saddam Hussein the ultimate terrorist weapon, a missile with a nuclear warhead. I often remember seeing on TV on September 11th that awful skyline of New York City, that beautiful city, and with those buildings crumbling down. And, I thought, you know, if they had that ultimate weapon, a missile with a nuclear warhead, we would be looking at nothing but a piece of charcoal. We wouldn't be talking about 5,000 or 6,000 people. We would be talking about a million people. There are nearly 30 nations that either have or are attempting to acquire ballistic missiles today. Some of these countries can reach the United States and we have no defense against the ICBM (Intercontinental Ballistic Missile). We're naked. And some of these countries are trading technology and, perhaps, even systems with countries like Iran, Iraq, Syria, Libya, North Korea—and I don't want a Saddam Hussein to say, "If you go after Osama bin Laden in Afghanistan we'll launch a nuclear missile at the United States." Let's remember what Saddam Hussein said after the Persian Gulf War. He said if he had waited for ten years to go after Kuwait, march on Kuwait, the Americans would not have been there because we'd have a missile that would be able to stop them from doing it. And here it is, ten years later today.

And so we have asked in the Senate Armed Services Committee just who is crazy enough to assure his own destruction by doing something like deploying a missile against the United States. Well, after September 11th, we know. The missile threat is real. I do not believe our intelligence is reliable enough to accurately predict how close some of these nations are to deploying these systems. I remember the National Intelligence Estimate of December 1995 stated that Korea, North Korea, would not be able to develop a missile that would threaten the lower 48 states for at least 15 years. Then, on August 30, 1998, they fired a three-stage Taepo-Dong missile.

So, in summary, I'd say first, in this new era of national security, Congress must renew its efforts to make national security our number one job because it hasn't been before. Second, we must set new spending priorities to provide the resources needed. We must relook at the organization and the structure of our present system. Third, we must take action to strengthen the intelligence community and the cooperation so desperately needed between and among members of that community. And, finally, we must continue to support the transformation of our military without taking unnecessary risks to our present capabilities and develop a strong missile defense system. And I once again thank you for allowing me to come here today and talk about what I consider to be the most important subject in America today. (Applause)

MR. McWETHY: Our next speaker is Doug Feith. He is Undersecretary of Defense for Policy. He has this broad array of responsibilities that make his presentation especially interesting. Responsibilities include the formulation of defense planning guidance and force policy, Department of Defense relations with foreign countries, and the Department's role in the U.S. government interagency process. He spent 15 years pulling together a law firm that has his name on it. And prior to that, he was also in government, a protege of Richard Perle. This is the guy who you can see bleary-eyed coming back from Andrews Air Force Base after shuttling back and forth between Washington and Moscow. Whatever agreements or understandings President Bush and President Putin come to, they have Doug Feith's fingerprints all over them. Doug?

MR. FEITH: Thank you, John. Professor Pfaltzgraff, General Shinseki, other members of the U.S. armed forces, and ladies and gentlemen. When the World Trade Center and the Pentagon were attacked on September 11th, the speculative world of defense planning changed instantly into the high-speed, here-and-now, no-time-for-theory world of military operations. Just days before September 11th, the Defense Department completed a major reassessment of U.S. defense strategy, known as the Quadrennial Defense Review. And, in light of current events, in light of the war on terrorism, I'd like to recall a few key thoughts from the Quadrennial Defense Review, which was prepared under the direction of Secretary [of Defense Donald] Rumsfeld in the six months or so preceding the war.

The first key thought is that planning should recognize that even with the best intelligence and the most careful analysis, we cannot avoid surprises. We have to take to heart Samuel Goldwyn's observation that it's difficult to make forecasts, especially about the future. In our planning we should prepare to handle the inevitable surprises. Now this may seem like an obvious point, but much national security policy over the years has been based on the crucial (though not admitted openly) assumption that we can, for example, create and preserve strategic stability through arms control or otherwise know and control the future. The Quadrennial Defense Review exhorted everyone in the Pentagon to expect to be surprised, which, of course we all duly were on September 11th.

A second key thought of the Review was that we need the ability to take military action quickly anywhere in the world. We need forces that are lighter, capable of being moved quickly and easily; forces that are highly effective—that is—lethal, even in relatively small-scale deployments. The Review recognized that we won't necessarily be able to count in the future on having six months, as we did during [Operation] Desert Shield in 1990, to flow around a half a million troops into a single theater. It recognized that we may have to fight more quickly with fewer and lighter units in multiple locations simultaneously.

The third key thought of the Review related to forward basing. The Review recognized that it is valuable for the United States, it is an important strategic asset of the United States, to have access to bases abroad. It also recognized the likely circumstance that we would find ourselves having to operate without bases where we need them. Both points are important. That's why the review stressed the importance of long-range precision strike capabilities.

Now, since the September 11th attack and since the start of the war on terrorism, we can note a few additional points about the role of the U.S. military. First, the importance of homeland security. The Quadrennial Defense Review noted that this is going to be an important function in the national security field. It flagged the issue of what we've referred to as emerging threats, terrorist threats, to the United States and the responsibility that the Defense Department is going to have in territorial security. Nevertheless, no one I think anticipated how large, how complex and how difficult the territorial security responsibilities of the Defense Department were going to become as a result of the September 11th attack. We are just now defining the appropriate military roles. And we, I think, should not assume that the Department's role in this area is a temporary condition. On the contrary, the challenges of territorial

security are going to be with us for
the long term.

Second, as we see quite vividly
from this morning's news and the
news in recent days from Afghanistan,
our armed forces are learning innovative ways of working with local forces
to achieve important results. These are
lessons that have implications for how
we organize our forces and develop
our capabilities and plan operations.
We are thinking about the best ways to
use our comparative advantages and to
work with local forces to change the
picture on the ground. This is also
going to shape the way we deal in
peacetime with friends and allies
abroad and lay the basis for cooperation in war through our peacetime
security cooperation policies.

Mr. Feith

Third, I want to focus specifically on an aspect of the war on terror-
ism, and that is the recognition that terrorist organizations, if they are to do
large-scale harm over a sustained period, require a territorial base for their
operations. This is why you have heard Secretary Rumsfeld and the President
and other Administration officials stress so heavily the importance of state
support for terrorism. If we are going to succeed in the war on terrorism, we
have to fight terrorism at the wholesale level. There are simply too many terrorist organizations and cells for us to be chasing after each individually. We
need a territorial approach, we need to recognize the importance of state support to the operations of terrorist organizations. And we have to see to it that
other governments deny terrorists the territory from which to operate. That
means that some may have to be persuaded; some may have to be compelled.

Eliminating the territorial base and state support for terrorism will also
help us address the problem that was highlighted by Senator Inhofe, which is
the nexus of terrorism and weapons of mass destruction. The list of countries
that support terrorism and the list of countries that are pursuing nuclear,
chemical, biological weapons and missiles are remarkably coincident.

Now, as you've heard and as you saw in the film that preceded this panel,
the Administration has been stressing that the war on terrorism will draw on
all of the instruments of U.S. national power. These different instruments reinforce one another. We can see from this morning's news that the use of military force can create the conditions for more effective collection of intelli-

gence, can create the conditions for diplomacy. Likewise, intelligence is crucial to the effective application of military force. And diplomacy can also be crucial to the achievement of military ends. So, I would like to encourage more thinking among all of us on the issue of how these different instruments of national power can reinforce one another and make each other more effective.

I also want to point out that each of these instruments has its limits. And that also is important to recognize. There are limits to what we can accomplish through diplomacy. There are limits to what we can accomplish through the use of military power. In the war on terrorism, for example, we recognize that victory will be determined as much by what happens on the battlefield of ideas as on the military battlefield. And so I will conclude by observing simply that our concept of national security policy has to take all of these instruments into account, not the least being information and the need to change the international environment, to change the way people think about terrorism. Thank you. (Applause)

MR. McWETHY: And, now for the State Department point of view. Avis Bohlen is one of the State Department's veteran diplomats. She has served all over the world, joining the Foreign Service in 1977. She was most recently Ambassador to Bulgaria during its continuing journey toward democracy, a very challenging post. She has had a number of assignments in Paris. Those are fairly suspicious, Avis. I don't know that Paris is more challenging than Bulgaria. That's probably true. She has been deeply involved in arms control at many different levels, in many different positions in the State Department. She is currently Assistant Secretary for the Bureau of Arms Control. In her long and distinguished career, she has been dealing with first the Soviets and now the Russians again in that forum. So, Avis, the microphone is yours.

MS. BOHLEN: Thank you very much. It is a great pleasure to be here this morning. John Bolton was called to join the Secretary [of State Colin Powell] with the President down in Texas and is very sorry not to be here with you today. But it is my pleasure to be here, and I will try to sound as coherent as I can about this very important issue.

September 11th catapulted us into a different world or at least a different mode of thinking. But, if we look back over the last ten years, and even farther back in some respects, we realize that this different world has been taking shape for a long time. For a number of years now, we have been dealing no longer with an easily identifiable foe with large identifiable forces, easily spotted by our intelligence.

We are not dealing with foes who behave in ways that we find entirely rational—that is, according to obvious national identification of national interests. Clearly, the world has moved beyond what we all were accustomed to for such a long time. The threats that we face today are multiple and, as has already been said this morning, quite unpredictable. To quote a very relevant section from the Quadrennial Defense Review: "While the United States cannot predict with confidence which adversaries will pose threats in the future, the types of military capabilities that will be used to challenge U.S. interests and U.S. military forces can be identified and understood."

As in the September terror attacks in New York and Washington, future adversaries will seek to avoid U.S. strengths and attack U.S. vulnerabilities using asymmetric approaches such as WMD terrorism, operations against our information systems, and ballistic and cruise missile attacks. We no longer face a single primary threat. There is no way to calculate with any certainty the likelihood of one threat against another.

Ms. Bohlen

And we need to defend ourselves against the full range of threats. This requires a great deal of flexibility and it also requires a comprehensive strategy that, as both Senator Inhofe and Doug Feith have suggested, really cover the full range of U.S. government and U.S. national capabilities and require a much better degree of integration than we have achieved in the past.

We obviously need to have the military forces appropriate to the task. We're no longer in the era of huge tank armies, but as Senator Inhofe said, we still need ground forces. Some have suggested that missile defense is no longer necessary because it wouldn't have protected us against September 11th. This is clearly a false premise. It shows precisely that the threats that we will face are not predictable. If we think how horrible September 11th was, we can imagine how much more horrible it would have been if it had been a missile with a nuclear warhead. And how could any President defend himself against the charges that he had neglected to work on the defense for this threat?

But beyond the military forces and the intelligence, we need a broad range of policy responses to the challenges that we are dealing with today.

The fight against terrorism should embrace a full panoply of instruments. We spend $12 million a year on the fight against terrorism. Henceforth, it needs to cover the whole field of homeland security with its many challenges. It also extends overseas to attacking the sources of financing for terrorists. Most importantly, it will challenge our diplomatic skills. What September 11th and the fight against terrorism have shown us is that that we need to give a great deal of attention to policies to deal with these multiple threats. One very important element will be nonproliferation. This continues to be an important part of our policy. We need to try to persuade or induce proliferating governments to change course, as well as to deny proliferators the supply of equipment, material, or technology from abroad. We need to use U.S. threat reduction programs to secure, eliminate WMD and missile capabilities left over from the Cold War. We need to strength international nonproliferation treaties and promote new ones where they meet U.S. interests, as well to upgrade the means of verifying these treaties and commitments. Effective nonproliferation makes the job easier for those who are crafting counterproliferation measures. Our policies seek to ensure that our forces face fewer, less capable weapons from fewer countries, so that our missile defense and counterproliferation will have smaller challenges to deal with.

We need to strengthen our diplomatic instruments. Senator Inhofe mentioned the need for linguists. There are large areas of the world where we do not have the trained resources of Pashto and Dari speakers. We need to strengthen those capabilities. We need to strengthen specialists in this area. In order to put together an effective counterterrorist strategy, we need to work on cooperation with friends and partners throughout the world. And this is what we have done. The course of events since September 11th have showed us that laying the ground work diplomatically and politically for the military actions that we have undertaken was an absolutely essential precursor. There are some lessons here. We need to think strategically about who our partners and friends are going to be in the world. Three months ago, we would not have thought that we would be in a close embrace with Uzbekistan, Tajikistan, and Pakistan, but these countries have—or have again, in the case of Pakistan—become very important to us. I think we would all agree that some of the problems that we're facing today lie in a decade of neglect of Afghanistan and Pakistan after we thought they were no longer as important or when we decided that the primary element in our relationship should be, as in the case of Pakistan, the nuclear one. So we need to learn again as we did during the Cold War to think in strategic terms, to think in terms of the countries that are going to be important to our effort. This needs to be a long-term effort. It cannot just be an ad hoc alliance.

We should, above all, not lose sight of those countries that have been our friends and allies over decades. The NATO Alliance, Japan, South Korea, Australia—those partners will remain absolutely crucial to our effort to put together a good counterterrorism effort. And this is not only because of their support for what we are doing. We need their support, not just for the military effort, but even where they are not participants. We cannot do things like cutting off the financing for terrorists without cooperation from the other developed countries whose banking systems have also been used. We have had really quite amazing successes to date on this front, and I think this is because we have been able to build on existing institutions to achieve cooperation.

There are other instruments that we can use, that we must use, to make the diplomatic instrument more effective. Both Doug Feith and Senator Inhofe talked about the need for better integration. This is certainly true in an area which is a principal activity for the State Department overseas, and that is issuing visas. I'm sure you have all read in the papers of the problems we have with our system of delivering visas. This is not an imperfection in embassies. It is because embassies are not, in some cases, given the full information that may be available to other agencies. There is a vast amount that we can do to improve this. We also need to revive—and are in the process of doing this—our efforts at public diplomacy. Over the past decade, our public diplomacy budgets were cut again and again. We are now seeing that we have paid a price for this throughout the world. We need the specialists who know the areas, who know how the message will come across. We need to not just be giving the line of the day, but making a broad-gauged effort that will go at the cultural roots of what we are dealing with and that will also convey a broad picture of America. So, diplomacy remains an essential tool in this new world, diplomacy in all its many facets. And we need to integrate our efforts better. We need to look where our efforts need to be improved and indeed, in some cases, plussed up. Thank you very much. (Applause)

MR. McWETHY: Thank you, Avis. Now Paul Bremer, a man who has spent most of his life on the tail of terrorists, tracking them, analyzing their movements, trying to figure out how the U.S. ought to deal with it. A month ago, exactly a month after September 11th, Ambassador Bremer was named Chairman and Chief Executive Officer of Marsh Crisis Consulting Company, a subsidiary of Marsh and McLennan Companies—so he's starting up a company a month after the crisis of September 11th. He is also Chairman of the National Commission on Terrorism. He was appointed to that by then-Speaker [Dennis] Hastert in the House of Representatives. Paul Bremer was a Foreign Service officer serving in Afghanistan, Malawi, Norway, and the Netherlands. I don't understand this, Paul. You were first appointed Ambassador in 1983 when you were what? Ten years old? It is amazing. He has completed a recent report on terrorism, and in it I'm sure he will describe for you how he saw most of what has happened to the United States in the last two months. He saw it with great clarity. He saw it coming. He was knocking on the doors of various government agencies and finding it a tough sell. Paul Bremer. (Applause)

AMBASSADOR BREMER: Thank you, John. Professor Pfaltzgraff, General Shinseki. It is a great pleasure to be with you today. As John's introduction sort of suggested, like everybody in this room I was shocked by what happened on September 11th, but I was not surprised. And I was not surprised because the

National Commission on Terrorism, a bipartisan commission set up by Congress which I chaired, reported a year and a half ago that we would be experiencing large-scale, mass-casualty terrorism in the United States and we would likely see biological terrorism here, as well, in the months ahead. We made a number of recommendations to the President, then President Clinton, and to the Congress when we issued our report a year and a half ago. Not one of those recommendations was put into force before September 11th.

Now, I think, in fact, so far this morning we have underestimated the impact of September 11th. I would argue that what we saw on September 11th represents the threat to American national security for the next decade or so. And that we are now at a flex point in American foreign policy very similar to the point we were at in 1946 and 1947, when the then-postwar leaders of the United States had to find an organizing principle around which to organize American foreign policy. They came up with a policy of countering Soviet Communism, which of course was pursued over the next 50 years with great patience, resilience, relentlessness and skill, and that's the kind of strategy we need now.

Why do I say that this is the new threat? First of all, the trends in terrorism for the last decade led any serious student of terrorism to predict mass-casualty terrorism. The terrorism we saw in the 1960s, 70s, and 80s was terrorism which was motivated largely by narrow political objectives, often groups, particularly the homegrown groups in Europe where Marxist-Leninist groups that basically were seeking goals such as getting American bases out of Germany or attenuating American relations with our NATO allies. Or often they conducted terrorism to get their colleagues out of jail or to publish a political screed. Most of these groups, including many of the Middle Eastern groups which were active in those years, used terrorism to get the press to pay attention to their cause because they believed they had a broad cause that had public support.

And so their objective was to kill enough people to get the press present but not so many as to turn off the public. And in effect, therefore, these old-style terrorists had a self-imposed limit on the number of casualties that they would kill. Sometimes they killed hundreds, but on the whole it was a question of killing 10 or 20 people, maybe a few more in order to get the press present. Now, the West came up with a strategy under the leadership of President Reagan in the early 1980s to defeat this kind of terrorism. It was based on three simple propositions. First of all, you don't make concessions to terrorists because if you do that you start down the slippery slope of blackmail.

Secondly, terrorists are criminals. They conduct criminal acts and, therefore, we should bring terrorists to justice. And thirdly, it cannot be allowed in the international community that states use terrorism as an instrument of national policy. Those are the three pillars of the strategy developed by the West under American leadership in the 1980s. And I would argue it was a suc-

cessful strategy in dealing with the
old terrorists. But what happened was
by the end of the 1980s, and particularly in the 90s, we saw a shift to a
new kind of terrorism. And the new
terrorists are not motivated by narrow political goals. The terrorism
which we started to see in the late 80s
and in the 90s is a terrorism that is
motivated by sometimes hatred,
sometimes revenge, and often ideological or religious extremism. And
the occasional group is motivated by
an Apocalyptic vision of the future,
such as the Japanese group, Aum
Shinrikyo, and its attack with chemicals on the Tokyo subway in 1995.
Well, groups which have these kinds
of motives are not self-restrained in
the number of casualties that they
inflict, and in fact, they may want to
inflict more casualties. And this

Ambassador Bremer

accounts for the paradoxical fact that during the 1990s the number of international terrorist incidents went down while the number of casualties went up.
Also during the 1990s, we noticed that fewer and fewer terrorist incidents
were claimed by a particular group, and that an increasing percent of terrorist
attacks involved suicides.

In 1998 when I was Ambassador-at-Large for Counterterrorism, I commissioned a study of terrorist incidents from 1968 to 1998 to try to find out
how prevalent suicides were among terrorists, and we found that in those
years, less than 2 percent of terrorist attacks involved suicides. The old-style
terrorists did not want to be caught. They did not want to die. The new-style
terrorists are very different indeed. And I would argue that this new style of
terrorism has rendered irrelevant two-thirds of the old strategy we had. Why
do I say that? Well, I still think it is a good idea not to make concessions to
terrorists, but the question of making concessions to people like bin Laden
and Al Qaeda never comes on the deck. There isn't anything to discuss with
him. He's not asking anything of us except maybe that we cease to exist. But
there is no negotiation to be had, so there's no question. Making concessions
is irrelevant.

Secondly, while it is always a good idea to bring terrorists to justice, the fact
of the matter is that for someone who is willing to fly an airplane at 500 miles
an hour into a building, he is not going to be deterred by the prospect of a cou-

ple years in jail. And so, the President has it right when he says we need to turn our thinking around and instead of talking about bringing terrorists to justice, talk about bringing justice to terrorists. So, we are left in effect with only one pillar of the old strategy standing, which Doug Feith hit on this morning, which is state support. And I'll come back to that in a minute. But even this, in my view, does not adequately describe why terrorism is such a threat to the United States. For that you have to look at the geopolitical environment.

The end of the Cold War left the United States in a position of geopolitical dominance, which is without equal and without comparison any time in recorded history. Sure, there have been other countries which have, at their time, been dominant. But if you look at the examples, look at Rome, dominating but dominating only the littoral area around the Mediterranean. The Tang Dynasty in China was dominant, but it dominated basically the eastern half of Asia. Even the British, who dominated the 19th century, found that there were counterveiling forces available in Europe and in Asia to countervail British imperial power. American military, political, economic, and even cultural power today is without any precedent. And, while it is hard for many Americans to believe, that sets up a lot of problems for us. There are a lot of people who hate us for that dominance. There are a lot of people who resent it, and there are a lot of people who want to change it. But if you want to attack American power in this moment of domination, how can you do it?

Well, one of the clear lessons of the Gulf War was that even a lavishly equipped conventional army and Saddam Hussein's army at the time, as many of you here know was the fifth largest army in the world, equipped with modern Soviet tanks, artillery, and air force. Even the most lavishly equipped conventional army in the world was no match, not even close to a match, for American military force and that was already ten years ago. And so, the lesson is, as the Senator pointed out from the Quadrennial Defense Review, that if you are going to attack America now, you have to use unconventional means, "asymmetrical warfare," in the terms of the Pentagon. And terrorism is the ultimate asymmetrical warfare because it allows the weak to attack the strong.

Terrorists benefit from two specific asymmetries. First of all, we have to defend across the entire range of our vulnerabilities, whereas the terrorists can choose the single spot to attack. He can bring all his force to bear on one single place while we have to defend across an entire range. And secondly, terrorism benefits from a gross asymmetry in costs. If a terrorist wants to attack an airport, he just needs an AK-47 assault rifle and a couple of clips. But to defend that airport against that attack will cost literally millions of dollars. The best estimate of September 11th is that it cost something in the range of a half a million dollars. It has caused at least $100 billion in damage and the number is still rising. So, terrorism benefits from a dramatic asymmetry. And the lesson of the Gulf War suggests that not just terrorists, but other states will see that this is the way to attack the United States.

And so for these two reasons, the secular trends in terrorism and the geopolitical situation we find ourselves in, I think it is no exaggeration to say that what we saw on September 11th is, in fact, the face of the new national security threat to the United States. I do not see any country or group of countries which will be able in a traditional sense to counteract American power for the next 10 to 15 years and, therefore, this is the threat we're going to have to deal with. Of course, we're going to have to worry about some places where conventional military force could be used against us, for example, particularly in the Korean peninsula. But from a broad point of view what we see now is what we're going to be facing.

Now, what are the implications of this analysis? First of all, we need to be absolutely clear about our strategic objective. In my view, the strategic objective now, and Doug Feith touched on it, is to deny terrorists territory. Because as he said, if a terrorist group can operate in a benign environment, such as Lebanon was in the 70s and 80s and Afghanistan has become, then terrorist groups have the luxury of training, recruiting, planning, testing their kinds of operations—the kind of elaborate operations we saw on September 11th. Deny them that territory, and they have to start worrying about police coming through the door at 2 o'clock in the morning, they have to worry about people eavesdropping on their communications, they have to worry about a lot of things that we want them to worry about. It becomes much harder to conduct the kind of elaborate attack we saw.

Therefore, we must deny terrorists territory. This is going to be a long campaign, as the President has said. It is going to take a lot of patience. And we are going to have to operate across the entire spectrum of American capabilities from military, covert action, diplomacy, public diplomacy, going after finances, the entire range of activities. We have had, I think, so far a significant success in the first phase, which is the Afghan phase of this, where we had two objectives: defeating the Taliban and overthrowing them and killing as many of bin Laden's people as we can. And I think we've had significant successes there. But we have to move on because this is just the beginning. Next, we must move to close down the al Qaeda cells that are located in some 60 countries of the world, including the United States. It was good news in Spain that the Spanish have wrapped up an 11-man cell in Spain that has been doing recruitment there for bin Laden's organization, and there have been similar efforts in other countries.

Secondly, we have to go after the other states that provide this benign environment for terrorists. There is a good starting point, which is the State Department list of states which support terrorism, five of which as Doug pointed out, are also states which have both ballistic missile capabilities and nuclear, chemical, and biological programs. In my view, we must after the Afghan phase start to go and have very serious discussions with these groups, hoping that we can compel those states to stop their support for terrorism with diplomacy, but being ready to use force if we have to. I would start with Sudan, by the way, which has expressed an interest in trying to work with us on terrorism and I would say to them, "We are pleased that you want to work with us on terrorism. The test is that these six terrorist camps that are still operating in Sudan must be closed down by Tuesday midnight or we'll do it for you. And if you wonder what happens to what the President on September 20th called 'hostile regimes,' here have a reference to what happened in Kabul."

I think we have to be absolutely serious about it and we have to go, in my view, beyond what the President has said. He repeated in his address to the UN that we are going to go after terrorist groups with a "global reach." I think that's wrong for two reasons. It is not enough, first of all, because in fact the group other than al Qaeda, the group that has killed more Americans than any other terrorist group in the world is Hezbollah, so Hezbollah has to be on the list of terrorist groups we go after. But more importantly, we cannot simply have an international coalition against terrorists if we say we're only going to go after terrorists who kill Americans. We have got to be consequential in our thinking. We have to worry about the Spanish fight against the Basques, the British fight against the Real IRA and so forth, the Colombian fight against the FARC (Revolutionary Armed Forces of Columbia) and the ELF (National Liberation Army).

So, it is not enough to say we are going after groups with a global reach. We have to say we are going to stop any states which are supporting terrorism. And, incidentally, that includes Mr. Arafat, who allows three major terrorist groups, including Hezbollah, to operate pretty much at liberty on the territory of the Palestinian Authority. That's got to stop, and I'm pleased to see the President has basically said there is going to be no meeting with him until such time as he takes serious action. Sooner or later we will come to the problem of Iraq. Whether we come to the problem of Iraq because of intelligence indicating Iraqi involvement in September 11th or not, we are going to have to finish the job we left unfinished in 1991 because Saddam Hussein considers himself to still be at war with us. He has now had three years with no inspections by the UN. It is safe to assume he has reconstituted his chemical and biological programs at a minimum and perhaps his nuclear program. He has used chemical weapons against his own people and against the Iranians, so he has no particular qualms about using these weapons when he gets them. He is the major threat to regional stability after we deal with radical Islam in Afghanistan. The implications for all of this are that we are going to have to work with what I would call an à la carte coalition.

We will find, as we move beyond the Afghan phase, that some of our allies will not want to join us. Others will. Some will want to work with us on a military basis. Some will join us in diplomacy. That's fine. We should be prepared to welcome support where we can find it, but not let our foreign policy be driven by the least common denominator. It is useful to have support from other countries. As Churchill said, "The only thing worse than fighting with your allies is fighting without them." And so it's useful where we can find allies and friends and we should look for that. But we should not be driven off the importance of the strategic clarity of our objective: Deny terrorists territory.

The impact of September 11th, I think, is already clear on American international relations in many ways. We've seen in just the last 24 hours the culmination of a dramatic shift of Russian foreign policy, really a shift that you almost have to go back, but I would defer to Avis who's more of an expert, you really have to go back to Peter the Great, almost 300 years, to find a Russian leader who so decisively said he wants to be part of Western civilization. The Chinese have joined us, admittedly for good Chinese reasons, in the fight in Afghanistan. India sees an opportunity to emerge and consolidate its importance in the subcontinent. We have seen both Japan and Germany in their own ways break out of the post World War II constraints that had been placed on them with the Japanese Navy sailing for the first time away from Japanese home waters and the Germans for the first time deploying fighting forces outside of Europe.

There will also be, as the Senator pointed out, an important impact on U.S. government organization and programs. We must have a much more aggressive attempt at getting intelligence about terrorism. This was a colossal failure of intelligence and of law enforcement on September 11th and an important failure in our border security and immigration programs. All of those things now have to be fixed. I'm pleased to see that the CIA has, indeed, adopted a more aggressive approach since September 11th, that the President has announced, in addition to signing the Antiterrorism Bill, has announced yesterday the institution of military courts to give expeditious trials to terrorists who are caught, and that the Attorney General is moving with others to try to find better ways to protect our borders through more aggressive border and immigration controls. And, as Avis Bohlen pointed out, the important thing here is to get a seamlessness in the intelligence so that people issuing visas overseas have access to the databases they need.

Now, we're not going to, even if we do all of these things, we are not going to eliminate terrorism. Terrorism has been around as long as mankind has been around. So, we're always going to have terrorism. But by being aggressive and denying terrorists territory, by being serious and relentless in the program we've engaged in now, both in Afghanistan and in the phases to come, we can reduce terrorists' ability to operate on the scale we have seen. And we can get it back down to a level where terrorism becomes more of a criminal problem, which can be dealt with by normal intelligence and law enforcement operations and where it does not dominate American foreign policy. Thank you. (Applause)

MR. McWETHY: At the risk of losing everyone, I would like to do something that I think is essential after sitting in your chairs for an hour and a quarter. I'd like you to stand up and allow your blood to circulate back up to your brain so that we get into the more interactive part of this presentation. You'll notice I'm not giving you the opportunity to go to the washroom, but don't want to lose you completely. OK. Blood back at the top half of your anatomy? I'd like to give the panel members a moment to do a little interacting. It's rare that a journalist has an opportunity to do anything with a group of this esteemed nature.

I would like to ask one question of the panel, and then I will let them interact by themselves. And it goes to the issue that I raised at the beginning, and that is why do they hate us? Paul Bremer talked about it. Obviously, when you have cultural, economic, and military dominance the way the United States does, there is resentment. But, what part of the policy as we work our way through has to also address how the United States is perceived in the world and how does the U.S. do a better job of explaining its values and sell-ing what it represents in the world, as opposed to the images which the world often has of us as created through Hollywood or the news coverage of civilian casualties in places like Afghanistan? How do we incorporate that into a game plan? Any panel member want to take a stab?

AMBASSADOR BREMER: I'll start. The question—John misstates the problem. The problem isn't to persuade other people what our values are. It is our values that they hate. I am often asked when I speak, "How could these guys who conducted these attacks have lived among us, sent their kids to our schools, gone to the Friday night football game, shopped in our malls for years, and done what they did on September 11th?" And, the answer is that these people hated us more every day they were here. Because their proposi-tion is, and if you can just read bin Laden you'll understand it, they hate us for what our values are. They hate us for our freedoms, they hate us for our uni-versal suffrage, they hate us for the fact that women go about unveiled and can get college educations and serve in high positions in government, they hate us for our material success, they hate us for the fact that we separate church and state, and they hate us for, perhaps most of all deepest down, the fact that our society has appealed to their young people. And so there is, as I said earlier, no negotiation to be had with those kinds of people. It is not an issue of we do something. Now, I'm all for us pursuing public diplomacy and presenting the best side of American life. I did it myself as a diplomat for more than two decades. So I don't deny that. But we have to be clear about what we're up against here. We're not going to persuade the people like bin Laden that he's sort of missing the point about America. He's got us. He figured us out. He knows exactly what we are and, therefore, he hates us.

MR. McWETHY: Isn't there a background of support that is created on the streets of even our most friendly allies, a background of sentiment about the

United States that lends support to the more fanatic end of the spectrum? And, isn't that where American efforts has to be directed at huge numbers of populations that view the U.S. in negative terms and allow people like bin Laden and his operators to freely go? Avis?

MS. BOHLEN: Well, just to follow up on what Jerry says, I absolutely agree with him that there will never be any persuading of the Osama bin Ladens in this world. But, I think where we need to direct our efforts are precisely the sort of second level that you suggested. He is able to exploit a kind of vast resentment that is out there among many of the people who support him. And he succeeded in having every group attach their grievance to his star. And, I think this is something that we can influence. First of all, we can seek to analyze and understand what those grievances are, and, secondly, I think we can have a public message that does appeal to the people that are not the inner core of Osama bin Laden, but some of the people who support him in the Islamic world today.

MR. FEITH: What Ambassador Bremer said sounds right: Much of the hatred cannot be appeased. I would though, add, just a few thoughts: There are some people among the religious extremists engaged in terrorism who have a fairly definite political agenda. And that agenda is not necessarily directly focused on the United States. It is focused more on politics in the Muslim world, and in the Arab world. The United States, I think, for some of these groups is almost like the bystander that gets damaged. We suffer collateral damage in the attacks that some of these groups are directing at their real targets, which are the rulers of Saudi Arabia, Kuwait, Egypt, and other governments in the Middle East.

Second point: While I think that there are people who cannot be dealt with and cannot be appealed to and we simply have to defend ourselves against them and defeat them, there nevertheless is a battlefield of ideas on which we have to engage. Efforts are being made by our enemies to recruit for their cause, to change the thinking of young people, especially in the Muslim world—to teach them that, for example, suicide bombing is martyrdom rather than murder. And it is in our interests to engage on that battlefield of ideas.

Everybody recognizes that strategy is a concept that is broader than just military action. And I think it is widely understood that morale is a crucial element of strategy. Well, I would say that one of the things we should have learned from the Cold War is that morality can be a key element of morale. It is one of the strategic vulnerabilities of our enemy in this war on terrorism that the killing of innocent people is morally repulsive to decent people around the world. So we have important strategic advantages in this battlefield of ideas, and we do have to engage there without in any way suggesting that on the battlefield of ideas we're actually going to be persuading our committed enemies.

I think that's an important point that Ambassador Bremer highlighted. We have to recognize that we're on that battlefield of ideas not to persuade our enemies, but to persuade the people that our enemies are trying to recruit into their cause.

SENATOR INHOFE: Well, I think one thing on the list that Paul used as to why they hate us, he got close to it, he didn't quite get there, and that is they are taught to hate us. These little kids that are in school, they are taught to hate us. And this isn't anything new. I'm old enough to remember when this was going on in the Second World War. Hitler used the same strategy. Castro, when he went to Cuba. First thing they do is get the kids and teach them we're the evil ones. They learn to hate us because they are taught to hate us. Now, that's a challenge for the information age, I think, for us to try to do something to get to these kids and show them the other side.

MR. McWETHY: We have microphones out in the audience. If we have some questions from the audience, raise your hand. A microphone will come to you and I'll start on this side if there are any questions over here? There is one. A gentleman in the red tie. Wait until a microphone gets to you. State who you are and who you work for if you would, please.

AUDIENCE MEMBER: My name is Jim Longley. I'm actually a former Congressman, but currently work in the field of missile defense. I want to just pick up on your question and ask a question based on two recent facts. One is I happened to notice about a month ago that when the old U.S. Embassy in Kabul was sacked that it was broadcast live in the Middle East, which implied that, A, someone had a camera on the scene, and B, someone had the technical logistics in place to transfer that imagery back. And it was somewhat ironical this morning to pick up the papers and read of the jubilant Muslims in the streets of Kabul celebrating the downfall of the Taliban. Coincidentally, we'd accidentally, I gather, dropped a bomb on the local headquarters of Al Jazeera. But, to pick up on your question, I wonder whether we have yet to learn that communicating in our language, in our terms with reference to our culture or whether we understand the importance of conveying in the Middle East that Muslims themselves are disgusted with the behavior of these folks. And, I just ask whether organizationally or policy-wise we're starting to appreciate that.

MR. McWETHY: Good question. Avis?

MS. BOHLEN: I think that is a very valid point and I think it is appreciated. And over the past few weeks I think we have sharpened up our public diplomacy efforts. We now have people who are—one of the problems was the time lag so that we were responding to things that, for example, Jazeera might be broadcasting early in their day, but everybody was already asleep by the time we were responding. So we now have an office in Islamabad. We have an office in London that is dealing with some of those sort of technical problems. But I think more broadly, it has been part of our message from the outset, and the President himself has stressed, that there are several Islams and that the Islam—that the face of Islam—that Osama bin Laden represents is not the face of true Islam, and I think that message has found resonance everywhere. If you look at the number of countries that, as somebody was saying earlier, killing innocent people is abhorrent to every religion, including the Muslim one. So I think that is part of the message. I hope we can—I don't know what we're doing to get the pictures of the people getting their beards shaven and the women casting off their burqas if Jazeera is not up, but I'm sure CNN will be there very quickly.

MR. McWETHY: Those images are being broadcast. Anybody else? Question on this side? Sir, right in front?

AUDIENCE MEMBER: David Litt, Political Advisor from the State Department U.S. Special Operations Command. I think the State Department has been making some major changes in the way we do business over the last several months. One of the key changes that we have been able to do is to adjust the way that we organize for strategic planning. I would hope that in the future as this comes to be, that we will also be able to look out ahead as the Army, Navy, and the Air Force have done to establish a strategic visioning cell to look beyond the horizon, beyond the headlights into the dark, into what are the strategic flagship capabilities that diplomacy can bring. One of them, it seems clear to me, is this whole concept of persuasion and compulsion, which we really need to be the primary front line experts on. And I guess the major question I have to you all is probably, as you all have said, Hollywood has been the major contributor to perception management about the United States. And recently, we've seen Hollywood beginning to—or emerging and suiting up and trying to get in the game of perception management on behalf of the United States. What do you all think about that prospect?

MR. McWETHY: We have a politician here.

SENATOR INHOFE: Well, there's no question about the impact that they have. And I—when you were asking that question, I was thinking, I think I'm more concerned about the impact they have within our country as opposed to outside our country in terms of developing perceptions. Sure, outside our country, they talk about how brutal we are, and we see all these things graphically in front of us. But so do our kids see this and they get to believing this is what it is all about. And I think they say that nothing good can come from something like September 11th. I've observed and I think I might have alluded to but not specifically said that up here that it has turned a lot of these people who are elected people—Mr. Longley, you know something about that—into changing their attitudes. People who would never vote to support national missile defense and that would never vote for modernizing the F-22, Joint Strike Fighter, any of these things, are turning around as a result of it. And, I would like to think that if we can turn around Hollywood, that would be another benefit that would have come from September 11th.

MR. McWETHY: Anybody else want to take a crack at Hollywood? Avis?

MS. BOHLEN: I don't want to take a crack at Hollywood, but I want to take a crack at long term strategic planning, which is something ever since I've been in the State Department, which is now getting on for three decades, it's something that we've spent a lot of time trying to figure out how to do and I am not sure we found the perfect answer. But I think it is, obviously, it is very important to look out there in the future. And I think at the base of the public diplomacy message has to be understanding other cultures that we are talking to, understanding of why this monstrous message has appeal, and you have to build your public diplomacy message on that. And, I think that is what the State Department, among other agencies, has to contribute. And, I think it has to be, as I said earlier, it has to be a long-term effort. You can't come in and out of—what regions have turned out to be of great strategic importance and expect to either understand what is going on or to be able to have an impact. So, I think that's an important long-term message.

MR. McWETHY: Yes, sir? In the blue shirt.

AUDIENCE MEMBER: Avon Williams. I'm with the Office of General Counsel for the United States Army. I noticed that, Ambassador Bremer, you endorsed having terrorists tried in courts of military justice. And I direct this question to both you and Mr. Feith. I understand some of the legal rationale for that, but of course, there is also a political rationale. And I was wondering if you might speak to that a little bit more extensively, especially with respect to not only the terrorists who we might capture in our operations overseas, but also the people who are currently in custody in the United States.

AMBASSADOR BREMER: Well, I'm not an attorney so I can't answer the second half of that. I don't know whether the Executive Order the President signed would retroactively affect people who are already in custody. I don't know the answer. Maybe Doug does. The reason I'm in favor of it is because justice, to be, you know, effective, has to be swift, and there is a precedent for this kind of military tribunal in the United States. It has been held constitutional by the Supreme Court. And, I think it can avoid a lot of the show trial aspects of terrorist trials, which has sometimes been a problem and which would certainly be a problem in the case of some of the terrorists we're after now. So I view it as a healthy idea. They will have full access to defense lawyers, which I might add in most of the countries they are coming from would not be the case. So I'm in favor of it.

MR. FEITH: I'm only half informed on the subject, so I don't want to comment on it now. Excuse me.

MR. McWETHY: Anybody in the back? Yeah. Way in the back. A gentleman in the last row.

AUDIENCE MEMBER: I'm Bob Brannon, a National Security Fellow up at Harvard's Kennedy School. My question concerns this new and evolving relationship that we seem to be nurturing with Russia, something that's playing itself out even as we speak today. What do you think Russia wants from us? And second, what do you think the risks might be to our national security inherent in nurturing this new relationship?

SPEAKER: You're the expert.

MS. BOHLEN: Well, I think that I would certainly agree with Jerry Bremer that that's been one of the most important developments that we have seen coming out of September 11th on the sort of political diplomatic front. My own assessment, for what it is worth, is that Putin—and I think this is an effort that really he personally directed—made a strategic choice following September 11th. He decided that this was his gateway to bringing Russia back onto the world stage in a constructive and positive way after a decade of wandering off in the wilderness more or less. I think he saw vindication for what he has been saying about the Islamic fundamentalists in Chechnya, which is I think a message that we were inclined to discount before September 11th as justification for what they were doing in Chechnya, which is reprehensible in many ways. But he was saying there are associates of Osama bin Laden with the Chechen rebels and the big threat is the threat of Islamic fundamentalism to the south. And I think he felt that message was vindicated. But thirdly, I think emotionally he wanted to be with the West in this fight. He didn't want to be with the enemies of the West.

What does he want from us? I think he is seeking above all a kind of integration into the West broadly defined. I think he would like closer relations with NATO. I think he has responded very sincerely and what the President has said about constructing a new relationship, and not just a new strategic relationship, I think that is something that has resonated. So he sees this as a chance to really put his relations with the West and with the United States, especially, on a new footing. And, there are a number of specific things. I think Jackson-Vanik is just extraordinarily important to the Russians. They see it as a symbol of the past that still continues to exist. The risks, I think, would be that he is not able to deliver his establishment. I stress Putin's role in this because I think there are some skeptics in Russia. I think there is still a lot of old thinking around, and I think that could impact on a lot of different issues. And I think we can't make ourselves hostage to Russian desiderata in this relationship. But I think it is a very positive development overall. I don't know if

MR. McWETHY: Senator?

SENATOR INHOFE: I think I had to jump in on this one because I think what they really need is help in getting out of this economic problem that they have over there right now. John mentioned in his introduction I flew an airplane around the world that was reenacting the Wiley Post flight on its 60th anniversary. That was 10 years ago. And I remember going across, all the way from Moscow all the way to Provodania, but we got about halfway across and you look down and you see—and many of you military guys know what I'm talking about—you look down and you see that vast wilderness, you see those natural resources, you see the wealth that's down there that's just there and it's untapped. And, of course, being from Oklahoma I'm sensitive to the petroleum opportunities and elsewhere.

Here is my concern. While they have very serious problems with their economy right now, they at the same time have been able to use their brainpower and their technology to develop systems that we haven't been able to develop. I mean right now—I mentioned in my opening remarks—we don't have the best of everything anymore. Now, you talk to some of the people in the Air Force, the best air-to-air vehicle we have is the F-15. They have the SU-27. It is better in certain ways and it is on the open market today. The same I could say about the F-16 and the air-to-ground comparing it to the SU-30. Now they're developing, along with the, you know, the Euro-Fighter and the Rafael come along. They're coming along with their—in Russia with the SU-35 and the SU-37. We've got to get ourselves modernized because if they get desperate enough they will continue to market that around the world, places where we don't want to be inferior in the sky. And they have that capability. So I think anything we can do to be of assistance to help them develop their resources so that they won't be dependent upon selling those vehicles places that could inflict harm on us would be to our benefit.

MR. McWETHY: More questions way in the back on the right.

AUDIENCE MEMBER: David DeGiorgi, EED Systems. To the question of why they hate us. There have been dominant powers through history and there's always the antipathy of those dominated towards those who are dominant. But it seems that the depth of this antipathy, the breadth now, is something that's almost unprecedented. And I'm wondering if there is something in the cultural context which is behind this that's allowing this to occur. There was a caption on the cover, I think it was the cover story, of the *New York Times* magazine this past weekend and it spoke of a woman in one of the Middle Eastern countries in her late 30s who had asked her, as I recall, asked her husband for permission to go and train for Jihad. This is not a twenty-something radical but a thirty-something housewife. What is it that—in their cultural context I think there is something deeper than just the dominant power.

AMBASSADOR BREMER: Well, you are right, Mr. DeGiorgi. Dominance always does provoke hatred and resentment. I think there are a couple of factors. First of all, we can't ignore the impact of the communications revolution that has been brought to many parts of the world in the last decade where people can communicate with each other through Al Jazeera, for example, or can see the parts of the American lifestyle they don't like by just watching cable television. It is true that you cannot explain a lot of this kind of terrorism that we're talking about by focusing on the traditional so-called root causes, the economic poverty and so forth. People who killed themselves on September 11th were universally from the upper-middle class, they were well educated. So, the consequence of going after the root cause there is to say we shouldn't have any wealthy Saudis around. It doesn't seem to me like that's a very good operational way to go at the terrorism problem.

The American culture offends lots of Americans, as the Senator pointed out, and it offends lots of people. I think—my own view—is the reason we are seeing a broad move towards fundamentalism in all of the three major monotheistic religions in the world in the last decade is because many people feel disrooted, deracine, from their fundamental beliefs, and they see that American culture, or what they conceive to be American culture purveyed often by Hollywood, is at the root of that particular evil. It's something that takes them away from the root of their religion. And this is one reason why bin Laden does have a broader appeal. But he's not just appealing to lunatics and criminals. He's appealing to people who really have a way of saying we need to turn back to the fundamentals of Islam. Now, by turning back he means really pretty far back, but it isn't, therefore, too surprising that you see that when you consider that there have been lots of people in the Christian and Jewish religions who have also said the way the world is developing, the modern world to me seems to be offensive to what I take to be the core beliefs of my religion. And how you deal with that to me is a—I mean this is a sociological problem of immense size that is not particularly a terrorism problem; it is a problem of how societies organize themselves. And there isn't an awful lot that any one person can do about it.

But let me make a point about Islam. The President has been careful, and so have his top leaders, to say over and over that this is not a war against Islam. And that is right. It certainly is not a war against Islam. But there is, today, a war within Islam, and it is between the people like bin Laden who want to define Islam the way that bin Laden defines it, essentially as turning back to the, what he takes to be, the roots of Islam even though they are misinterpreted, and between the moderate Islamic leaders who would not like to see him define Islam that way. And we have a huge stake in the moderate Islamic leaders winning that fight, a huge stake, because if, in the end, bin Laden and people like him can hijack Islam and define it the way bin Laden wants to define it, then this will become a war of civilizations. This will become a war against Islam. So we have a very big stake in encouraging moderate Islamic leaders from Detroit to Jakarta to stand up and say what bin Laden says about Islam is wrong. These people, as Doug pointed out, are not martyrs. They are apostates. They are not going to go to heaven and enjoy 72 black-eyed virgins. They are going to go to hell.

MR. McWETHY: Doug Feith?

MR. FEITH: It might be useful to approach this issue of terrorism also at a different level from a different angle. We see as much terrorism as we do not simply because the world has fanatics and irrational people. I think it is because if one looks back over the history of the last 30, 40, 50 years, there have been enough rewards for terrorism to persuade even rational people that it may not be a bad way to pursue specific political ends. The gentleman who asked about strategic thinking and diplomacy triggered the thought in my mind that if we really want to be strategic in our diplomacy, it is probably a good idea to remind ourselves of the importance of certain principles. When we talk about using every instrument of U.S. national power in this war on terrorism, we should be aware that our principles are among our crucial instruments of national power. There is a temptation often to sacrifice principle to short-term diplomatic convenience, cutting deals with terrorists to try to solve a particular problem. But the consequences are that decade after decade you are cutting deals with terrorist after terrorist. Some people start out being terrorists and then kill enough people over a long enough period of time that they come to be regarded as statesmen.

The problem with cutting deals with terrorists is that over time you create an incentive for people to engage in terrorism. We have had a declaratory policy about terrorism: that we don't reward terrorism, we don't deal with terrorists, that terrorism is an unacceptable means no matter what the cause. We've had a declaratory policy like that for many years, but the United States and many other countries in the world have had a policy in various contexts of embracing and rewarding terrorists. And, this should stop. And if we stop it is going to mean is we are going to have to pay the price in immediate inconvenience: not having the interlocutors that we are searching for in some places, because if you're really not willing to reward terrorists, if you are going to weed terrorists out of the community, then that means you are not going to have people to negotiate with on occasion. But if we're going to have a strategic approach to diplomacy and a principled approach on the war on terrorism, then we're just going to have to make that sacrifice.

MR. McWETHY: One might ask as you are doing your coalition-building the United States is also making accommodation to nations that we have specifically not had relations with because we don't like, not their terrorism policy, but almost every other policy that the United States has held dear. So when you talk about principles in this war you sacrifice one set to fight another set.

MR. FEITH: Well, that's an interesting point. But not every disagreement about policy is a matter of principle. Adjusting policies at given times to take into account the exigencies of the moment, that's national security policy making. You have to have a certain amount of flexibility. It would be a mistake to view every policy issue as a matter of principle. But I think it is sustainable to say that people who purposely murder innocents for political purposes have violated a principle and have disqualified themselves and should be viewed as people who have discredited rather than advanced their political causes.

AMBASSADOR BREMER: But John is quite right, that for example, as Avis pointed out, we had a very strong dislike for the human rights policies of Mr. Karimov, the President of Uzbekistan, which we were quite rightly, in my view, willing to put aside for the time being. And that's what diplomacy's about. You are always going to have trade-offs. There are no easy decisions. There are always going to be tradeoffs, and we made the right tradeoff in Uzbekistan in my view.

MS. BOHLEN: You can't have a sort of one-note relationship with countries.

MR. McWETHY: Young woman right there.

AUDIENCE MEMBER: Beth Dixon, a student at the Fletcher School. My question is really for Ambassador Bremer, but I'd like to hear from all three of you possibly. You mentioned the next state you envision the U.S. working with is the Sudan, the state of Sudan. And I'd just like to hear a little more about how you envision our relationship with them given their fundamentalist Islamic regime and the civil war they are currently waging against the south.

AMBASSADOR BREMER: My strategy for Phase Two, and since I don't work for the government you needn't be frightened by it, my strategy is you go after the weak links before you go after the strong links. And what I would like to see our government do is build the momentum on the back of success in Afghanistan, which I think is within sight now, and go to the weak links. And the two weak links, in fact, among the states are Libya and Sudan, both of which are still considered states which support terrorism, both of which have indicated since September 11th an interest in trying to get off that list and get right with us. And I would take advantage of that as a diplomatic opening. But I would give them essentially an ultimatum. I would say, "We are willing to work with you. We're willing to have you part of this coalition, but you're going to have to do X and Y, and you're going to have to do it by a fixed time and, by the way, there is no negotiation about it. And, we're prepared to act, if necessary, unilaterally and, if necessary, with all the force that America can bring to bear to be sure you comply with these requests, or we will consider you, in the words of the President, a hostile regime." And I would try to build some momentum by knocking off some of these relatively weaker links in the terrorism international, and build momentum forward towards the Palestinian Authority, Lebanon, and Syria and basically leave Iraq for the end unless there is evidence that Iraq was involved—unless more evidence, there is evidence— unless evidence is conclusively shown that Iraq was involved, I would leave it to the end. I'd work with the small guys forward. And with the Sudanese one of the things one would have to say is you got to stop slave trading. It is the only government in the world that I know of where the government itself actively still is involved in slave trading. You've got to stop the war in the south. But I think there is an opportunity with Sudan and I think we ought to seize it.

MR. McWETHY: We have ten minutes. Wait a minute. Anybody on this side? Sir?

AUDIENCE MEMBER: Good morning. I'm Bob Ivany from the United States Army War College. During the last several weeks, there has been a lot of discussion about what is the true center of gravity, that is, the strategic center of gravity, in this war against terrorism. That is the one point that we should direct all our military, economic, and political efforts. I would just like to ask the panel for their view as to what that true strategic center of gravity is.

MR. McWETHY: I'm sure Doug knows the answer to that.

MR. FEITH: I had suggested that it is focusing on the territorial base for the terrorist operations. I think that—as Ambassador Bremer pointed out—

one is not necessarily going to be able to prevent all people ever from conducting terrorism. But I wouldn't say that victory means that nobody will ever
commit a terrorist act again. The ability of terrorist organizations to plan large-
scale actions over a long period of time depends to a very large extent on their
having a base of operations that they can do undisturbed work from. And I
think that if we approach the terrorist problem that way, we can avoid the
problem of dividing our attention among numerous cells and organizations all
over the world. We can't chase every snake. There is a value in draining the
swamp, rather than trying to chase every snake. That's another way of saying
that we should go after terrorism on a large scale by focusing on the territorial bases.

AUDIENCE MEMBER: Dick Diamond from Raytheon. I was trying to
square what the panel had said about the unprecedented premier position of
the U.S. with why they don't like us in the Muslim world with what
Ambassador Bremer said about sooner or later we've got to get back and finish
the job in Iraq. And I was wondering about the linkage there. I was trying to
think of one of those former empires that would allow a festering sore like that
on its border for 10 years with no particular protector in the world, with clearly roughish acts. And I'm wondering what the panel thinks are the linkages
between the fact that the Islamic world disrespects us for the fact that we have
imposed sanctions on the Iraqi people for ten years, but have been powerless
to sort of overturn the government. And I wonder how much the fact that we
have unable to deal with Saddam has allowed those countries that harbor terrorism to think that they can get away with it and be outside the reach of the
U.S.

MR. McWETHY: Any hands going up?

AMBASSADOR BREMER: I'm happy to answer it. I think you are right. I
think you've put your finger on an important fact, which is that the decade of
policies we've had towards Iraq have been probably the worst combination of
all. We have managed to impose sanctions which don't hurt the government
we're after and hurt the people and allow, therefore, that fact to be broadcast
throughout the region while not having finished the job we started in 1991,
which, therefore, undercuts the respect for our power in the region. It would
be hard to conceive actually of a worse policy, except one which started an
inspection regime and then stopped it, which is also what we did. It is a mark
of the fecklessness of American foreign policy towards Iraq over the last
decade that we still have to talk about it. It is a major problem we are going to
have to return to. Whether we return to it as part of this campaign because it
is shown that Iraq was involved in this terrorism or whether we deal with it
because it is the major threat to regional security, sooner or later some

American government, whether this one or the next one, hopefully this one, is going to have to deal with the threat that Iraq poses.

MS. BOHLEN: I'd just add to that. I don't want to get into a whole discussion of this which is an immensely complex subject, but I would just point out that I don't think really that Osama bin Laden was motivated to do what he did, or emboldened to do what he did, by the lack of whatever we didn't do in Iraq. And, secondly, the same countries that are criticizing us for both for not finishing the job and for causing babies to starve will be the first to turn against us if we take more consequential action.

AMBASSADOR BREMER: I don't agree with that at all, Avis. I think if we decide [to undertake operations] in Iraq, we will find much more support in the region than we will in Europe. I think the Europeans will be nervous. But, I think if we show—and that's why what we are doing in Afghanistan is so important. We need to show that America is prepared to use all that power we have relentlessly and ruthlessly to pursue our objectives. And once we establish that fact it becomes easier to deal with Sudan and Libya, as I mentioned earlier, and it becomes much easier to deal with Iraq because people in the region will realize for once we're serious.

MR. McWETHY: Final question from the audience. You're it. Is there one back there? I'm sorry. Way in the back.

AUDIENCE MEMBER: Scott Flower from the Association of United States Army. Thanks, Mr. McWethy. All of you have alluded to information and intelligence. I would like to ask if this was a problem that existed before September 11th and it's been brought into sharp focus. I would like to ask each of you what you would do to improve intelligence operations within the government and, without being flip or irreverent, I would like you to avoid using the word "share."

SENATOR INHOFE: I'll start off. You know, one of the criticisms I had when we were talking about our intelligence back in the early 90s when we had the problems at our energy labs and, you know, just very obvious things that could have been prevented. And I'm sure the problems that are there are problems that are overseas also. When we went through just because we thought it might be demeaning to someone, we stopped using color-coded badges at our labs, we stopped doing background checks, we stopped doing a lot of the things that we had done before to stop the compromises that are taking place only to find out that there have been some 16 compromises in our labs, and now the Chinese and others have almost everything that we had that we were holding in confidence. You know, I look at this and I don't know how the program is going to go from this point forward, but I'm hoping that somebody out here cares about what we're doing conventionally if you'll forgive me, John, for just deviating a little bit here.

There are some things that we can do that we ought to be doing, and they are very obvious. I mean you talk about Iraq. We allowed them to kick out our weapons inspectors. Now we don't know what's over there. We have our kids going over right now on deployments from the East Coast where they're not properly trained. We have the USS *Roosevelt* over there right now. They did not get live-fire training because we allowed a bunch of lawbreakers to kick us out off of the live range at Vieques. We have the—I think the *JFK* is going to be deployed in January, and I think we should be looking at this saying, "All right. Let's make this is a mission that we're going to make sure that they are trained," because when they get over there they are actually involved in combat. And people have to understand that everything that's happening in the world isn't all happening in Afghanistan because we're at war elsewhere, too.

We have obvious things that we can do. Go up to the 21st TACOM (Tank and Automotive Command). You see that they are using M119 trucks that have a million miles on them and you could use just the amount of money you pay for maintenance every three years to buy a new fleet. You know, some of the obvious things that are out there that we need to deal with on a conventional score. And, that's why I said in my opening remarks, let's not sacrifice our conventional capabilities with all these theoretical things and with fighting these wars that—against terrorism. We've got to be prepared for the future, but we also have to use our resources that we have right now to defend America and defend our young troops that are over there who are fighting with inferior equipment. I forgot what the question is, but that's the answer. (Laughter)

MR. McWETHY: It's a great answer. Spoken like a true Senator. More evidence of why you are where you are, Senator. (Laughter) I'd like to give everybody just a brief moment to sum up.

MR. FEITH: My brief answer to the question would be: more and better human intelligence.

MS. BOHLEN: I would second that. I think we—the first thing we have to do is to decide our priorities. And I think we clearly have given a low priority to this particular area where we now have troops fighting over the past couple of years and I think we need to take a look at those priorities. It means money in the U.S. government and I go back to building the cadres of specialists that can help us with language, with understanding, and that's whether they are State Department or intelligence people. And, I'm sorry, I would like to say sharing, but…

AMBASSADOR BREMER: You can't have a counterterrorist policy without good intelligence. And the only good intelligence—really the only good intelligence against terrorist groups—is human intelligence, as Doug mentioned. The CIA, over the last two and a half decades, has evolved into a risk-averse culture. A problem that was exacerbated by guidelines which President Clinton put into effect in 1995 that made the recruitment of terrorist spies more difficult and in fact discouraged case agents in the field from doing it, as our commission pointed out. So, we need to have better collection. We need better analysts. A lot of talk today about better linguists. That's—there's no question. And we need better dissemination of intelligence. If you don't like the word "sharing" then the word I'd use is we need to have a seamlessness in the intelligence and law enforcement information world where intelligence is moving back and forth across what used to be Chinese walls between these two. And, again, the Anti-Terrorist Bill that the President signed two weeks ago goes a long way to starting that process.

MR. McWETHY: I'd like to thank the panelists for giving time from their very busy days. It's a wild time. Also, I'd like to make note of how many Army officers are here, and the top leaders of the Army. That's very impressive to spend your day kicking around ideas like this. General Shinseki, General Keane, General Meigs, all of my friends and colleagues from the Army. We are finished. This is your first go-around. You'll begin again in about 15 minutes I think. (Applause)

LUNCHEON ADDRESS

THE ECONOMIC INSTRUMENT OF NATIONAL POWER

Mr. Sean O'Keefe, Deputy Director, Office of Management and Budget

Summary

• *The United States is experiencing an entirely new economic reality since September 11. The aftermath of the terrorist attacks sparked a spirited debate regarding our priorities, economic capacity, and wherewithal to deal with a range of national policy questions. History has shown that similar debates, while grounded in economic realities, are primarily political in nature.*

1. In the late 1980s, it was a working assumption that the persistent structural deficit was unavoidable for the foreseeable future. It was argued that a constitutionally mandated balanced budget was the only means to end deficit spending. Sustained growth during the 1990s negated this assumption.

2. As of September 10, the latest debate focused on the size and allocation of the budget surplus and protecting social security by placing it in a "lock box." In reality, however, all excess revenue was used to service the national debt. Therefore, the discussion was also political, not economic.

3. The President has consistently stated that his intention is to maintain a balanced budget unless we encounter war, recession, or national emergency. On September 11, we met all three criteria and shifted our national security dialogue from resource availability to a political debate of priorities and requirements.

• *There is no question that the United States has the economic capacity to meet our current and future national security requirements. Despite the current recession, our $10 trillion economy is robust, resilient, and very resourceful. The greatest policy imperatives of our new economic reality are not questions of resource, but of organization and prioritization.*

1. The first issue is meeting the rapidly rising requests from federal agencies for funds to deal with the September 11th aftermath and future homeland security needs in a period of declining revenue.

2. The second challenge is defining homeland security in broad organizational terms, as well as specific programs and resources—and deciding at

what level the federal government should be involved.

3. The third effect of the attacks will be a continuing debate about future strategy and force structure. Of particular concern will be whether and how a transformation of policy and/or the military is needed, and how the pursuit of such goals should be prioritized with respect to legacy forces and procedures.

Analysis

In his address, Mr. O'Keefe pointed out that the United States has the economic capacity to meet current national security challenges. The current debate on resources and priorities, like similar discussions in our recent history, is a political issue, not an economic challenge. In the late 1980s Americans assumed a deficit was inevitable and could be reduced only by a constitutional amendment to require a balanced budget. But in recent years, the debate centered not on an inevitable deficit, but on how large the *surplus* should be and the need to protect Social Security revenue. Since September 11, the debates on the surplus and the "lockbox" have given way to a new set of imperatives.

America must now determine how best to respond to the immediate challenges posed by the war against terrorism. The $40 billion supplemental authorization bill, requested by the President and approved by Congress shortly after the September attacks, gave the President unprecedented authority to allocate resources and meet the nation's immediate needs. But the $1.25 billion requested by federal agencies since September for consequence management and homeland defense illustrates the magnitude of the current homeland security challenge. Congress and the Executive Branch must now determine the appropriate role of the federal government, including the military, in homeland security in order to determine the resource requirements.

Mr. O'Keefe suggested, in light of the September 11th attacks that the national security strategy be altered to address potential changes to the military's transformation objectives. These and other resource demands strain our economic capacity. However, the $10 trillion U.S. economy is indeed resilient, and debates are ongoing about how best to stimulate the economy to return to the unprecedented growth rates of the past decade.

Mr. O'Keefe reinforced themes heard in the conference's first panel: the yet-to-be-defined requirements for homeland defense, determination of the extent and pace of transformation, and the need to prioritize the requirements resulting from the terrorist attacks. Mr. O'Keefe emphasized that we cannot assume this current economic reality will persist. Just as the economy experienced a period of recurrent deficits and sustained surplus in the last two decades, the future will continue to be dynamic. The nation is at the start of a new economic period. The events of September 11th require national security leaders to move beyond theoretical concepts and begin the hard, yet necessary, debate on our current requirements and priorities.

Transcript

DR. PFALTZGRAFF: Ladies and gentlemen, may I have your attention, please? I know that everyone has been enjoying a very good lunch and a very good conversation. I know at our table that has been the case and I'm sure elsewhere as well. But now we must get back to even more serious work and discussion and turn to our luncheon speaker. I have great pleasure in introducing Sean O'Keefe whom I have known for many years. His present position of course is that of Deputy Director of the Office of Management and Budget and he has just been nominated, I should add just this morning, to be administrator of NASA (National Aeronautics and Space Administration). In his present position, he oversees the preparation, management, and administration of the federal budget and government-wide management initiatives across the executive branch. He brings some very special qualifications to the discussion of the economic instruments of national power, which is the area that we asked him to focus upon in his remarks at lunch today.

Sean O'Keefe has had a long and very strong interest in national security and specifically in defense policy. In 1992 and 1993 for example, he served as Secretary of the Navy. He served as Comptroller and Chief Financial Officer of the Department of Defense from 1989 until 1992. He also has been a staff member of the Senate Appropriations Committee dealing with defense issues. Just before assuming his present position, Sean was a Professor of Business at Syracuse University. I should say he holds a degree from that school as well. He was Director of National Security Studies overseeing executive education programs for senior military and civilian Department of Defense managers. Last but not least, Sean O'Keefe is the author of numerous publications on defense and public policy issues. Therefore it is with very great pleasure, personal and professional, that I welcome Sean O'Keefe as our speaker here today. (Applause.)

MR. O'KEEFE: Thank you, Bob, for a very thoughtful, warm introduction. It is reminiscent—I believe it was the Lyndon Johnson line that my father would have been impressed and my mother would have actually believed it. I think as he walked resume items to include this morning's announcement it dawns on me that most folks who would consider such a checkered set of experiences would lead to the conclusion that I have a difficult time holding a job. My wife reminds me of that with regularity. I am always trying to determine what it is I want to do when I finally find the opportunity to settle into something. But nonetheless it has been a varying set of experiences, and I appreciate spending the time with some friends here who I have known over the course of lots of years of professional experience in the national security field and certainly in the resource management business as well. The topic of an economic instrument of national power is a daunting challenge. The

Mr. O'Keefe

assumption would be you have some extensive or thoughtful treatise on what the economic prowess globally could be or in the United States very specifically to bring to bear on the question of national security in international affairs issues or a range of different applications. I am not so qualified to give you an economic treatise of that variety. As a matter of fact, all of my colleagues and friends at Syracuse University would be aghast if they thought I was impersonating an economist, in this particular situation. But I remind them that economists are merely those who aspired to be accountants but didn't have the personality. So as a consequence let me focus a slightly different bent on this.

And speak to the economic instrument of national power that we possess, that we bring to bear that has changed so dramatically in the course of the last two months. And how that will bear on the overall kinds of issues and problems that we have to sort through. First and foremost it is important to kind of reach back just a little bit of time, not more than about ten years, and consider and think in terms of what the burning national debate was not, more than ten years ago. It was a working assumption that there would be no prospect at all of anything short of a continued sustained persistent structural deficit. The commonly held view among politicians, statesmen, policy makers, economists, and the like was that it was simply a fact of life that we were stuck in a grind of persistent annual deficit spending, and that would be our condition we would have to sort with year in and year out. Which always required therefore some sense of concern of exactly how you deficit finance as well as how you would service that debt that was accruing during of course of that time. Spirited debate at the time also, albeit a minority view, was that in time given the right circumstances of economic performance, that we would grow our way out of that problem. Well, that minority view proved to be more the truth or more the reality than any other forecast at that time.

It isn't too long ago to recall the nature of the debate was consistently to debate annually the question of a constitutional amendment to require a balanced budget. We've achieved that without that very extensive action on the part of the Congress, but nonetheless, it was that debate that brought around that particular view. And were it not for the extraordinary expansion we experienced in the 1990s arguably we would have remained in that deficit spending condition for some period. Just by way of statistics, it was a position in which we annually spent on the order of magnitude of $200 to $250 billion more than what we took in as revenue. That was again an accepted condition by some; by others it was to be argued and worked out of and statutorily dealt with if need be. As it proved that no statute is ever going to have quite the effect that the economic performance could have. Nonetheless, in the course of the last few years we have been in an interesting debate. One I frankly don't recognize at all having spent time in Washington in the deficit debate days, of an argument over exactly what size should the surplus be.

On September 10th the debate that was brewing mightily and the arguments that we were engaged in with tremendous amounts of enthusiasm with our friends on Capitol Hill was whether the size of the surplus should be enormous or merely just immense. There was a term that was used with absolute regularity, in every newspaper, every single day, typically on the front page somewhere, referring to a lock box. I haven't heard that term since September 11th. For the argument was and the debate was that we should set aside a percentage of what we bring in as revenue each year for social security revenue, as if somehow it went into some separate special account for that purpose. Indeed, and I think as most know, the condition is that all proceeds given the unified budget were used for the purpose of paying down the national debt, including social security revenues in excess of payments to individuals. So the nature of the debate and the argument was a political argument. Not an economic one. Indeed, I would suggest that the nature of the debate and argument ten years ago and the argument of balanced budget amendments and everything else were also on the order of a political debate as well.

The conditions have changed dramatically since September 11th, and as a consequence of that there is now a new set of imperatives to be sure. Some of which are real, some of which have a very profound effect on our economic capacity, our capacity to produce, and to afford and the wherewithal to deal with a range of national policy questions. And some of it is much like the nature of the debate 10 to 15 years ago over the issue of balanced budget amendments, or lock boxes, a very political argument. And again, that is not a derogatory term. It is the nature of policy, debate among individuals over the question of what political arguments will be. So as a consequence I think we're experiencing an entirely different circumstance. One that is very much not like the deficit days, certainly not like the surplus experiences of arguing over how much should be reserved for some other set of purposes optimally when indeed it is reserved for the same purposes we've always used them for.

But instead now it is an argument and debate, a spirited one, a very earnest one, over exactly what should be the nature of our priorities and what is our economic capacity to afford. The President has been very specific in arguing that his intention would be to maintain a balanced budget unless we encountered war, recession, or an emergency. Well, shortly after September 11th unfortunately we have hit the trifecta. We've encountered all three of those conditions in the course of this span of time. And our greatest challenge I think can be summarized in three areas and I'll leave this for food for thought and I'll open it for questions, comments, and dialogue but I hope we provoke some thought on how we sort through these three items in specific in terms of the kind of imperatives we need to deal with.

The first issue, I think, is very much a question of how to respond to the immediate challenges that emerged since September 11th. There is no question our economic capacity to afford and to provide for, inasmuch as we are, to be sure, in a position dramatically different than that we experienced on September 11th. We're now looking at two successive quarters of negative gross domestic product expansion as a result, that's a double negative, an actual contraction of the economy, as it were, of slightly less than 1%. As a result of that we are clearly on our way towards what is defined by classical economists as a recessionary period. Not a big surprise, but nonetheless has an enormous effect on what the overall revenue would be and what the projections will be for the foreseeable future. Nonetheless we are still dealing with a $10 trillion economy. One that, while you see a contraction which doesn't portend the continued expansion that we've experienced over the course of the last ten years, it nonetheless is a very robust, very resilient, extremely resourceful economy in that regard. . . Okay, three imperatives, I think, can be narrowed to [inaudible]. It is how to sort through the immediate aftermath of disasters of September 11th.

The Congress in a historic expeditious manner enacted a supplemental appropriations measure for emergency response within days of the event and provided the most broad-based sweeping authority that any President in the United States that I have ever heard of or anyone else I have been associated with had ever considered possible. What it did was provide the authority to the President for 20 of that 40 billion to respond with virtually no notification to all the things that are happening at that time. For debris removal in New York City, the repair of the Pentagon, immediate assistance for the victims involved, a range of different circumstances that required immediate response. It was quite remarkable and quite unprecedented in terms of the authority granted by the Congress to the chief executive of the United States. But in doing so there was a range of expectations and aspirations that grew beyond that. Forty billion was considered to be an absolutely preposterously large number, more than adequate to cover anything imaginable.

Not so fast. Within a matter of about ten days the federal agencies and departments of the federal government generated requests sufficient to absorb about 125 billion. Well, it doesn't take a high math expert to realize there is no way you are going to stretch that to a factor of three. So the expectations and the demands are well beyond what anybody would reasonably expect, and for largely issues, problems, and concerns that are immediate consequences of the aftermath of September 11th. As in immediate remediation that's required, but also a range of different objectives that are recovery oriented. Intended to be more long term in their permanency. Think of it in terms of security measures. You can either establish some temporary security measures that are labor or personnel intensive, or you can erect a more comprehensive force protection if you will a kind of regime that will take more in terms of resources, as well as time, effort, and energy. But all of that is accomplished in a larger set of expectations. This is not restrictive of the federal department and agencies.

The Congress of the United States in an effort to respond to a range of things have been considering actively a range of proposals that, based on our last count, total easily $200 billion dollars, all of which have some direct consequence or linkage or in some cases very indirect consequence or linkage depending on your circumstances to the immediate events in the aftermath of September 11th. So that is one set of concerns is the immediacy of the kinds of problems—what is it we really require, what do we want to do? Quite frankly the response from the President has been let's press on, move on with the initial supplemental funding, and do what we need to do to deal with the immediate problems and then let's sort through this and determine what those requirements are down the road. And as in nowadays, down the road means weeks, not months or years. It is a continuing process that develops on a real-time basis.

The second challenge I would suspect, and it is going to be a real refinement of the kinds of challenges that will place great pressure on our economic instrument of national power, is how we define what the requirements are for homeland security. This is something that there have been lots of commissions, every one in this room is well aware of panels, commissions, blue ribbon groups, all kinds of folks who have talked about what the consequences of homeland security should be and how it should be defined—more broadly in terms of an organizational context or in terms of very specific programs and resources. That to be sure is going to be the focus and the concentration of attention over the course of the next several months and the next few years in terms of how we redefine what we've talked about in an academic or, if you will, theoretical context. We now see the graphic consequences of the challenges of something as basic as intragovernmental coordination between federal, state, local law enforcement first responders. That's a term that's now rolling off the lips of those journalists.

If you had said that two months ago, they wouldn't have had a clue what a first responder was. Now it is part of the lingo. And that is part of the challenge of sorting through what level and activism does the government want to be involved in, the federal government specifically in these sets of challenges. You are seeing it played out in the context of right-now debates on the aviation security bill for example. Very spirited difference of view over how extensive that regime needs to be and exactly what component should be consumed in that. There are those who would believe if you make that as complex and as in-depth as some would like the aviation security provisions to be, you would guarantee that one passenger will board each aircraft. It will be a very efficient way to do it, but it will be restricted to one. Because while everybody else will be left in line as the plane takes off getting through the security regime.

Those are the kinds of problems we'll dealing with in addition to what is the range of requirements that are necessary, numbers of people required, whether screeners will be federal work force officials, all kinds of different implications like that. And those have enormous consequences in terms of the overall cost as well as a strain on our economic capacity at a very time when our economic capacity is being challenged. So how this becomes defined is a more broad-based construct than what has typically been viewed by many as a counterterrorism response. This now becomes a much more expansive kind of debate. It includes and encompasses a wide range of capabilities. Yet to be defined. And could be very consequential in terms of its organizational implications as well as to be sure of the resource implications that will flow from it.

The third and final piece I think has been a continuing debate, certainly in the course of this Administration, is what ultimately will portend as a consequence and revisions to the strategy review which may be necessitated as a result of the events of September 11th. The concern over what transformation should look like, what constitutes transformation, definitionally, and in turn how rapidly you should go about doing that and can you afford to abandon legacy procedures and approaches and force structure and programs in your pursuit of some transformation is a continuing raging debate. But one that translates into if you maintain both, it will be more expensive than it is today to be sure. Therefore again putting a greater and greater strain on what the overall consequence and economic impact will be in this fragile period in which we're trying to respond to that.

And again with these three pressures coming to bear, the immediacy, redefinitions of homeland security, and a refinement, a thinking through of exactly what the national security strategy may portend or import as a consequence of these dramatic revisions in turn will all place enormous resource requirements on what is right now our fragile economic condition and how we provide for this. Again, a great point to take heart in is again we're dealing with a very resilient capacity of a $10 trillion economy, for which the Congress of the United States right now is brewing over whether a $100 billion stimulus package will be sufficient to jump start. You do the math.

It is one that is very much an issue of how do you provide impetus stimulus capability that will at least move or prod along some elements of what may be sluggish in this economy, but the very notion that somehow we can do something along the lines of what we experienced as classical or more traditional definitions a economist would view as Keynesian economics by either spending or specific tax provisions that will have a dramatic impact on what the economy will do, this is comparatively a spit in the bucket. But it is nonetheless one that has some.

[inaudible]...thought and debate where we can engage in more of a dialogue where we are not talking at you. I want to thank you for the opportunity to be here, it is a great pleasure to be here with the Fletcher School.

DR. PFALTZGRAFF: It is a great pleasure to have you Sean with us, why don't you have some ice tea or water and we can offer you, we have some cold soup here too. In any event we have a few moments for discussion or comments. Who would like to ask the first question? Please raise your hand.

AUDIENCE MEMBER: I am an analyst with Credit Suisse First Boston. In light of, sir, the comment that you made regarding expanding the expectations, we have heard all kinds of numbers of where the defense budget could be going as a trajectory could be going as a result of the next 5 or 6 years, can you limit our expectations, or sort of lay a groundwork at least for what the expectations should or can be?

MR. OKEEFE: The short answer is no. I think it is yet to be determined. The more central question that is going to drive a set of answers to the question of how big this is going to be or how attractive whatever else, depends largely, but not exclusively, on the proposition I laid out earlier which is to the extent that you decide is that there is a consensus, that's quite a leap of faith in itself, that we could actually define what would constitute transformation, identify programs, initiatives, specific policies, there are lots of ideas on that front but exactly how that is going to gel in a very specific way is still at the formative stage. There is still a lot more debate and discussion going on that is certainly beginning to coalesce around a number of different ideas or initiatives. But if you pursue those, concurrent with the maintenance of a legacy type of position, it is going to translate into substantially more resource requirements. The alternative is you pursue both and do both poorly. And that's part of the challenge to pursue this kind of agenda or strategy concurrently but nonetheless is an imperative brought home and made more clear to us by the September 11th events. That said, I think that we are looking at again the difference between how I began this discussion of how we once viewed the question of surplus whether it is enormous or just merely immense.

AUDIENCE MEMBER: I'm Suzanne Carlton, Department of the Army.

MR. O'KEEFE: Hi, Suzanne.

AUDIENCE MEMBER: Recently I saw a group of CEOs in corporate America offering to come to the aid of the military and the government in whatever way their corporations could assist this new transformation, so to speak, we are trying to achieve. Is anything being done to channel that sector and overcome some of the procurement legislation all the things that does to a very slow process to help quickstart companies that are hurting to channel their energy to help the country move along here.

MR. OKEEFE: Absolutely. I think that is a very good point and frankly I have been stunned in the course of the last couple of months by the speed and agility with which this federal process can move when properly focused in this regard but it takes specifics, that's the catch. And I'll give you two points. I think they are really worth driving home. First one is there is a specific set of cases. I'll give you one really right off the bat, it came up just the other day kind of example, in which the Federal Bureau of Investigation has been for some time working on an effort to substantially upgrade its information technology systems for information that I think you could use any amount of your imagination to determine what it is that they would use that capacity for.

I'll leave it at that.

But the purpose is to speed up that process and move along. Every single effort from a contractual standpoint with every corporation, with every contracting official, whatever who have identified specific circumstances in which they need to move that particular contract action along accelerated to meet a very ambitious timetable that the FBI Director I think appropriately laid down for its initiation and initial action, all of which are well within the parameters of existing law. And all it takes is identifying what those limitations are, and then moving on expeditiously to move all of the impediments and the usual challenges that would otherwise occupy our time out of the way because we now have an objective that is so clearly understood that you can use existing law. And indeed, the concern initially was raised, we have to get a law to waive the following requirements on a very cursory examination ascertained as how there is absolutely no legal statutory impediment whatsoever to do what they want to do. It is all within the parameters of existing law. It is all a question of focus. It is astounding to see how well that can be deployed.

Second one is, there is a very specific provision of law that the President has proposed which establishes a procedure for the elimination of specific statutory impediments to efficiency. To doing what it is we think managerially as managers within the federal establishment are necessary in order to do this. And he named it himself, the Freedom to Manage Act. What it sets up in a very simple, no-frills way is a process by which each year if there is identified a specific set of provisions of law that get in the way of doing the work much like your question poses as a context, that we can put that under an expedited procedure for immediate Congressional consideration for which they will be required within a very specified period of time to vote to sustain that particular requirement or statute or repeal it. Very rapid process for that consideration. That kind of discussion would never even be enjoined as a serious debate or serious question of public administration were it not for the events of September 11th I would suggest. Now it is focused the mind and attention in a way that says we don't want to have something that is an impediment that serves a very narrow set of purposes, it statutorily is in place, it would otherwise impede a response for the protection of the citizens of the United States.

Here is the rub. What I found fascinating in a cursory request and review from departments and agencies is among the things that are perceived to be statutorily impeding much like this FBI analogy, most of it melts away as soon as you say I have a process to get rid of it. Suddenly you've come to find out that it really isn't a statute at all. It may be some interpretation of some report language long ago forgotten as to why it got there that suddenly has crept into in the way we do business, simply because that is the way we've always done business. As so a result, no one is even left alive who can remember what the genesis of it was, but that's the way we are doing it. In which you come to find out like the old Pogo cartoon would suggest, we have met the enemy and it is us. More often than not the impediments to this kind of circumstances are not statutory, they are not regulatory, they are typically because we've interpreted for a set of reasons legitimately with good faith, rarely in malice, that ultimately has us in a process for which that has served that purpose.

This particular provision, I think, the President really hit on something hereby proposing this Freedom to Manage Act provision is going to be useful for the purpose of specifically repealing a set of provisions of law that are impediments, but more importantly, it is going to work in those 99% of the cases in which those impediments don't exist at all, but it now gives you a means, a way to answer that particular process and assertion each time it is raised that we can't do efficiently because the law says we can't. Now you have a rhetoric that says show me the law. And if you can't show me the law, then do it. And that's a very different mindset, interesting cultural managerial mindset change of how I think we are going to be doing business in the future.

Thank you for the question.

DR. PFALTZGRAFF: Thank you very much, Sean, for this outstanding presentation. We should end on this upbeat note, if there's not a law, let's do it. We thank you for being with us and understand that there are many more questions, but the art of good public speaking is to stimulate so many questions that you cannot possibly answer them in the time available. And you've done that brilliantly. So we thank you very much for being with us today. May I suggest also that we should move rapidly back into the theater where the afternoon session will begin in approximately ten minutes. In fact at exactly 1:30. (Applause.)

PANEL 2

THE ROLE OF MILITARY POWER
IN A COMPLEX ENVIRONMENT

Chair: Dr. Robert L. Pfaltzgraff, Jr., President, Institute for Foreign Policy
    Analysis

The Honorable Curt Weldon, Republican, Pennsylvania, Chairman,
    Procurement Subcommittee, House Armed Services Committee

General Wesley Clark, U.S. Army, Retired, former Supreme Allied
    Commander, Europe

Rear Admiral Kathleen Paige, U.S. Navy, Systems Technical Director,
    Ballistic Missile Defense Organization

Lieutenant General Edward G. Anderson III, U.S. Army, Deputy
    Commander in Chief, U.S. Space Command

General Barry R. McCaffrey, U.S. Army, Retired, former Commander in
    Chief, U.S. Southern Command, and former Director, Office of
    National Drug Control Policy

Panel Charter

The United States possesses the strongest military force in world history.
Nevertheless, as the recent terrorist attacks have demonstrated, adversaries
have studied our successes, noted our strengths, identified our weaknesses,
and developed asymmetric means to attempt to destroy our resolve and undermine our strength. Our armed forces, in conjunction with the other instruments of national power, must remain vigilant to deter, dissuade, and take
necessary action to defeat such adversaries.

The ability to apply decisive military force at the appropriate time and place
is indispensable for the United States to provide for its security. The U.S. military must maintain a high level of readiness and operational flexibility. Among
other things, this calls for information dominance as a key element of power.
The quality of information in advance of the use of military capabilities and as
part of situational awareness during the conflict is essential if we are to minimize
the fog of war. In the broadened security spectrum of the twenty-first century,

the U.S. military faces a broad range of potential missions, extending from deterring the use of weapons of mass destruction against our deployed forces, our homeland, and our allies/coalition partners to the ability to project and maintain forces capable of operating for prolonged periods overseas in hostile environments. Such diverse contingencies make necessary a military capability that is lethal, mobile, agile, and flexible. In order to build and maintain such a force, we must draw the appropriate balance between the readiness of present capabilities and the modernization that will be needed to create tomorrow's military.

Among the threats faced by the United States is the possibility of a ballistic missile attack. Therefore, the United States places high priority on developing and deploying an effective missile defense system. This includes the defense of the U.S. population as well as of military forces and extension of protection to our allies. The importance of missile defense arises from the increasing proliferation of missiles and WMD warheads to larger numbers of states and other actors as well. The timelines for deploying a missile defense appear to be narrowing as missile and warhead technologies become more readily available to additional states and perhaps nonstate entities. Missiles represent a potential capability for asymmetrical warfare against the United States and its allies/coalition partners.

Our armed forces, no less than the private commercial sector, have grown more reliant on space-based assets. The overall U.S. dependence on space is increasing at a rapid pace, especially as a result of the need to acquire and transmit information whether in the military arena or in the private sector. In many cases, commercial satellites are utilized to carry military information. At the same time, the vulnerabilities of the United States—in space and from space—are multiplying. This includes space-based communications, reconnaissance, and surveillance systems. This trend will only accelerate in the coming decades. As a result, space will become an arena of growing importance for national security. This fact presents numerous issues for consideration in this panel session such as the relationship between operations in space and overall U.S. security strategy and the priorities to be attached to space. These include the challenges that the United States is likely to confront to its civil, commercial, defense, and intelligence interests in space.

In the early twenty-first century, the U.S. armed forces are undergoing their most extensive transformation in more than a century. Our armed forces are being shaped by a Revolution in Military Affairs. This trend includes new generation weapons systems based on innovative applications of information-age technologies. As such change proceeds, the U.S. military must also be prepared to respond to threats and challenges across the spectrum, including the use of military forces in support of operations other than war. The effort to feed Afghanistan's population, even as the United States engages in military operations, represents an obvious present example. In other words, the U.S. military is being called upon to undertake an unprecedented number of

Left to Right: *The Honorable Curt Weldon, Lieutenant General Edward G. Anderson III, Rear Admiral Kathleen Paige, General Wesley Clark, Dr. Robert L. Pfaltzgraff, Jr., General Barry R. McCaffrey, and Dr. Jacquelyn K. Davis*

diverse tasks. This panel provided an unusual opportunity to address issues directly related to the appropriate balance between modernizing for the future and remaining ready for today's challenges across that spectrum.

Discussion Points

  • In light of the broadened conflict setting, what are the most important readiness requirements for the United States military?

  • What impact will Operation Enduring Freedom have on military readiness?

  • What are U.S. military modernization priorities in light of the events of September 11?

  • What are the requirements for application of decisive force as a key component of national security strategy?

  • What role will missile defense will play in U.S. national security policy? What will be the role of allies?

  • What are the R&D and acquisition priorities for missile defense? How will the types of missile defense—ground-based, sea-based, space-based—fit together?

• Why is space an integral part of overall national security strategy, including elements such as space situational awareness, surveillance from space, and C4I?

• What types of capabilities will the United States need to provide assured access to space and improved homeland security?

Summary

The Honorable Curt Weldon (R-PA), Chairman, Procurement
Subcommittee, House Armed Services Committee

• September 11th should not have been the wakeup call. The call should have come in 1993 after the first bombing of the World Trade Center, in 1998 with the embassy bombings in Africa, or in 2000 with the bombing of the USS Cole. The American people must understand the nature of the threats to our security and that the federal government's number one constitutional responsibility is to provide for our national security.

• The declining defense budgets of the last ten years coincided with dramatic increases in troop deployments—37 major deployments in eight years. These operations were funded by cuts in readiness, modernization programs, and research and development. And the failure to enforce arms control treaties—particularly with Russia—facilitated virtually uncontrolled proliferation and gave potential adversaries access to technology they could not have developed on their own.

1. The United States is always going to have to play a lead role because of our stature. However, we should review our deployment criteria and ensure that we are placing troops in harm's way only as a last resort, when necessary to attain our national objectives.

2. We have short-changed our military over the past decade, and this funding shortfall has severely damaged our military facilities, spare parts, and troops' readiness. One possible solution is to eliminate excess infrastructure commensurate with the post-Cold War decrease in force structure. However, the Base Realignment and Closure (BRAC) process has proceeded slowly and remains politically charged.

• We must understand how to deal with the high technology threats of the 21st century by using all of the existing intelligence resources, which have largely been "stove piped" in the past, to provide a common intelligence picture.

• Our first responders must be properly prepared and trained, especially in terms of integrated, emergency communications systems. However, they will always need backup, and the National Guard plays a crucial role in that requirement.

General Wesley Clark, U.S. Army, Retired, former Supreme Allied
Commander Europe

• As a result of the war in Vietnam, our senior military leaders were determined that we would not become engaged without the strategy, the resolve, and the means to be decisive. But after the Cold War, the world became less structured; our armed forces were committed more and more in ambiguous and difficult situations.

• Since 1993, we have been engaged in "modern warfare," which is characterized by unclear objectives and an uncertain end state. With no extended period for preparations and build-up, combatants must continue to plan, adapt while fighting, and operate with multiple strategies.

1. As long as our armed forces are superior and unchallengeable, we will retain the capacity to use our military in limited ways and achieve tremendous leverage. We do not have to be militarily decisive to be strategically decisive if we bring to bear the other elements of national power effectively.

2. In the early stages of a campaign, there is a heavy reliance on air power, and it is difficult to commit ground forces. Throughout a campaign, there is a heightened fear of civilian casualties driven by the risk of losing legitimacy and support.

3. We must have allies and coalitions, not only for military access but also support. We need to give allied governments time to change their procedures, in order to be able to share intelligence and take action against fundamentalists on their own soil. And we need to reinforce the efforts of moderate Muslims to oppose Islamic extremism.

4. The information campaign is essential, in particular projecting a different image of America. We must build this image by reducing our consumption of the world's resources and helping build the safety net for those left in globalization's wake.

• The U.S. military needs to adapt to the challenges of the 21st century.

1. Long-range precision strike capability has improved our global reach and is essential to our current and future force structure.

2. We need lethal, agile, and survivable ground forces, consisting of high quality, dedicated personnel. We need the full spectrum of capabilities, including special forces, light forces, intermediate brigades, and heavy forces.

3. We must train our forces to exploit public affairs and information operations. Our military education system should teach the application of pure military force and the integration of the military with other instruments of national power.

• The 1990s revealed heavy requirements for nation-building. The United States has a responsibility to help, but military deployments are not the most effective long-term solution. Troops are effective in ending hostilities, but not in fixing states. We need an agency—not the State Department or Defense Department—to help develop legal infrastructure and set the conditions for economic development.

• Americans are not rushing to volunteer and perform public service. We need to build a new sense of community to keep people interested and engaged and to get young people to stay in school and serve.

Rear Admiral Kathleen Paige, U.S. Navy, Systems Technical Director, Ballistic Missile Defense Organization

• We must defend against terrorist use of ballistic missiles, and due to the nature of this threat, we must anticipate being surprised and place the uncertainties in the hands of our adversaries.

• The DOD has refocused and revitalized the missile defense program from one focused on a single-site national missile defense system to a broad-based research, development, test, and evaluation effort aimed at deployment of missile defense.

1. Until very recently, we had a clear demarcation in missile defense programs between strategic threats and theater, or shorter-range, threats. We now view threats along a continuum, which will change our concept of operations in both our theater and unified commands.

2. In the past, we have had a collection of independent programs managed by the three services. Now missile defense will be managed as a single, integrated program that will exploit the various synergies of a unified architecture.

3. We want to be able to intercept incoming ballistic missiles in the boost phase, during midcourse, and in the terminal phase as they approach their target. Technically, each phase offers both targeting opportunities and challenges.

4. We are planning a variety of basing modes to create systems that can operate from the ground, from the sea, from the air, and conceivably even from space. We are using a variety of technologies and approaches, focusing heavily on research, development, testing, and evaluation.

• We must move from a threat-based model to a capability-based approach to provide management and engineering flexibility. We will deliver incremental capability by employing mature systems and integrating emerging technologies as they become available.

1. We need to deploy current technologies with the capability to field future upgrades to those systems seamlessly.

2. We must preserve program flexibility to incorporate future technological breakthroughs.

Lieutenant General Edward G. Anderson III, U.S. Army, Deputy Commander in Chief, U.S. Space Command

• We must treat full-spectrum information operations as a key warfighting capability and develop the organizations and processes to employ it effectively. Joint Vision 2020 highlighted information and decision superiority as keys to suc-

cess in military operations. The QDR stated that space and information are emerging as warfighting core competencies and no longer just enablers. A global area of operations requires a global reach that space capabilities can provide. Our ability to control space and cyberspace will determine whether our combatant commanders will achieve complete situational awareness.

1. We must make maintaining space and information superiority a priority while denying these capabilities to our adversaries. Space control is vital, given our increasing reliance on space assets, including commercial assets. Developing these systems and integrating them with our existing capabilities will provide us a global perspective with worldwide connectivity and real-time situational awareness.

2. U.S. Space Command is building real-time situational awareness for all combatant commanders using traditional space capabilities such as missile warning, satellite communications, and navigation and timing. In addition, it is providing terrestrial and space weather as well as intelligence, surveillance, and reconnaissance.

• *Space and cyberspace can make major contributions to the military during its transformation. There are many promising technologies that can translate into warfighting capabilities and integrate into joint and combined forces to enhance our information and decision superiority.*

1. We need a mix of terrestrial and space-based systems that complement the high-demand, low-density assets in our inventory. We must develop the ability to model, simulate, and analyze; build a comprehensive terrestrial and space-based surveillance system; create systems to protect our satellites from environmental hazards and hostile acts; and develop the ability to deny the enemy the use of his assets.

2. Since our cyber systems will become prime targets, indications and warning systems are our top priorities in information superiority and we must address the DOD's role in national information infrastructure protection.

• *In the war against terrorism the United States and its allies are fighting a sophisticated enemy on a primitive battlefield, an enemy who has effectively used the mass media to spread his message. However, even in this unsophisticated environment, high technology, such as space and cyberspace capabilities, have a very important role. Providing timely, usable information over long distances gives our warfighters the decisive advantage.*

General Barry R. McCaffrey, U.S. Army, Retired, former Commander in Chief, U.S. Southern Command, and former Director, Office of National Drug Control Policy

• *The United States is operating in a new world order: the survival of the force is at stake and American people have paid with their lives for an enemy attack*

There are five principles that bear on how we organize our military.

1. The first defense responsibility for the U.S. armed forces is to prevent the employment of weapons of mass destruction against the U.S. or our allies. We must ensure that our nuclear attack capability is credible, secure, trained and modern. We need sound international treaty constraints, strategic intelligence, and missile defense capabilities.

2. We must control the oceans' choke points and ports and maintain the appropriate naval and other forces to do so.

3. We need a strategic conventional attack capability, which includes air and sea components, cyber warfare, special operations forces, and ballistic missiles, which are synchronized with the other elements of U.S. national power.

4. Enhancing the capabilities of expeditionary operations in order to transfer substantial amounts of combat power to theater by air is essential.

5. We must sustain the readiness of our air and land forces to provide political stabilization through deterrence.

• *The United States will spend whatever resources are required to construct an adequate national military strategy and develop the necessary foreign aid and foreign intervention tools. Sometimes it is inappropriate to discuss exit strategies when we talk about U.S. military strategy.*

1. Despite advances in technology, our military must sustain the lethality of combat forces to fight and win the nation's wars.

2. We must reorganize our headquarters and ensure that the majority of our senior leaders are in the frontier.

3. To multiply force structure, better training and better quality people are more important than more units. Attaining these goals should receive our funding priorities.

4. We need much better protection of America's 7,000 miles of national frontier. We need a 40,000-strong national gendarmerie to patrol the borders, since we do not want the armed forces involved in domestic law enforcement policy.

5. We need to modernize the Coast Guard to ensure its capabilities, strategy, and doctrine are adequate for its missions. Although it is an incredibly effective force, its ships and aircraft are aging.

6. We must construct domestic defenses that are responsive, adequate, and decentralized. Governors, mayors, and city councils will need the appropriate non-Title 10 force structure—including military police, light infantry, field hospitals, signal capabilities, and new biological-chemical reconnaissance and decontamination—in every geographic entity.

Analysis

The United States military faces an unprecedented set of opportunities and challenges in this new era. Our forces are without a peer competitor and can expect to sustain this advantage for at least the next ten to twenty years. However, the nature of warfare is changing: our adversaries counter our strengths through asymmetric means. The military must reorganize and exploit technological advances to maintain its preeminence while simultaneously sustaining current readiness to deter and defeat today's threats.

Since the end of the Cold War, the military conducted over 37 major deployments in the context of what General Clark terms "modern warfare." Our military objectives are not always clear; and, as General McCaffrey observed, it may not always be appropriate to define an exit strategy. However, the unparalleled power of the United States supports strategic decisiveness without necessarily being militarily decisive. To continue to be successful in the future, we must integrate the employment of our military with our other instruments of national power—diplomacy, economic, and information.

Military doctrine continues to evolve and embrace space and information operations as key warfighting competences. Full spectrum space and cyberspace operations can provide timely, useful information to combatant commanders. Lieutenant General Anderson stated that, as technology continues to develop, U.S. Space Command is working to provide real-time situational awareness to give our warfighters a decisive advantage in any future conflict. General Clark reiterated that a critical component of information operations is the communication of our values, goals, and objectives to influence external populations. We must ensure that we are projecting the appropriate image of America and educating our officers to exploit the full range of information operations, including public affairs.

As the United States continues to modernize and improve the effectiveness of its armed forces, our adversaries counter with asymmetric means, such as ballistic missiles, to undermine our might and challenge our resolve. General McCaffrey and Rear Admiral Paige highlighted the need for a sound missile defense capability to combat this threat. Admiral Paige discussed the DOD's current efforts to revitalize and integrate missile defense programs into one broad-based effort aimed at deployment of a missile defense system. This flexible, incremental model incorporates both mature and emerging technologies. This capability allows the United States to anticipate surprise, if not the specifics of the actual attack, and forces our adversaries to face the uncertainties of the U.S. reaction in terms of time, method, and location.

We must maintain the lethality of the current force to achieve the directed military purpose or mission while modernizing and preparing the future force. As General McCaffrey stated, the armed forces must prevent the use of weapons of mass destruction (WMD) against the United States and its allies, control the oceans' ports and choke points, sustain a strategic conventional attack capability, enhance expeditionary capability, and provide stabilization through deterrence. To perform these missions, General Clark advocated long-range precision strike capabilities and the full spectrum of highly capable ground forces, from special forces and light forces to intermediate brigades and heavy divisions.

The modernization effort was challenged in the 1990s by decreasing defense budgets and a significant increase in the frequency and number of major deployments, a paradox that necessitated a shift in resources from modernization and research and development to near-term readiness. This lack of investment undermined the effectiveness of the current force. Congressman Weldon recommended improving readiness by reviewing our deployment criteria and reducing our excess infrastructure while stopping the uncontrolled proliferation of WMD. General McCaffrey believes these same resources should be used to improve the quality of people and training to enhance our current force structure most effectively.

The United States must continue to operate with allies and within coalitions to ensure military access and support and to sustain the public endorsement and legitimacy of our actions. However, we must work with our allies to encourage further investment and modernization in their forces to improve interoperability and reduce the current gap in military technology.

As we wage the current campaign against global terrorism, we must also review the ability of our forces to defend the homeland and respond to future threats. Our first responders must be properly trained and equipped, and it is essential that the National Guard provide effective support to their efforts. The National Guard must be organized to provide this support. General McCaffrey recommended that the National Guard be restructured and reorganized to provide governors and local officials more effective and responsive capabilities. We must also review our intelligence organization and capability to ensure we are providing decision-makers at all levels a common intelligence picture.

Transcript

SPEAKER: Ladies and gentlemen, Dr. Robert Pfaltzgraff.

DR. PFALTZGRAFF: Ladies and gentlemen, it is with great pleasure that I welcome our Panel Two, which will be coming on stage momentarily. I would like at the outset to make a few opening remarks about this panel and to tell you that we have prepared, as you see in your programs, extensive questions and issues that we hope each of the panels will address. And I would urge that if you have not already done so, that you read the panel charter that we have for Panel Two because we have seen all too vividly in the last two months the important role of military power and its synergism with the other instruments of power. We have this afternoon a large number of issues to address. For example, how we apply decisive force based on appropriate strategies. And force is, of course, central to our ability to focus national power, the theme of this conference.

This panel has the greatly challenging task of surveying this important landscape and doing it in the limited time available this afternoon. We will be dealing with a whole range of topics as listed in the charter. They include how we reconcile the requirements for present-day readiness with the needs for modernization for tomorrow in this broadened and complex security setting; how we develop a clearer conception of the modernization priorities that we face in light of the events of September 11th; and, how to apply decisive force as a key component of national security strategy and, in particular as discussed this morning by so many of our speakers, all of our speakers mentioned this, the role of space as well as the role of missile defense in the national security strategy that we have before us. All of these issues will be addressed by the panel this afternoon.

So, I would invite the panel to come on stage at this time. I would like to introduce the panel members in the sequence in which they will be speaking, and to remind them that we hope to keep their remarks to about 15 minutes so that we have ample time for discussion. It is with very special pleasure that I introduce the opening speaker in our panel this afternoon. He is the Honorable Curt Weldon. As I have had the opportunity on many other occasions to do, I introduce him as my Congressman, because I happen to live in the Seventh Congressional District of Pennsylvania and, as I always remind him, I call him whenever I have a constituent interest, and I had a constituent interest this afternoon, as you can see. He was elected to the United States Congress, House of Representatives, for an eighth term in the year 2000. He has been a member of the House since 1987, and he has taken very important leadership roles on a whole range of issues ranging from national security to the environment. He has served as Chairman of the Military Research and Development Subcommittee. He has overseen the development and testing of key military systems and weapons programs. He has served as Chairman of the Readiness Committee. And, he now serves as Chairman of the Arms Services Procurement Subcommittee. He has worked with Russian leaders on a wide range of issues and, of course, he has been a strong supporter over many years of missile defense. So, it is with great pleasure that I welcome my Congressman, Curt Weldon, to this podium this afternoon. (Applause)

CONGRESSMAN WELDON: Thank you, Bob. And, good afternoon ladies and gentlemen and distinguished panel members that I have the honor of serving with. And let me congratulate everyone who has been involved with establishing this conference and for allowing us to come together in I think what has turned out to be a very important discussion about where we are and where we are going as a nation in terms of our military preparedness.

As Bob mentioned, I've served on the Armed Services Committee for 15 years and have now served as Chair of three of the three key subcommittees. My discussion topic is to focus on the competition between readiness and modernization. And, to set the stage, I want to tell you about a trip I took a total of 25 members of Congress on this past August. Four went with me and the other twenty-some met us at various sites. I want to see the true state of our military readiness by visiting our bases. Over a four-day period we traveled to 15 states and visited 24 bases. When we arrived at the bases, we didn't go to the dining rooms to have a nice luncheon. We went to the very specific purpose to see the problems that exist on our military bases, not just at the bases we visited, but as examples of problems of our bases around the world. And, what we saw was beyond any of the ideas that we had as Democrats and Republicans working defense issues.

We saw military bases with raw sewage under the barracks because of a lack of funding to repair the basic infrastructure. We saw water systems and sewer lines that were inoperable. We saw a young mechanic up at a base up in Idaho working on B-1 planes where he had a backlog of spare parts that was 365 days. He had just worked six days 12 hours a day to cannibalize one B-1B to keep the other one in flying in the air. We went down to some of our busiest naval stations, air stations down at Miramar and down at North Ireland and saw runways that had major problems with the potential of debris getting up into the actual plane engines and causing significant damage. It was at that same site that we saw a young sailor who was working out of a metal container that is typically used to put cargo on a ship. But, that had been his site for the previous year and a half to locate spare parts for the helicopter inventory with no electricity and no power because he had no other place to work.

We traveled to another base where we saw a young woman who was so frustrated with her room that had been assigned to her that she went out with her own money and bought caulking and a caulking gun to caulk one-inch cracks in the walls of her own room and did the same for the rest of the rooms on her floor. But perhaps the most telling signal to me about our readiness was when we went to Hunter Army Air Field in Georgia on our way back to Washington and there encountered a young colonel, a very proud colonel, proud of what he was doing, who had just returned from 16 months in Bosnia. And, he said to us, "You know, we're proud of what we do here and we are prepared to go"—and they have gone by the way. He said, "But let me tell you my frustration. I just served 16 months in Bosnia. I had better housing and better food service in Bosnia than I do back here in the States."

The point is that we have short-changed our readiness over the past decade. In fact, at every base we visited where our meetings and operations accounts should run approximately four to five percent of the replacement cost value of those infrastructure plants, we didn't see one base that even approached one percent in terms of annual budgeting. So all of our infrastructure in terms of our facilities and spare parts and the readiness of our troops has, in fact, been neglected.

The second major problem that we encounter today is a ten-year period of declining budgets for research and development. During the six years I chaired the Research and Development Subcommittee, each year I would see requests to cut the S&T (Science and Technology) accounts and the R&D (Research and Development) account lines by approximately 25 percent. Exactly the wrong time to be cutting what is, in fact, the seed core of the future. At a time when I was the chairman of the R&D Committee, I was looking at emerging threats. Four key areas: The emerging threat of missile proliferation; the emerging threat of the use of weapons of mass destruction, the emerging threat posed by narco-drug traffickers and the emerging threat of cyberterrorism. All of them involving

Congressman Weldon

terrorism. At a time when we in the Congress were looking at these emerging threats, all of which are high-tech threats and all of which should require a significant increase in the research and development account lines, we were going the opposite way. A terrible mismatch in terms of our needs. And so when you consider the fact that in our 200-year history, our research and development in the military has usually led the way for the civilian improvements in our quality of life. The first jet agent, the first airplane, the first laser—use of laser technology, the first use of the internet; all were developed by military research. And, now with the information revolution, we see a change occurring with the private sector. In particular, information technology companies are in some cases equal to, in some cases ahead of where we are going in terms of our military and defense capabilities. And yet during this period of time we, in fact, were shortchanging on our R&D account lines.

Well, the bottomline logical solution here is to partially look at cutting our infrastructure because of the decrease in the size of our forces. You can't keep the same number of bases when you cut your Navy from 585 ships to 315 ships, which it currently is today. Or, you cut the force levels of the other services. But unfortunately, the Congress was burned by a, and what we have considered to be, a misuse of the base closing process in 1996 in privatizing two bases in place, one in California and one in Texas, even after the Base Closing Commission had recommended they be closed. But the Congress has been unwilling for the past five years to consider another round of base closing. That action, coupled with a lack of confidence by the Congress on the financial accounting methods of the Defense Department to give us good numbers in terms of savings realized when facilities are closed has caused the Congress to be log jammed and not willing to consider closing additional infrastructure sites. When you add these parameters together and couple in one other, it is in my opinion, a recipe for disaster.

That other factor is the uncontrolled proliferation that occurred in the 1990s. We have arms control regimes because they are supposed to keep the bad guys from getting the kind of technology they could not build on their own. That's why we have treaties. I monitor these treaties on a regular basis and lack of compliance with them. In fact, as many of you know, I am the point person for our relationship with Russia, and I have traveled there 27 times. I did a study through the Congressional Resource Service in 1998 that assessed 37 specific violations of arms control agreements, primarily by 11 Russia and China, over a limited period of time—six years. In those 37 cases of violations of existing arms control treaties where we saw evidence of chemical technology, biological technology, nuclear technology, missile technology, conventional arms in violation of treaties be proliferated from two countries, Russia and China, and end up in the hands of Iran, Iraq, Syria, Libya, and North Korea. The proliferation of that technology that should have been controlled by arms control agreements gave the bad guys and the current unstable terrorist groups in the world the opportunity to avail themselves of technology they could not have developed on their own. It was no surprise to us that India and Pakistan saved Iran with their nuclear technology and their medium-range missiles. After all, we saw that technology flowing. We saw China send them 11 missiles to Pakistan, and 9 to Pakistan for the nuclear program. And we saw Russia transferring missile technology to India on a regular basis.

I was in Moscow in January of 1996 when the *Washington Post* had just reported a front-page story that Russia had been transferring guidance systems, accelerometers, and gyroscopes to the Iraqis to improve their missile accuracy. When I went to Ambassador Tom Pickley in our Embassy in Moscow, I said, "What was the Russian response? That's a clear violation of the MTCR." His response was, "Congressman, I can't ask that question of the Russians. That's got to come from Washington." And, the response President Clinton sent to me in April of that year, he said, "Congressman, we take the allegations in the *Post* very seriously. It would be a serious violation of the MTCR, and if it occurred, if we can prove it, we will take dramatic action. But we don't have the evidence." Well, folks, when I give speeches around the country, I usually carry the evidence with me. I carry a Soviet accelerometer and Soviet gyroscope that were clipped off of Russia Soviet SS-N19 long-range missiles. At that time, one of our agencies that shall remain nameless had over 100 sets of those devices in its control. We had evidence that the Russians had been transferring technology to Iraq, not once, not twice, but three times and we did nothing about it.

The proliferation regimes that we were a party to in the 1990s broke down largely because we did not want to impose the required sanctions mandated by the treaties. That's why the Congress passed their (inaudible) Sanctions Bill in 1997 despite the direct lobbying by Vice President Gore and President Clinton it would be bad for our relationship with Russia. I was at both meetings in the White House with Vice President Gore where Joe Lieberman, Bob Kerry, Carl Levin, John McCain, John Kyl, Lee Hamilton, 12 of us sat in a room where for one hour we were lobbied to vote against the bill. The Bill passed the House with 398 votes, passed the Senate 99 to zero because the Congress was so full of a lack of trust that our arms control treaties were being enforced. We were also not told at that time that there had been a secret deal cut with the Russians in 1995 that Congress was not aware of to allow Russian entities to continue to sell technology to Iran until the year 2000. When you add those parameters together; the lack of funding of our readiness, the lack of closing down bases to free up more funds, the lack of investment in research and development, the lack of enforcement of arms control treaties, you put us in the category we're in right now.

During a time of declining defense budgets with massively increasing uses of our troops—37 major deployments in eight years—none of them funded in advance, all of them having to be paid for out of a decreasing defense budget. When we rob money from modernization programs, when we take money from the readiness accounts, when we apply across-the-board cuts to research and development and science and technology, just to keep the troops operational, you begin to understand the train wreck that I think we are in the midst of. What we've now got to do is rethink the way we approach our national security. As the new Chairman of the Procurement Committee, I'll be hosting a series of out-of-the-box hearings in the first quarter of next year because we have to do things differently. Yes, we are getting increased funds largely as a result of the American people realizing after September the 11th that defense and security should be our number one priority.

But that alone will not solve the problem. We've got to think out of the box of how to reconfigure our military, how to deal with the high-tech threats of the 21st century, how to understand the use of intelligence in new ways creating data fusion centers so that we can create profiles of the bad guys using all of the 32 classified systems that existed up until now have largely been stove-piped. Only when we understand that the number one responsibility of the federal government is to provide for our national security, according to Article One, Section Eight, of our Constitution, and convince the American people that it requires a sustained level of funding, and only when we allow ourselves to understand we must reduce the size of our infrastructure, we must enforce arms control agreements or they mean nothing. We must support increased funding for science and technology because high tech is the future of the kind of threats we're going to face, and we must take care of the troops back home because the quality of life of our troops is always going to be the top priority. Only when we understand and address those issues will our military be capable of supporting the kind of sustained efforts that we are now currently involved in. I'm concerned that the support of our military, not because of our troops. Their morale, in spite of the readiness of our bases, in spite of the lack of spare parts, in spite of aging platforms and lack of modernization, their morale is still at the top. Our young people are ready, willing, and able to do the job the Commander in Chief assigns them. But the question is how long can that continue?

What frustrated me the most, and I say this in closing my comments, was when I traveled the country last year and did 200 speeches in 25 states. In each speech that I gave I talked about the state of our military. I talked about the emerging four threats. I talked about the fact that we weren't paying for readiness, that we weren't dealing up-front with the need for modernization, with the need for science and technology and R&D funding. And yet every major national poll in the country last year showed defense dead last, dead last. The American people demanded more money for education, they demanded more money for health care, but they were not convinced that defense was a priority that we should focus on. We've got to understand that for us to deal with the challenges of the 21st century we've got to also reeducate the American people.

September the 11th should not have been the wake-up call. It should not have happened that in 1993 when bin Laden bombed the World Trade Center, and I went up at that event because I also work disasters, America yawned because it wasn't a large loss of life. When a few years later when our embassies were bombed in Africa, and 200 people were killed including 12 Americans, America yawned again because we thought it would never happen on our soil. Again, it was bin Laden. And then we sent 26 young sailors home in body bags from Yemen, from the USS Cole because, again, bin Laden attacked us. And what did the country do? We yawned, because it wasn't on the radar screen of the national media. It wasn't the kind of issue that we would correlate with an increased need to fully fund our military's requirements. On September the 11th, America screamed.

The country demands to know why we hadn't taken the steps to prevent and respond to this terrible act of aggression. What we have to do is let the American people understand the nature of the threats that are out there and the need for the federal government, as its number one priority, to fully fund those requirements. And that continues to require us to cut the waste and abuse out of our defense budget and it is still there. But by and large, unless we address those issues I've outlined, unless we come to terms with the reality of the broader approach to our security, we will not be able to meet the modernization needs to buy the new platforms and new equipment that a 21st century military has to have. Thank you. (Applause)

DR. PFALTZGRAFF: Thank you very much, Curt, for this very important Congressional perspective on the issues that we face this afternoon. I wanted now to turn now to our next speaker who has had, indeed, very important and recent experience in focusing national military power, indeed in focusing international military power. As we all know General Clark, Wes Clark, was Supreme Allied Commander Europe (SACEUR) from July 1997 through May 2000. He also was the Commander in Chief of the U.S. European Command. In his position as SACEUR, he was the overall commander of approximately 75,000 troops from 37 NATO and other nations participating in the ongoing operations, the peace enforcement operations in Bosnia and Kosovo. He, of course, has had numerous other assignments and appointments in his distinguished military career, and he is now the author of a very fine new book on his military experience. So, it is with very great pleasure that I welcome back to this meeting, General Wesley Clark, USA, retired. (Applause)

GENERAL CLARK: Bob, thank you very much. It is good to look out in the audience such as I can see. It is a little hard to see from up here, but I do see a lot of old friends and colleagues out there. And I'm just delighted to be here. I think this is an important forum. Now, I'm not in uniform. I'm standing before you as an impoverished investment banker. And it occurred to me when I was in England, we did a British edition of the book about three weeks ago when I was there, with—I went to Royal Staff College down at Shrivmon And one of the members of the faculty said he was just a humble academician. So I put that in my list of oxymorons. You know, military intelligence, political leaders, humble academicians, impoverished investment bankers.

I don't want to talk about investment banking and the economy directly. What I'd like to talk about is our armed forces and where we are right now. We are in midst of a new struggle in a new time. Most of us here are familiar with the post-Vietnam Army at some point. For those of my generation, Barry McCaffrey and John Abrams and Monty Meigs and Jerry Hendricks and everybody else I can see out there, we came out of Vietnam determined that we would never again let our Army be committed where we did not win. We were not going to be patsies. We were not going to be abused. We were not going to be thrown in there without a strategy, without the resolve, and without the means to be decisive. We built that Army. We built it on a big five, the opposing force principle and training, we built it on our combat training centers, we built it on battalion and brigade command selection boards, we built it on OPMS and EPMS, and we proved that Army in Desert Storm and in Just Cause and, in fact, it was decisive.

But with the end of the Cold War something began to change and as we lost the structure in the world, we found our armed forces committed more and more in ambiguous and difficult situations. It wasn't that we weren't prepared to be decisive in Korea or a replay of Desert Storm, but we weren't called on to do that. We were called on to go in to Haiti and restored democracy. And the Fauds five V150 armored fighting vehicles—five—were the most photographed, analyzed, and tracked armored vehicles in the history of modern warfare. We knew exactly where they were and what they were capable of.

We went into Bosnia. It wasn't an exactly conventional warfighting mission. In fact, it's a mission we really would have preferred not to have had. And I was one of those on the Joint Staff who was quite concerned about this. We tried to limit the mission so it didn't grow and didn't creep and didn't get us in trouble, as we took the lesson from Somalia. But, we went in there. And then we went into Kosovo. And, by the summer of 2000, we had seen that we really were—our country really was, as a result of what we had done in the 1990s, as a result of the buildup of our military forces, we were historically dominant in a way no nation has been for 500 years. Our armed forces were not only the strongest, they were unchallengeable. Our economy drove the world economy. Our culture was the wellspring of movies and art and fashion around the world. Our consuming power plus our ideas just drove it and our language. English was the language everybody wanted to learn. We were the incredible—incredibly lucky beneficiaries of globalism. And, of course, after September 11th, we also discovered we were the victims of it.

What we're engaged in and what we have to operate within is a new form of warfare, which I've been calling "modern warfare." It's characterized by the patterns that we saw in Kosovo and the patterns we're seeing today. It starts with some degree of difficulty in defining a clear end state. It is hard to figure out exactly what your objective is or where you might end up. It includes planning and adapting as the fighting goes on. No six-month window to get ready. You've got to continue to plan even as you fight. You have to operate simultaneously on multiple strategies. There is a heavy reliance up front on air power. Why? Well, because it's usually the most available means of making a military statement, and it has considerably improved over the years in its ability to strike targets precisely with high destructive capacity and rapidly. There is an inordinate fear of civilian casualties because we know that with civilian casualties you lose legitimacy. You lose your base of support. There is a difficulty in committing ground forces because, well, they are not there, or somebody else can do it, or it takes too long, or you may suffer too many casualties from it. There is a requirement to use coalitions and alliances and there is a heavy reliance on public affairs.

That's what modern warfare is. That's what we found it to be in Kosovo, and remarkably, that's what we are finding it to be in this current conflict. And so, the problem is how do we be decisive if it is not through D-day, island hop-

ping, and the conventional means of
using military power that are cele-
brated in American movies and in
American history. In a word, it seems
to me that modern military warfare
gives you the capacity to be militarily
decisive in a different way. You can
violate the principles of war. You can,
and still win. And you can still be
decisive. You don't even have to be
militarily decisive to be strategically
politically decisive if you line up the
other elements of national power correctly: the legal, the diplomatic, the
economic on top of the military. How
can this be? Because as long as we are
superior and unchallengeable with
our armed forces the way we are
today, we can use our armed forces in
limited ways and achieve tremendous
leverage if we bring to bear the other
elements of national power.

General Clark

So, what is happening in Afghanistan today is a case in point. We go in
with air power, we go in with special operating forces, and we use the
Northern Alliance on the ground. And, inevitably, the Taliban falls, at least
in the area where we've been able to target them. Why? Because they can't
stand the weight of the air power, and with ground forces there to help provide the targeting and bring that power to bear, it is tactically decisive in
those areas.

But I think the broader picture of the campaign also suggests that in order
to be decisive, we have to fully take account of what modern warfare is. We
have to understand that this is a struggle not only in Afghanistan, but it's also
a struggle in a number of other countries against terrorism, and to win this
struggle we have to win it from the outside in, and the bottom up, and slower
is actually better. Why? Well, all the conditions that make fighting in
Afghanistan so difficult—the geography, the culture, the language, the tor-
tured history of the land—are reversed when we're dealing with our own
country here. We know the geography, we speak the language, we understand
the culture. The police officers are even friendly most of the time in this country. And, surely, we can from here and Britain and Germany and France and
Italy pull together what we need, take apart the terrorist network cell by cell,
individual by individual, from the bottom to the top and take away Osama bin
Laden's capacities to act.

To do this, though, we've got to have allies. We've got to have people working with us and they have to make changes in how their governments function. That's why we need the coalition. Not just for military physical access, but because if we are going to fight modern warfare we've got to have support. And so we've got to give time for these governments, the governments of Germany, and France, and Italy, and Greece, Saudi Arabia, and Egypt, to change their procedures, to be able to share intelligence, to be able to take action against fundamentalists on their own soil. That's not enough.

This is also a struggle for Islam. We are going to have to find those hundreds of millions and their leaders who believe Islam is tolerant and peace loving. And they're going to have to take their own stand against Osama bin Laden and his interpretation of what Islam is. And we are going to have to reinforce them. And that's going to take time.

And even that's not enough. I've heard a lot of people say they want to drain the swamp, and by that they usually mean where we're going after Afghanistan. Is it Somalia, is it Iraq, is it Libya, is it Syria, is it Iran? How many? How soon? How often? But I think it's more than that because that swamp is out there as a result of—partly as a result of us. We are five percent of the world's population. We're taking 25 percent of the consumable resources. And that's an unsustainable condition in the long term. And so, part of winning the modern war is winning the information campaign, and a big part of that is what we're trying to do now, which is project a different image of America. But you can't project an image that doesn't reflect reality. And so, it means we're going to have to tend to the reality that's out there.

Even beyond the Islamic world the conditions of poverty, disease, despair and hopelessness in Africa and elsewhere will affect us. We can't have the benefits of globalism without helping build the safety net that lets us have those benefits.

What this means for the military, I think, is this. First, I think precision strike's been a real blessing and I think we ought to continue to pursue it. We need global deployment and global capabilities, but air power is limited. It can only do so much. And what we saw in Kosovo wasn't the unlimited potential of air power; it was equally or even more so the limitations of air power to look inside, to look behind, to look underneath. We've got to have effective, capable ground forces. They've got to be able to get there. They've got to have high-quality, dedicated men and women who have the courage to be there on the ground. It means that whole spectrum of capabilities starting with special forces and going to the intermediate brigades and up to heavy forces. And I'm very much supportive of the direction that the Chief has taken the United States Army in its transformation. I think it's critical, and I think it needs to be supported and it needs to be resourced more intensively than it is today. And I hope that some of these additional resources will go into that transformation effort.

But I think even that's not enough. I think we've got to do more in terms of public affairs and training for our officers. Because what we find is that the public affairs and the communication of ideas can be strategically decisive in a global age. We've got to have that capacity. We've got to train our people to work with it.

And beyond that, we've got to go back and look at the development of our officers and noncommissioned officers. During the 1970s and 1980s, we made a tremendous effort to strengthen the skills of the muddy boots army. It was essential. We had, prior to that, battalion commanders who didn't know their systems. They couldn't fight their own tanks. They weren't technically competent. We can't ever lose that. But we can't be satisfied with that. Because there is no other source in the United States government for the strategic vision and the capability to assemble the military power with the diplomatic and the legal that the United States armed forces and their officers can bring together. That's what we should be teaching in our staff colleges, in our war colleges and in our general officer courses not only how to apply pure military force, but how to bring it in and use the other elements of power.

Let me just ask you a question. Why isn't Osama bin Laden indicted as a war criminal? He declared genocide against the United States. It's an order, his order, to kill all Americans, military and civilian, anywhere in the world. Sounds like genocide to me. I got a call a couple of days ago from the International Criminal Tribunal of Yugoslavia concerning Mr. Milosevic. He is on trial for genocide and other crimes against humanity. Why isn't Osama bin Laden? In many respects, the crowning, decisive blow of the Kosovo campaign wasn't the deployment of the Apaches, the preparation of ground forces of the air campaign. It was the fact that Milosevic was indicted. And when he was indicted all hopes that he had for compromise and finagling and cutting a deal were cut off.

I think the men and women who lead the armed forces and those who are coming up in it have to understand that in modern war you can get tremendous leverage from military power if you line it up with the diplomatic and the legal on top of it. To me, that's the charge for how to be decisive today. Keep the armed forces unchallengeable, force your adversaries to fight asymmetrically and line up the legal, the diplomatic, the economic and the military against them. That's the key to decisiveness. Thank you. (Applause)

DR. PFALTZGRAFF: Thank you very much, General Clark for this concise and very important statement about military power. It fits brilliantly into the discussions this afternoon. Let me now introduce our next speaker.

We turn now to a discussion of missile defense, the very important topic on the national security and military agenda. We have to discuss this topic with us Rear Admiral Kathleen K. Paige, United States Navy. She is the Systems Technical Director of the Ballistic Missile Defense Organization. She is a 1970 graduate of the University of New Hampshire and was commissioned to the United States Navy in 1971. She has had many tours of duty since then. They include Technical Director, AGEIS Program Office, very important for our discussion this afternoon; Chief Engineer, Naval Surface Warfare Center; and Baseline Manager for the Combat Systems Division of the AGEIS shipbuilding program. I might add that she has also had an assignment as Director, Theater Air and Missile Defense and Systems Engineering. She is also a graduate, I might add here, with a Master of Science degree from the Naval Postgraduate School in Monterey, California, and is a graduate also of the Defense Systems Management College and the Cornell University Program for Executives. So, it is with great pleasure that I welcome Rear Admiral Paige to this panel and to this discussion this afternoon. Admiral Paige. (Applause)

ADMIRAL PAIGE: Good heavens. Thank you for that generous introduction. One thing that wasn't mentioned is that I am an Engineering Duty Officer, and so the way I have spent the day typically for the last 30 years of my Navy career has been working with engineers to build ships, combat systems, and, more recently, ballistic missile defense systems. So, this really is a very rare opportunity and I will even say a welcome one to join you and participate in such a policy forum.

I have structured my remarks this afternoon around a statement from the Quadrennial Defense Review. That statement says that DOD has refocused and revitalized the missile defense program from one focused on a single site national missile defense system to a broad-based research, development, and test effort aimed at deployment of missile defense. I'll describe the key elements of this new program and how it responds to the transformational nature of the military as defined in the QDR. Next viewgraph, please.

We have a refocused and revitalized missile defense program, ladies and gentlemen, because of President Bush's strong commitment to missile defense and because of the long-standing support from key Congressional leaders, which has allowed us over the many years to maintain at least some degree of momentum so that we have an opportunity to be prepared now that the nation has recognized that ballistic missiles are, in fact, a terrorist threat. Now, I show here a quote from President Bush. He has talked often about missile defense. I selected this particular quote from the 27th of February for a couple of reasons. You read the quote and it is prescient in so many ways. It presages the potential for a September 11th type of attack. It recognizes that the ballistic missile is a terrorist weapon. And it is essentially an outline for what we see in both the Quadrennial Defense Review and in the structure of the new missile defense program. Next viewgraph please.

Now, in that quote President Bush addressed threats that are more widespread and less certain. That's really key to much of what we see in the QDR and in our new program. The QDR provides a model for responding to such a threat environment. I've listed in this view graph some of the quotes, some of the tenets from the QDR that apply to defense in general and, specifically, to missile defense. The tenet that I'd like to discuss first is the imperative that we move from a classic threat-based model to a capability-based model. And Congressman Weldon set me up perfectly for this next discussion. Next viewgraph, please.

Admiral Paige

This next view graph gives you an idea, graphically, of the world's population of ballistic missiles, almost 30 years ago in 1972. Next view graph. Here we are almost 30 years later and just the graphic impact of the growth, the proliferation in that threat around the globe, to me is awesome. Now, certainly understanding the scope and general characteristics of the threat remains vitally important, even as we say we are moving away from a threat-based approach to addressing a capabilities-based approach. But that's because what's even more sobering than what we know about the threat is the number of times that we have been surprised by specific, very critical aspects of the threat. These are what we tend to call the "unknown unknowns," and listening to Mr. Weldon, unfortunately, there is also a category called the "I don't want to knows."

Let me give you just two examples of things that were truly unknown unknowns that surprised the intelligence community and, therefore, the military community. First was in 1993, when North Korea launched a Nodong missile. We knew it. We tracked it. We knew what we expected of that missile and its flight. We looked at the data, put it away, and moved on. Four years later, 1997, for a reason I don't recall, an analyst was reviewing those data and instead of stopping the review at the first sign of losing track on that ballistic missile that day, that analyst had patience and looked through some more data. And, guess what? Our tracking sensors started to track something again. It turned out that nobody had anticipated the range that that missile could have, and so when the sensors first dropped track, the analyst said, "That's as far as the missile went. We don't expect it to fly any further." But, in fact, it turned out that that missile overflew Japan, flying further than we thought the missile capable of flying. It was a fairly embarrassing diplomatic incident when we went back to Japan and said, "Remember that missile launched from North Korea four years ago? Well, Japan, that overflew your country."

It was a year after that realization that we had another surprise: on August 31, 1998. Again, it was North Korea, this time launching a Taepo Dong. We were prepared for a launch. In fact, we had some AEGIS ships stationed in order to track the launch. It didn't happen exactly when we expected. The United States ships had to go off on other assignments, but the Japanese AEGIS destroyer, *Myoko*, stayed on station and was able to track that Taepo Dong. What was that surprise? We had been told by the intelligence community that that missile didn't have three stages, that North Korea couldn't build a three-stage rocket. Guess what? It had three stages. It is the surprises that get you on defense. It is the surprises that we need to be able to cope with in this new approach to missile defense. Next view graph.

This is a different way to look at the threat. And it shows you the range of various threat types. Now, I mention this for a number of reasons. First of all, for—since the outset of the missile defense program, up until very recently, we had a very severe demarcation: we talked about strategic threats and then separately we talked about theater threats. And, those theater threats tended to be your shorter-range threats. Well, if you look at this graph, you'll see that we have examples of threat ranges that go from the short to the medium to the intermediate to the long range. We have now a continuum of threat ranges. And even those threats that are of a shorter range, we have seen launched from ships at sea just as we launch Trident missiles from sea. And so those missiles don't have to be of the classic intercontinental ballistic missile range to be able to reach our shores.

Another very personal way to view this graph, instead of looking at just the numbers and the lines, look at that short-range missile on the left. That represents a missile that can fly from Iraq to Tel Aviv. The medium-range missile next to it is something that can fly from North Korea to Japan. The intermediate range, further to the right, that's Libya to London. I had just arrived in London on the 11th of September, as the World Trade Towers and the Pentagon were being hit. And the largest parabola is the United States being hit from anywhere around the globe. So, being able to address a missile of any range is of critical importance. We can't make that strategic versus theater demarcation any more, and that's going to change the way we operate, the concept of operations in both our theater commands and in our unified commands.

Now, there's one other point I would like to make from this chart, and it is the fact that we are not going to restrict ourselves to being able to kill incoming ballistic missiles in only one or even two portions of their trajectory. We want to be able to kill in what we call the boost phase, soon after the launch of the ballistic missile, during mid-course, during that long period when it's flying out, as well as in the terminal phase. We want to do that for a couple of reasons, because technically each one has their advantages and opportunities, each of those regimes has their problems. Also, operationally, if we can take out a ballistic missile as it's launching, not only is that before it's been able to release its decoys and its chaff, those things that confuse the problem of killing the business end of the missile, but it also keeps the business end of the missile, that part that carries the weapon of mass destruction, the high energy explosives or the chemical or bio-agents, keeps them far from our shores. But it also gives us the ability to predict where will be that fallout and where is the best place to take the shot to prevent damage to the underlying countries or areas. Next view graph, please.

So to address that kind of threat environment, we have what is, in fact, a very different approach to missile defense. Yes, we've been working on missile defense for 15 years or more. We have proven many of the technologies. We're coming close to deploying the PAC3, the Patriot Ballistic Missile Defense System, which is able to kill in the terminal phase. But to date, we have had a collection of programs, each managed as independent programs, by each of the three services. From now on, they'll be managed as a single integrated program where you can bring the synergies to bear, you can create an architecture that gives you the power of overhead sensors, and command and control opportunities, and that gives us the flexibility that you need when you play defense, when you are in the reactive mode. We're also providing a lot of variety. You also always want a lot of arrows in your quiver, as large a magazine as you can have.

So what are we planning? A variety of basing modes, systems that can operate from ground, from sea, from air, and conceivably even from space. A variety of technologies, and very different concepts and development approaches. And, again, trying to bias the deck in the defense's favor, the ability to exploit complementary phenomenologies. Another very different aspect of the new program is that it is focused on research development, test, and evaluation. These systems must earn their way into the procurement budget before we commit the procurement dollars to them. They do so both by proving themselves in tests and proving that they provide value added to a larger architecture. And the last thing that is very different about the former approach, we're addressing protection not just for the United States and for our deployed forces, but for our allies and friends. And not just protection for our allies and friends, but true cooperation and collaboration with our allies and friends. Next view graph.

We talk a lot about being capability based instead of threat based. That's discussed in the QDR. It is the hallmark of the new missile defense program. And what does that mean? Well, bottom line is that means we have the management and the engineering flexibility to provide us an insurance policy against all of those unknown unknowns. Next view graph? And how do we go about actually delivering and fielding capability so we have protection available around the globe? Capability-based means you don't wait 20 years to have what you think at the outset is the ideal system, and it is a has-been by the time it is delivered. The plan is to be able to deliver incremental capability where we pull together the mature capabilities that are consistent and coherent in their architecture, that are integrated via a cohesive battle management and command and control system, and we test it thoroughly, and if directed, deploy it. Two years later, we upgrade that capability.

Now, an important point that I would like to make here is that this requires us to be operating basically in three epochs. We need to have a very focused effort in executing well the immediate programs and engineering that we have on our plate today. At the same time, we need to be maturing technologies so that when we field the existing capability, we are prepared to start engineering and integrating and fielding the upgrades to those systems, because the offense doesn't wait. But we're not going to just continue to evolve what we know and stay with what we know.

In parallel with that, we need to give equal emphasis to the "wild blue yonder," so when you get to the point of those later year block developments, it may look very, very different than the initial block that's fielded, concepts that will just turn the whole idea of missile defense on its ear. Radically different. We're open to those ideas. And that's the only way that we will be able to address those unknown unknowns. Next view graph.

In the end, our ability to deter or defeat the ballistic missile threat as charged in the QDR comes down to understanding that defense is a reactive, not an elective, function. If we're going to succeed against the adversary's playbook, we must have a very robust playbook ourselves. We must execute well with constancy of purpose. We need to put the guessing games, the insecurities, into the laps of those who would do harm to us, to our allies and to our friends. Thank you very much. (Applause)

DR. PFALTZGRAFF: Thank you very much, Admiral Paige. There is much that you have said that we should take on board. One thing that I liked in particular you said that we cannot make that theater/intercontinental distinction any longer. We need to think about that as we think about missile defense requirements and the terrorist threat.

We now turn to our next speaker, Lieutenant General Edward Anderson, United States Army. General Anderson is Deputy Commander in Chief and Chief of Staff U.S. Space Command, and Vice Commander, U.S. Element, North American Aerospace Defense Command, that is NORAD. In this capacity, General Anderson helps lead the unified command responsible for directing space control and support operations, including missile defense as well as the computer network defense and the computer network attack (CAN) capability. General Anderson has also served as Director for Strategic Plans and Policy in the Joint Staff, the assignment he had before his present assignment.

And I might add that previous to that he served as Commanding General, United States Army Space and Missile Defense Command. So, it is very—with great pleasure, with very great pleasure, that I welcome General Anderson who has spoken at previous meetings of this kind to give us yet another dimension, which is looking at the space dimension. Ed, great to have you back.

GENERAL ANDERSON: Thank you very much, Bob. General Shinseki, fellow flag officers, both active and retired, distinguished guests, ladies and gentlemen, it is a great pleasure to be here and certainly a great privilege to be a part of this very distinguished panel. General Eberhart sends his regrets. I can assure you that would very much like to have been here. He recognizes the importance of this particular forum and particularly as they address such current and relevant issues. I must add congratulations to General Shinseki and the Army staff and to my good friend Dr. Bob Pfaltzgraff and the IFPA staff for once again another magnificent and superb job in putting on the Fletcher Conference.

As Bob indicated, I've been asked to speak about space in military operations. As I think you all know, U.S. Space Command, and as Bob indicated in his introduction, is not only responsible for space but it is also responsible for computer network defense and computer network attack, which we have formed together into computer network operations. And so, I have chosen to expand my remarks just a little bit to not only address space, but to address cyberspace, which I do think is a relevant issue for discussion here today. Next slide, please.

I am going to add my effort at trying to describe what this new environment is that we're going to be in, using these measures up here. We had a taste of that this morning, a very good sense of that this morning. Certainly, as we all know, the President has clearly declared war on terrorism worldwide and, of course, all of our CINCS are prosecuting that through Operation Enduring Freedom. And what we have found is—all of us have found is that Operation Enduring Freedom certainly presents some unique challenges, particularly to us as warfighters. If we consider a traditional war—and I admit that it's hard to define "traditional war"—to be along the lines of what we used to refer to as two-major-theater wars, then I think we would all certainly agree that this is a nontraditional conflict that we are embarked on. The adversary is certainly not a peer competitor and certainly not a super power. And although he has global presence and certainly he has global reach, he does not have the conventional, dedicated nation-state support that we would expect. In other words, a single nation supporting him. But he certainly has nation-state support as you'll recall from the discussion this morning. He may be fighting on an age-old battlefield. I mean we even see the reports of cavalry being used in Afghanistan, and so on and so forth. But leveraging the latest, he is also leveraging the latest in commercial information technology. And clearly, as evidenced by the tragic events of the 11th of September, this adversary employs asymmetric weapons as part of his strategy as well. And this adversary clearly understands that information is a powerful and potent weapon, as he has effectively used mass media to spread his message.

So in this war we are fighting, I would suggest to you, a sophisticated enemy in perhaps a not so sophisticated battlefield environment. But just because it is not a sophisticated battlefield, that does not mean that high-tech capabilities, such as space capabilities and cyberspace capabilities, don't have a role. As a matter of fact, I submit to you that they have a very important role in Operation Enduring Freedom. Next slide, please.

It is interesting to note that Joint Vision 2020 outlined that the two keys to success in military operations were information and decision superiority. In other words, our ability to control space and cyberspace, I would offer to you, will determine whether our combatant commanders will be capable of achieving complete situational awareness, ultimately leading to information and decision superiority. In U.S. Space Command, our warfighters are working hard to build real-time situational awareness right now, for General Tommy Franks and ultimately for all CINCs. And we use traditional space capabilities of missile warning, satellite communications in order to link our warfighters over large distances, navigation and timing to allow our warfighters to know where they are and at the same time to allow our precision weapons to function, we provide terrestrial and space weather, an important factor in our operations, as well as intelligence surveillance and reconnaissance.

In addition to those standard space capabilities that we are all well aware of, we are also working to provide to General Franks coherent change, detection capability, in other words, our ability to observe change over time, tracking of blue forces as well as providing time critical information which would enable our warfighters to bring the right mix of either kinetic or nonkinetic weapons at the right place at the right time. In the area of information superiority, we are partnering with DOD agencies, other government agencies, the Joint Staff, the services, as well as law enforcement agencies and our allies as we continue to provide cyberspace protection of both our critical DOD information and our communications infrastructure.

But all of these efforts have led us to believe that there is a new perspective that is required, as well. And so, we have embarked on an effort to provide support to General Franks and CINCCENT and ultimately the other combatant commanders in developing a full-spectrum information operations campaign for both CINCCENT and for the global counterterrorism campaign. So, as the QDR said, and obviously we agree, that space and information are warfighting core competencies, they are not just enablers as we have traditionally been accustomed to, and we learn that every day. But that's today. What about tomorrow? Next slide, please.

What we are seeing in Operation
Enduring Freedom is much the same
as we have seen since Desert Storm,
and that is that there has become a
greater reliance on military and commercial space and information systems. And we certainly do not expect
that trend is going to diminish. But it
is not just passing information that is
the important piece of this, it is providing usable information in a timely
manner over large distances that
allow our warfighters to be successful—to give them the decisive advantage. So the requirement to collect
and move real-time information, critical information, to our forces in the
field we expect certainly will grow.
But our potential adversaries are
watching what is happening in
Operation Enduring Freedom, just as
they watched what was happening in

General Anderson

Kosovo and just as they watched what was happening in Desert Storm, in all
cases where we enjoyed and currently enjoy information superiority. And they
will seek to deny that advantage to us.

The graphic on the right of this chart may serve as an indicator for you
just to look at the cyber events that have happened. And if you were to extend
that out one more year, as you may have read in the *Defense News* the other
day, our expectation is that number will double. So this is a situation that is
getting worse, not better. And certainly, in the future the battle for information will be critical. So, what do we need to do? Next slide, please.

While at the risk of stating the obvious we must, we believe, maintain
space and information superiority. We must make these a priority today, not
just in the future. We will be challenged. We've already seen evidence of that
and we can be sure of that in the future, as well. In the area of space superiority, space control is vital, given our increasing reliance on space assets to
include commercial assets. Now, if you look at the slide—at the right those are
the components that we use to define space control. And so, we must, we
believe, first and foremost develop a comprehensive and robust terrestrial and
space-based surveillance system. We need the protection systems on and for
our satellites, both to protect them from environmental hazards as well as from
hostile acts. We need the prevention capabilities to be able to deny the enemy
the use of his assets, as well as deny him from denying us the use of our assets.

And, ultimately, we need a negation capability, preferably a reversible capability. But to offer the combatant commander whatever options he may need, it may mean that there are other types necessary, as well.

Now, I am not trying to suggest to you and I hope you would not let me leave here with the thought that we are advocating that space can do it all. It cannot. And it would be tough to do all of what I've just suggested to you and certainly it would be very, very expensive. There must be a mix of terrestrial and space-based systems in the future and what we need to do is to develop the ability to model, simulate, and analyze just like we have for terrestrial systems, so that we can make those trade-off decisions in an informed way. In the area of information superiority, indications and warning systems are at the top of our list. Our cyber systems will become prime targets. We already know that. But we want to know it before they do it. We don't want to be in the reactive posture that we are right now. We must be in a proactive posture. We believe that it is now time to treat full spectrum information operations as a key war fighting capability, and to develop the organizations and processes to employ it effectively. And DOD's role in the national information infrastructure protection must be addressed. We all know that our own war fighting infrastructure is directly tied to the national information infrastructure protection capability. So it's all about information and who controls it. This will be important as we work to transform the force. Next slide, please.

Transformation of our military has already begun, we already know that, led by the Army as a matter of fact. Has been for some time. We would suggest that space and cyberspace can make major contributions to the force during this transformation. There are several promising technologies that are out there that we need to translate into capabilities, which we believe would ultimately enhance our information and decision superiority capabilities. For example, space-based moving target indicator. Gives you the capability to see deep behind enemy lines, no risk to a crew, no concern about landing rights, and certainly gives you a huge field of view—in essence, global. Another capability—hyper-spectral imagery. A new generation of imagery products which unlock vital information on the battlefield. Among other things, it gives you the capability to detect camouflage vehicles.

And certainly space-based laser communications to give us the opportunity to move bulk information both into and out of the theater of operations. So, as I say, we must translate these technologies into warfighting capabilities for our warfighters. And then, what we must do is integrate these capabilities into our joint and combined forces, to provide real-time communications between sensor and shooters and shooters and commanders, essential today and certainly very essential in the future. Certainly a global area of operations requires a global reach, and space capabilities can provide that. We must complement the high-demand, low-density assets that are so precious in our inventory.

I'm not trying to say that if you have space-based radar, you don't need JSTARS. That's not it at all. As I indicated earlier, we have to determine the mix. But, we do think that there is a capability to complement those kinds of systems. And we must expand computer network operations to full-spectrum information operations. We must take the next step and take full advantage of full-spectrum information operations. This will be a major challenge, I can assure you. But, as I say, space and cyberspace we believe will be able to assist in transforming the way we fight. Next slide, please.

So, in conclusion, one of the keys to success will be our ability to leverage our space and information capabilities while denying that to our adversary. Developing these capabilities and integrating them with sea, land, and air capabilities will be of utmost importance, both today as well as in the future. These capabilities will enable a global perspective with worldwide connectivity, real-time situational awareness which will provide effects-based solutions. Today, we are engaged in a two-front war, one front here at home and one front abroad. Space and information are key parts of that war today, and will be for every engagement in the future. Thank you very much and I look forward to your questions. (Applause)

DR. PFALTZGRAFF: Thank you very much, General Anderson for remind us and pointing out the indispensable role of space and, indeed, of cyber space and, of course, space control. Very important as we think about military power in the 21st century.

Now last, but not least, I turn to General Barry McCaffrey. General McCaffrey is the Olin Distinguished Professor of National Security Studies at the United States Military Academy at West Point. He is also President of his own consulting firm based in Alexandria, Virginia, and has been elected to the Board of Trustees of Microtek Systems and to the Board of Directors both of the Phoenix House Foundation and the Atlantic Council of the United States. All of us have known General McCaffrey in his previous assignments. In particular, I should remind you, but I really don't need to do so, but I will anyway, that he was Director of the White House Office of National Drug Control Policy from February 1996 until January 2001. In that capacity, he served as a member of the President's Cabinet and the National Security Council on drug-related issues. He, of course, came to that position after a long and distinguished career in the United States Army. So, it is with very great pleasure that I welcome General McCaffrey to this discussion this afternoon. And, of course, we have seen General McCaffrey very often on television recently. Now, we have a chance to see him in person. Barry, welcome. (Applause)

GENERAL McCAFFREY: Thanks very much, Bob. Thanks for that generous introduction. Normally what I do when I'm on TV is I go listen to Dave Cranes and then Wes Clark and then I know exactly what to say. Let me begin by thanking both Bob and Dr. Jackie Davis, because the two of you have been such a tremendous influence and part of their national security process. I thank you for helping organize a conference and for both of you for your continuing friendship over the years. Let me take particular note of Congressman Curt Weldon. You know, there are probably 30 or 40 Congressmen who bear a disproportionate influence in shaping the national security process. You know, and our former—one of our former chiefs was wont to say that those of us who are privileged to wear the uniform are only one aspect of a strong national defense. Clearly, the American people and also Congress. Why don't you join me in a round of applause for Congressman Curt Weldon. (Applause) It's always fun listening to Wes Clark. I started off listening to him when he was teaching political philosophy a few years ago when he was a major. I'd go drift by his class. He has been a brilliant dedicated officer and a life-long friend. Admiral Kathleen Paige, thank you for your presentation. And Ed Anderson I've known for years. I didn't realize—we were sitting up here, it was like being bugs under a light. I couldn't tell who was in the audience. Chief, thanks for your leadership, for your example. Bob Wood, DAMO-SS, smarter than most of us who have served in job. I saw Pete Cuvielo, the world's smartest living human being—my title, not his—for helping set up such a turnkey modern joint headquarters in Southern Command. Chuck Maham and others who lead the Army or the joint forces in our latest conflict.

A couple thoughts, if you will, about looking toward the future. You know, there is a good argument that many of us who are senior military officers are the most conservative people you'll ever run into. There is a reason for it. We've seen things screwed up from the time we came into the Army at age 21, you know, rolling or falling down ravines, horizontal sleet, mud, confusion. I didn't get the word. We know a thousand ways to screw things up. We've seen it go right a lot, too, and we're very risk adverse. We don't like—and many would argue historically the United States armed forces don't face risk very often. One could argue that except for the Jalu, Guadalcanal, and the Civil War we never faced situations where we think the survival of the force is at stake. And, until September 11th, we never thought the American people would pay with their lives for an enemy attack. It is a new world we're operating in.

Let me sort out for you five principles that I think many of us might want to bring to bear on what we're up to in organizing America's military. And the first one might be odd for an infantry officer to start off with. I used to introduce myself for years when I was a J5 certainly, either as the Jane Fonda of the Joint Staff. That's when I'd go to National Security Council meetings and say, "How come everybody in here wants to fight but me? Can't we talk to these people? Do we have to start by bombing them?" You know, that kind of dialogue. And, then the other line I would like to use frequently was to introduce myself as the Nuclear Strategic Deterrent guy for the Pentagon. I think we all

ought to remind ourselves frequently
that the principal defense responsibi-
ity for the U.S. armed forces, bar
none, is to prevent the employment
of weapons of mass destruction
against the US or our allies. Period.
Until we have done that we have not
fulfilled our responsibilities.

And that involves a lot of things
we don't talk about too much any
longer. One is strong, modernized,
carefully controlled nuclear attack
forces at an appropriate level. And
thank God the Navy and the Air
Force have not yet walked away from
that mission. It is not very visible.
But we need to put lots of money into
ensuring that our nuclear attack
capability is credible, secure, trained,
and modern. We clearly need sound
international treaty constraints. We
got it. Diplomacy is a huge piece of

General McCaffrey

preventing the employment of weapons of mass destruction. And our current
diplomatic conceptual architecture is outmoded and has to get rethought.
First-rate strategic intelligence is a piece of this huge primary responsibility.
Do we—you know, Kathleen Paige mentioned it. Do we actually know what
it is we are facing? And a lot of times it is painful to face up to some of these
threats. And, then finally, it seems to me we've got to do a strategic and
regional ballistic missile defense. I wrote an article for *Armed Forces Journal
International.* I was tempted to put in there "I'm one of the few military officers that are unequivocal in promoting BMD (Ballistic Missile Defense) as
part of the American people's security." And, part of it—I don't bear responsibilities like the Chiefs or many of the CINCs on opportunity costs of a billion
dollars invested in BMD, will it represent a threat to my own programs. But,
I think we back off it and we talk about our security responsibilities. That is
the first responsibility.

Secondly, the invisible aspect of national defense. It's controlling the
oceans chokepoints and their ports. We haven't been in a struggle, again one
would argue, except for Guadalcanal where we thought we would lose control
of the ocean's chokepoints. You know, we went and fought Desert Storm. It
was great fun. It was the first and probably last military campaign we will ever
carry out where with under 500 casualties the tragedies didn't outweigh the
gains. But a lot of—one of the major —many problems that comes out of

Desert Storm, postwar analysis, forget the role that the Navy that got us there, we go to war by sea. If it's ammunition, POL, or equipment it's got to go through a port. And we can get there rapidly with our new transformed Army divisions. I got all that. But we will fight only when we control the sea. So, we've got to keep whatever is appropriate as naval and other forces to control these chokepoints.

Three, we've got to have a strategic conventional attack capability. And I'm not sure we have adequately understood that this is a synergistic effect. It may well include strategic ballistic missiles. It certainly includes an air and sea component. It certainly includes cyber warfare. It certainly includes special operations forces as part of a strategic conventional attack capability. And again, to go back to Wes Clark's main point, none of this works unless it's in sync with the legal-diplomatic-economic leverage of the United States.

Fourth, expedition area operations air/ground. We've got a problem. We are going to have to understand, certainly the Army is faced up that in the last five years, we're going to have to build a very different kind of intervention capability to get substantial amounts of combat power into a theater of operations by air. Thank God for the C-17 and other ways of bringing combat power across a beach. If the Marine Corps walks away from understanding that their principal unique capability that we have to retain is the ability to intervene across a beach, we will be insecure in our national objectives.

Final one, air/land deterrents and stabilization. And there's, you know, the couple things we shouldn't forget. When you wake up in the morning you ought to say, "Thank God war in Korea didn't start today." There are still unpredictable people. We will fight for Korea. When we wake up in the morning we ought to remind ourselves there is still a reason for NATO deterrence forces to be on the ground, that we are still in Southwest Asia until next fall when we address what to do about Iraq. We'll be there. We have the requirement to maintain deterrence and stabilization.

I think one of the worst things we ever came up with was the notion of exit strategies. And for that matter, sometimes the words "end game" are inappropriate when we talk about U.S. military strategy. Certainly, a prime example in my view was Haiti. Eight million people, abject misery, right in the middle of the hemisphere, right in the middle of the Caribbean, huge economic and political and cultural and social implications to the United States. Had we stayed there for 25 years with special forces, it would not have been a day too long. We do not, it seems to me, constrain ourselves when we talk about immediate exit strategies.

Three cautions. Number one, particularly with some of the incredible brain power in the room. And, I borrowed this line from General Dick Cavasoes, one of my personal heroes and many of you in the room. "Who's pulling the trigger?" No one was ever killed with cyber warfare with information dominance. At the end of the day I want to hear who is the 23-year-old flying the F16. Who is in the tank, the Bradley fighting vehicle, what teenage boys are sitting around looking down the sights of an M249? Who is pulling the trigger?

Number two, we've got to rethink the way we organize our headquarters. You know, you've got to retire to have an idea on this subject. You've got to retire. But we ought to look and say, "Where are the generals?" I was thrilled when the Air Force, years ago, took all of their generals, many of their generals, ran them out of town and put them out with their flying wings. Generals ought to be on the frontier. Less of them ought to be in headquarters.

A third caution. If you want to multiply force structure, the first thing you don't do is buy more units. You buy better training. You buy better quality of people. We know that in an intellectual sense but we better let that observation guide our funding priorities. Training and quality of people magnify force structure, a notion that is inadequately addressed.

My daughter is a captain in the United States Army National Guard. You cannot imagine how proud I am of that fact. You know, she and her husband, a civilian lawyer, and I sort of have a triumphant in this. When she deploys, grandmother deploys. We are proud of the National Guard, a huge modernized sophisticated air and ground force. It is the wrong force to defend America in the coming 25 years. We've got to go out and look at it again and say, "How do we give 54 state and territorial governors the tools they need to defend the American people?" They don't need a tank division in New Jersey. Even worse, we've got these incredibly sophisticated ops research people who correctly will say, "Stockpile your F16 brigade in northeast, put your chemical warfare capability together in California, put your armored units together in the Southeast." What we need to give the governors is nonTitle 10 decentralized capabilities that were designed with a population or environmental algorithm in mind. The Governor of New York needs 10 recognizance decontamination battalions for chem/bio/nuke attack. The Governor of New Mexico needs one. We need to understand decentralized development of a National Guard force.

We need to go look at the American frontiers. It is unbelievable what happens on 7,000 miles of national frontier. We've got to create a national Gendarmerie. We took the border patrol, we took them from 3,500 people to 7,000. I used to tell the Attorney General the right answer is 20,000. Now, I say the right answer is 40,000 people in a national Gendarmerie to control our own borders. This is not a job for the U.S. armed forces, for the National Guard. We do not want members of the armed forces having a role in domestic law enforcement policy. We need to modernize the Coast Guard. It's an incredibly effective force. Its ships are ancient. Its aircraft are ancient. It needs to be structured with a strategic outcome in mind and a doctrine. They've done their doctrinal analysis. The U.S. Coast Guard is inadequate for its current missions.

Then, finally, it seems to me we need to go look at resources. You know, I was on one of the discussion shows debating one terribly smart person without much experience and another nitwit. And, you know, one of the critiques I got from another retiree when I got off it was to say, "You know, golly, you can't call for more resource expenses. Be politically aware. Be sensitive to the realities of the coming 10 years." If the American people want to survive into the late parts of this century, we will spend whatever resources are required to construct an adequate national military strategy and, in addition, will develop the tools in foreign aid and foreign intervention to keep the American people free. It was 40 percent in World War II. It was 6 percent during the Cold War. It is 3 percent now. We have inadequate resources to defend the American people. Lord protect the political leadership the next time we have a major incident and take 25,000 dead if we have been inadequately energized to do what is called for on an emergency basis in the coming two years to build an adequate defense.

I think it's moving in the right direction. Thankfully, we have, in my judgment, an incredibly good team currently leading the Department of Defense and, indeed, the Cabinet officers who are charged with this responsibility. But it won't happen without resources. On that note, thanks very much for letting me share these ideas with you. (Applause)

DR. PFALTZGRAFF: Thank you very much, Barry, for helping us to integrate the many themes that have been a part this afternoon, the need to think about global strategy, regional presence, deterrence, power projection, organizational issues, training and quality of people, and of course, to talk about the National Guard and the Coast Guard. We will have the Commandant of the Coast Guard on our next panel. So this is a good segue, indeed, into the next panel session on homeland security. Now, it is with great pleasure that I open the floor for questions. Please raise your hand and wait for the microphone. We have a few moments. We have, in fact, about 20 minutes for discussion. So, who would like to be the first to be recognized for a question? Right over here. Would you wait for the microphone please?

AUDIENCE MEMBER: Hi. My name is Erin Winegrad. I'm with Inside Washington Publishers. I was wondering if the rest of the panel could comment on General McCaffrey's comments about restructuring the National Guard for homeland defense and what capabilities they need and how they should be structured, placed around the country and the rest of it.

GENERAL McCAFFREY: Ask Admiral Paige first.

ADMIRAL PAIGE: Thank you, sir. I'm well equipped as an Engineering Duty Officer to talk about the National Guard. As a citizen and a taxpayer I'll say it makes great deal of sense to me and I'll pass the ball to that one.

DR. PFALTZGRAFF: Would General McCaffrey like to comment on his comment?

GENERAL McCAFFREY: Well, you know, the armed forces constructed a model where we literally can't fight conventional high-intensity operations from day one of the war without the active participation of the Reserve and the Guard. Air and ground Guard units literally are on our TPFDD (Time Phased Force and Deployment Data) from day one on. And, you know, so they are a valued part of the defense team. And, in some cases, you know, you look at—there are some parts of the Guard units that are far more competent, stabilized long term than their active component counterparts. There are just terrific capabilities. Military police companies are attached to my division in Desert Storm. Six of them, incredibly competent people. At the same time, I think we're facing a new era. We're not going to fight 17 divisions. If we do we can start them from scratch, but what is clear to me that will happen is we are entering a new era where we're going to have to look like Great Britain within five years. We're going to have to construct domestic defenses that are responsive and adequate and they've got to be decentralized. And, the governor and the mayor and the city councils have to have appropriate force structure.

We need military police, light infantry, we need field hospitals, we need signal capabilities that have generators and trucks that can move around. We clearly need new biochem recon decontamination. And they can't be all clustered in one part of the country. They've got to be in every geographic entity. We need combat engineering units. You know, when infrastructure goes down, that's it. And, when you actually look at what's out there in America, it's scary. State police organizations are 2, 3, 4,000 people. Incredibly competent discipline, but these are squads that move around. The border patrol is organized—and other INS, Customs, DEA, FBI, don't have squadrons you can pull out of Southern California and move into, you know, Eagle Pass, Texas. The infrastructure just isn't there. I mean, thank God the NYPD and New York Fire Department were the ones that were so tested by this enormous tragedy. They're as well organized as any army on the face of the earth. But, that isn't the case in, you know, Bopeep, Utah. And, there the Guard is literally the first thing the governor has to ask for in almost any emergency situation. You've got a problem with mail, you've got a problem with mass breakout at the state prison, you've got a problem with nuclear, chemical, or biological warfares, riots, the court system isn't functioning; that's who you turn to. We've got the wrong Guard formation. We're going to have to rethink it.

DR. PFALTZGRAFF: Next to comment on this issue is Congressman Weldon. Curt?

CONGRESSMAN WELDON: Well, the first responders in America are not the military. The first responders are the 1.2 million men and women who serve in 32,000 departments across the country and have done so for the last 250 years. They're the men and women of the emergency response community. I know. I was one, and it doesn't matter of the size of the town. I was the fire chief and the mayor of a town of 3,000 people. In 1975 we had the largest disaster in the country. Two ships collided in our port. One carrying Vinylacitate , the other carrying (inaudible). It was, in fact, a chemical weapons/incident. We had to handle it as volunteers and we did because you are properly trained and prepared.

We are never going to be able to have the military respond immediately to an incident that occurs, whether it's a hazmat incident on our railroads or whether it's a truck collision. We have to make sure that those men and women who will be the first in to respond are properly prepared and trained. Now, obviously, we've got to have the backup. The Guard plays a critical role there. As you know, the Congress saw fit to give the Guard training responsibility because they have the capability to integrate and bring in training systems. The (inaudible) is meant to be able to respond when you have that need. But, at its best, it can't respond for at least four hours. The largest determination of loss of life is in the first ten minutes. So, the people in that first in truck, in that first police car better understand the immensity of what they have. That means they've got to be properly trained and they've got to be properly prepared. That means we're asking them in the 21st century to do things they haven't done for the last 250 years. That means they've got to have basic chem and bio-detection systems. So unlike what happened in Japan in the sarin gas attack, the first responders don't get wiped out. They can make some preliminary decisions about what they have and know who to call to bring in.

I do all the disasters in the Congress. I chair the Fire and EMS Caucus. I go on them all. I was out (inaudible) the earthquake walking the freeway with the Fire Chiefs of San Francisco and Oakland and the Incident Chief in California. They were using dogs to sniff for people that still might be trapped in between the freeways. And I said to them, "Chiefs, why aren't you using thermal imagers?" This is ten years ago. And, they said, "Well, what are thermal imagers?" So you can look between as long as you have an opening to see if there's heat to get enough of the body of the victim, our military has that. We don't do a good job of letting our civilian first responders understand the capabilities we have. In terms of communications, we are totally unprepared as a nation. The military is well prepared. If you bring the military in you've got a great communication system.

Go out and talk to your first responders. Chief Morris in Oklahoma City, his biggest challenge when the Murrah Building was bombed was that he could not talk to any of the integrated agencies responding in the first few minutes to save lives. He couldn't use his radio system because the frequency allocation was all different. Some were on high band, some were on low band. The frequencies didn't match. So he went to portable cellular phones which immediately became overtaxed. So what did the chief of one of our largest departments in the country do? We wrote down his message on pieces of paper and had fire and EMS people hand-deliver them. And that's America in the 21st century. We do not have an integrated, coordinated emergency communication system for this country. And I can tell you, I'll have the Chief of D.C. meet with the Chief of Prince George's County, they can't even talk to each other.

We go out and train the first 125 largest cities and we give ourselves a false sense of security. Those same fire departments retrained to handle chem-bio incidents can't buy boots for their firefighters because their city budgets are cut. What good is giving a fire department a chemical detector or a biological suit if they don't have the funds in their budget to maintain it each year to guarantee the integrity of it? We've got to rethink the way we respond to homeland security. And, I can tell you right now, folks, we're not doing a very good job. That's not the fault of the military. It is the responsibility of Tom Ridge to steer us in a new direction. And, I'm telling you, it's an accident waiting to happen right now.

DR. PFALTZGRAFF: Next question. And, incidentally, we'll be hearing from Governor Ridge tomorrow, late morning. So, he will be with us. Next question? Yes. Please. Right back here. Wait for the microphone and then please identify yourself.

AUDIENCE MEMBER: Lieutenant Jed from the Coast Guard and I teach at the Coast Guard Academy. Thank you for all of your comments today. And my question is directed at the vision that each of you has described for the changing environment for our military in some part depends upon the ability to draw in the youth of America to sustain this vision into the future. How do you reconcile your vision with American children who are increasingly leaving high school without the ability to have the math skills or the reading skills or the technical capability to do what we would require of them in the future? For those that do have the ability, they are more attracted to high-paying civilian jobs to create video games or computer programming that takes them away from adding expertise to where the military needs it.

DR. PFALTZGRAFF: Well, who would like to address that question.

GENERAL CLARK: I'll address it.

DR. PFALTZGRAFF: Wes? General Clark?

GENERAL CLARK: Well, I'm very disturbed in the wake of September 11th. I thought I would find a real upsurge of desire to serve in the armed forces. I didn't find that anywhere. What I found was a lot of interest in it. And, I guess it goes back to the vision that a lot of young people have about America today. There seems to be an awareness of specialization. They are very interested in what we are doing and they sure hope we'll be successful. But, when I went to a couple of universities and I asked them, "What about you, sir?" They say, "Well, I'm studying engineering. I'm going to be an engineer," and so forth. I didn't get any sense that people are rushing to sign up for this. I think that's a commentary on the society that we live in.

It is not just the education or the technical skills, it's also the willingness to join and serve. And I think what we got on the 11th of September is a wake-up call. It says that what we've done in the past got us through the 20th century but we are going to have to look at it differently in the future. And I think in order to really overcome the challenge that we're facing, we need to build a new sense of community in this country. It needs to be built neighborhood by neighborhood, block by block, city by city because that's the way we are going to fight the fight against terrorist cells in our own country. You've got to use the tragedy that's affected us first to send information out to people. There is a lot of people out there who would like to know what bio-war really is. Now, I can tell you that if you watch CNN we have a couple of pretty good specials on it. I think they're even better than the NBC specials I've seen, Barry. But that's not the way we ought to be educating our people.

And again, this comes back really to homeland security. We need a top-to-bottom communications channel. The states can't afford it. I'm from Arkansas now, and I can tell you we love our National Guard in Arkansas and we'd like more of it. But we'd also like to have a whole lot more and for the fire department and the police department because we can't afford to do what we are required to do. We've got to have information out there and we've got to build a new sense of community around it. So, I think if we build a sense of community and we keep people interested in and engaged, we can get young people to stay in school and we can get young people to serve.

But, you know, we've reached—we saw on the 11th of September, we saw the results of what all my European and African friends would tell me. They say, "We come to America, we visit. We really like you all. It is a great country and we really enjoy and we follow all your elections and we know all your politicians, we listen to your movies," and so on and so forth. They say, "But you know, you don't know where we live. I have been all over America, I can't find any news about my country on any of your television stations. I can't—what I tell people in my country is they don't even know where it is. They don't know what the capital is, they don't know who the leaders are, and they don't know when the elections are. They just don't—you don't care about us."

So I think what we have to do is use September 11th and sort of go back and reformulate. And we start with a sense of community. We have to have a sense of community. We have to know who our neighbors are. When I got off the subway three days after the incident up in Penn Station and I looked around, people were looking at me differently than they have ever looked at me in New York before. Always before they look at you like a soccer player. You know, they're watching your belly button. "Am I going to get by his briefcase or is he going to bump me when I go by?" For the first time I saw people looking at faces and they were asking, "Are we part of the same community?" That's what we've got to come out of this with. And it has to be built from the bottom up. It's got to be started by the government. And it will lead to young people to want to stay and want to serve if we do this the right way.

DR. PFALTZGRAFF: Our next question is from right over here, please.

AUDIENCE MEMBER: My name is Gene Porter. Commendable attention to homeland security and doing things better in the local fire departments and so on. But we have a long history of preferring to fight our wars as far away from the U.S. as we can. I was struck by General McCaffrey's enthusiasm for keeping a battalion of special forces in Haiti for 25 or more years and the new QDR, which was cited several times by this panel, has a strong emphasis on overseas presence of U.S. military forces. So, I guess I'd like to ask the panel to comment on their vision of are we going to have a lot more U.S. military stationed or rotationally deployed overseas in order to continue to fight this war over the long haul?

DR. PFALTZGRAFF: Who would like to take this one on? This is a question that all of the panel members could say something about if they would like to. Maybe start with Congressman Weldon.

CONGRESSMAN WELDON: Well, I think we've got to be very selective in how we use our military. I was very troubled during the 1990s. If you compare that period of time to the period after World War II, I think we had 10 major deployments in four years. And all of a sudden in the 1990s we had something like 37 or 38 major deployments in a period of time where we're decreasing our defense budget by the largest margin certainly in this century, coupled with the uncontrolled proliferation causing us real problems. Congress doesn't necessarily object to America's deployment because we are still the only superpower and we have a role to play. Our question is do we give ourselves to insert ourselves in a place like Bosnia? Why do we initially commit 30,000 troops to that theater when, perhaps, a neighboring country like Germany commits 4,000 troops up front, or our key ally is Britain? The question is the relationship of our allies to those efforts. So it's not a case of whether or not we are deployed, it is how we are deployed and for what purposes.

I think America is always going to have to play a lead role because of our stature. But I think whenever we put our troops into harm's way we should have considered every other option prior to that. Many of us in Congress opposed the Kosovo conflict initially, not because we did not support our troops, but because we thought our State Department did not fully engage Russia to play the legitimate role they should have played to use their leverage to get Milosevic to step down. That was a question of where we could have used, and in the end we did use, Russia to bring in its power to force Milosevic out. Now, if we would have done that up front, perhaps we wouldn't have had to conduct that air campaign and put the troops on the ground in Kosovo the way we did. So, I guess what I would say is every policy maker, every member of Congress should put themselves in the mindset of understanding, which one of our panelists said, who's on the end of that gun? Who's shooting the bullet? Because that's the person we're affecting. And we should only deploy our troops when that's the last course of action to make sure that we're going to attain the objectives that we want.

DR. PFALTZGRAFF: OK. Wes? General Clark?

GENERAL CLARK: I think what we've seen in the 1990s is that there is a requirement for nation building. But it's not a requirement that falls primarily on the U.S. armed forces. But somebody's going to have to go out there and help other nations because the majority of the conflicts occur in states. With 6 billion people in the world, states don't meet the needs of their citizens. And what we've seen is we can no longer ignore it. Now, how can we fix it? Well, I think the most important assistance you give is trying to help a state establish a legal infrastructure. But if you want lawyers you can only get them really from the Guard and Reserve, and you have to mobilize people and send them out there, as we did in Haiti and in Bosnia. That's ineffective. What we need is an agency that's not a State Department and not a Defense Department, but that can go in and mobilize and put people in who can bring a legal infrastructure, help put in the place the conditions for economic development, help work an educational infrastructure. And we should be doing that rather than what is the easiest thing to do, which is deploying troops.

The troop deployment again and again turns out to be the easy thing. Troops are deployable. They are effective, at least when they first go in, in settling things. But, they are not very effective at fixing it. And so, you know, my concern with Haiti is not that we didn't stay—I could have supported staying—but the act of staying wasn't fixing what was wrong with Haiti. We didn't know how to fix it, we didn't have the means to fix it, and keeping troops there was simply a palliative. So we've got to move past that. But we do have to address the problem of those people around the world who want the things that we have as Americans. They want equal opportunity guaranteed by law.

And they can't have it. We can't do it with troops, but we've got to find some way to address that need.

DR. PFALTZGRAFF: We have time for one brief comment from Congressman Weldon and then I'm being told that we have only three minutes remaining. So—

CONGRESSMAN WELDON: Bob, just there are two other things that we could and should be doing. Number one, we need to set up a proactive effort using military technologies which has been done. In fact, I spoke with Admiral Watkins in the (inaudible) Commission yesterday on this issue. We need to use military technologies to help us understand weather conditions, things like the El Niño and La Niña effect, where you result in desert conditions or floods or tornadoes which then result in shortages of food. And which result in regional conflicts. Because if we can upgrade the understanding when adverse weather conditions in remote countries will cause economic problems, will cause pressures that then result in regional conflict, which then results in more, we can sometimes perhaps preempt the conflict which then results in us having to put our military into a theater. Now, this was done by a project in the intelligence community called "Medea," funded through the Mitre Corporation and the CIA. That kind of effort, where we use our military assets to help understand the conditions that may lead to war and help to deal with them in a nonmilitary way, I think is something we have to do in the 21st century.

The second thing we have to do is use our intelligence in a more timely manner. We are moving to integrate our intelligence. C4I is beginning to do that, but we're a long way. The Army has led the way. General Shinseki, you know what I'm talking about. The Army developed this Information Dominance Center at Fort Belvoir where they integrate intelligence systems to do massive data mining and profiling, profiling of the bad guys and the bad regions. We do not have a national capability for a national data fusion center. We should have had that three years ago, bringing together all 32 classified agencies from drug interdiction to the State and Commerce Department to the CIA, the NRO (National Reconnaissance Office), the NSA and all of those other agencies where the news controlled by the agencies themselves, but so that when we have a profile of a person like bin Laden or al-Qaeda, we can run that data through a massive high-speed computer using cutting-edge technology, like Starlight or Spires, the kind of technology the Army has developed, the kind of technology Special Forces Command has right now down at McDill [Air Force Base]. That kind of model needs to be beyond the military and needs to involve all of our intelligence capabilities. And it's not there today, and it certainly should be. Those two things that can help us avoid the eventuality of having to put soldiers on the ground.

DR. PFALTZGRAFF: Let me now on our collective behalf express thanks to this panel for the outstanding discussion that we had, the presentations which were superb. The only regret that we all have is that we haven't had more time for discussion from the audience. So, again, many thanks. (Applause) We shall now take a very brief 20-minute break, but you must be back in the room by 4 p.m. We will resume promptly at 4 p.m. with our next panel.

PANEL 3

HOMELAND SECURITY AND COUNTERTERRORISM

Chair: Dr. Jacquelyn K. Davis, Executive Vice President, Institute for
    Foreign Policy Analysis

The Honorable Gary Hart, Co-Chair, U.S. Commission on National
    Security/21st Century, and former U.S. Senator from Colorado

Ms. Michelle Van Cleave, President, National Security Concepts,
    Incorporated

Admiral James M. Loy, USCG, Commandant, U.S. Coast Guard

Major General John S. Parker, U.S. Army, Commanding General, United
    States Army Medical Research and Materiel Command and Fort
    Detrick

Panel Charter

Although the United States continues to face other security challenges, the September 11, 2001, attacks brought homeland security and counterterrorism dramatically and tragically into sharp focus within the government and in the public consciousness. As we conduct a broad and sustained campaign to eradicate global terrorism, we must focus all of the necessary instruments of power at home and abroad. Since September 11, homeland security has become the most immediate priority even though the United States has had to deal with previous terrorist actions. These have included the first attack on the World Trade Center in 1993, as well as the Khobar Towers terrorist attack in 1996, the car bombing of the U.S. embassies in Kenya and Tanzania in 1998, and the attack against the USS Cole in 1999. What these actions, together with the events of September 11, have in common is their escalating lethality.

Coping with terrorism, including the use of anthrax and perhaps other weapons, requires a strategy and organizational effort that cuts across traditional jurisdictions and approaches to security and creates the need for new capabilities and the more effective utilization of existing resources. It is also necessary to consider homeland security as encompassing not only a continuing effort to prevent and to counter terrorism at its point of origin, but also to

Left to right: *Admiral James M. Loy, Major General John S. Parker,*
Ms. Michelle Van Cleave, Dr. Robert L. Pfaltzgraff, Jr., and
The Honorable Gary Hart

deter and defend against other threats to population and critical infrastructure and to cope with the immediate and longer-term consequences of terrorist acts. How to detect, prevent, respond to, and recover from terrorist attacks has become a matter of utmost urgency. This panel focused on homeland security and counterterrorism. This includes the need to achieve the essential integration of effort from organizational efforts such as the newly created Office of Homeland Security and the Homeland Security Council, together with other initiatives to prevent future attacks. Linking response efforts at all levels of government—federal, state, local—and with the private sector is an essential part of the mandate for this panel. The newly created Council has as its mission the development and coordination of national strategy against terrorist threats.

The military campaign against terrorism is unlike any previous war waged by our armed forces, just as the domestic effort to prepare for homeland security is unprecedented. It encompasses consideration of the most appropriate existing assets for this effort, together with what additional capabilities we may need. How military forces can be used most effectively is a necessary focal point of discussion. The relationship between terrorist networks and states that sponsor them must be understood. The sources of support, including funding, safe havens, training camps, and other logistical aid, must be identihed and destroyed. There is widespread recognition of the basic fact that in order to defeat international terrorism, we must use all available political instruments and legal authority as well as intelligence collection and analysis resources. The methods by which terrorists select targets and plan operations must be understood as a basis for counterterrorist operations. Of utmost importance if we are to deter future terrorist attacks will be an enhanced ability to identify with reasonable certainty and then to deter impending terrorist actions by appropriate countermeasures.

As we respond to the current crisis, we must develop strategies and plans that can be the foundation for sustained action in the coming decades. We must provide a more secure society without undermining the civil liberties that define our way of life. How to cope with such challenges provides an important task for this panel.

Discussion Points

- What are the basic elements of a comprehensive strategy against terrorist threats or attacks?
- What are the potential roles and limitations of U.S. active and reserve military forces, the National Guard, and the Coast Guard in the homeland security mission?
- What are the lessons of September 11th for homeland security and counterterrorism coordination within and between the federal, state, and local levels? Between the government and the private sector?
- Will additional organizational changes be required to assure effective leadership and coordination from the national to the state and local levels?
- What are Congress' antiterrorism priorities? Would establishing a committee on homeland security be effective?
- What implications do the recent terrorist attacks have for the intelligence community and law-enforcement authorities, in terms of collection priorities and threat analysis?
- What types of military forces will the United States need to strengthen or develop to fight the war against terrorism?
- What is the appropriate balance between more effective counterterrorism policies at home and the preservation of democratic institutions?

Summary

The Honorable Gary Hart, Co-Chair, U.S. Commission on National
        Security/21st Century, and former U.S. Senator from Colorado

- *The U.S. Commission on National Security for the 21st Century was created in the fall of 1998 and was given a mandate to report to the next President of the United States. The commission published three reports, beginning by trying to describe the world that the United States would inhabit in the 21st century and concluding in the final report with 50 recommendations that were unanimously agreed upon by the Commission.*

1. The first finding was that "America will become increasingly vulnerable to hostile attack on our homeland and our military superiority will not entirely protect us. Americans will likely die on American soil, possibly in large numbers." While not reaching consensus on the timeframe, most members of the Commission felt it would happen soon.

2. The report called for the creation of a national homeland security agency, the recapitalization of America's strengths in science and education, and Congressional reform to reduce the dispersion of national security responsibility in the Legislative Branch.

3. The Commission recommended institutional redesign and suggested specific steps for the Department of State, the Department of Defense, the National Security Council, and the intelligence community.

4. The Commission encouraged the government to expand efforts to attract talented people to public service.

• *Our new security environment includes the following new realities:*

2. We no longer live within secure borders.

3. Traditional rules of war are not being followed by our enemies; they feel free to target our civilian population.

4. The distinctions between war and crime have disappeared.

5. In contrast to the conflicts that dominated the last century, conflict in the early 21st century will be more cultural than ideological.

• *The implications of these realities are:*

1. Convenience, but not liberty, will need to be sacrificed in the national security interest. Careful thought is needed to distinguish between Constitutional liberties and conveniences.

2. Civil defense is once again central to national security.

3. Rules of engagement and conduct must be reviewed within the context of American principles and values.

4. As war and crime merge, the distinction between law enforcement and warfighting is fading and could disappear.

5. Reducing cultural friction through diplomacy will be crucial to the future security effort.

• *This new environment requires immediate action to guarantee our national security:*

1. We must adopt a doctrine of preemption based on superior intelligence and give human intelligence a special, almost elite, status.

2. The roles and missions of the Special Forces should be more central to doctrine and planning.

3. The National Guard is the appropriate entity to protect the United States; therefore it should be trained and equipped for the homeland security mission.

4. We need a review of all national security related laws, structures, and institutions similar to the comprehensive evaluation conducted after World War II.

5. We must engage the American population in structuring the new security order.

Ms. Michelle Van Cleave, President, National Security Concepts, Inc.

• *In the aftermath of the recent terrorist attacks, there have been many demands on DOD resources. The Department has tried to answer many difficult questions by calling together groups of people to think in new ways about the next set of risks that we might be facing.*

• *The Quadrennial Defense Review identifies specific objectives to maintain sufficient military forces to protect the United States' domestic population, territory, and critical defense-related infrastructure against attacks emanating from outside U.S. borders.*

1. The QDR states that the military must be able to support U.S. civil authorities as directed in managing the consequences of an attack.

2. The Review requires the military to be prepared to respond decisively to international terrorism committed on the territory of the United States or an ally.

• *The definitions of homeland security and homeland defense should be clarified. There are at least three broad areas that could be considered homeland security.*

1. Active defense, which includes air defense, defending the borders, missile defense, and computer network defense.

2. Military support to civilian agencies, such as support for consequence management in the event of a WMD incident.

3. National security and emergency preparedness, continuity of government, and continuity of operations activities.

• *Ensuring that sufficient funds are available to combat the terrorist threats may require a theater engagement plan to unify defense resources within the United States and an operations plan to integrate homeland defense and theater operations.*

1. DOD is considering reorganization within the Office of the Secretary of Defense at the same time it is reviewing the Unified Command Plan.

2. To combat terrorism, we must create conditions that make it impossible for terrorists to succeed. This will require a full range of tools, including military capabilities that are effective at disrupting the terrorists' cells, support, communications, logistics, and safe havens.

Admiral James M. Loy, Commandant, United States Coast Guard

• *Protecting our ports, coastline, waterways, and the ships that use them must be an integral tenet of our homeland security strategy. These assets are more involved in our international commerce than airlines and trade centers, and are perhaps more vulnerable.*

• *Homeland security requires prioritizing difficult tasks and improving risk-based decision-making skills. Preventing another attack requires an understanding of the maritime dimension of homeland security. Sustained prosperity clearly depends on economic globalization; 95 percent of our international commerce transits our seaports.*

3. The biggest challenge facing our marine transportation system today is trying to ensure that legitimate cargo is not unnecessarily delayed by enhanced security measures. Government needs to keep ports open and minimize the disruptions and delays caused by federal inspections.

4. Conversely, ensuring maritime security suggests a requirement to restrict access to our ports to keep illegal migrants, drugs, weapons, and other contraband from entering and leaving the country.

• *The security failure of the September 11th attacks was not one of prevention, response, or consequence management, but rather a failure of "awareness." Awareness involves anticipating the threats well in advance and recognizing our vulnerabilities.*

1. Improved maritime awareness will allow us to adopt a risk management approach to reconcile the competing interests of security and prosperity.

2. International and domestic cooperation, both civil and military, is essential. We must establish international standards for all ports.

3. This approach should include point-of-origin inspections in foreign ports by U.S. or other trusted inspectors, in-transit transparency for cargo entering the country, one-stop coordinated inspections in the United States, and advanced detection equipment.

• *As both a military service and a federal law enforcement agency, the Coast Guard is uniquely positioned to fight the terrorist threat.*

1. The Coast Guard can help coordinate the efforts of various levels of federal, state, and local civil authorities, as well as of private sector industries to create a bridge among the various players within the civil interagency community and the Department of Defense.

2. The Coast Guard can provide legal authority, coastal assets, and command structure for military and civil agencies.

Major General John S. Parker, U.S. Army, Commanding General, United States Army Medical Research and Materiel Command and Fort Detrick

• *Countering bioterrorism requires that we enlarge our capabilities of research, think creatively, and educate doctors, health care workers, and the general public.*

2. We should welcome academic institutions, foundations, study groups, and manufacturing industry in their desire to contribute to the protection and defense against bioterrorism.

3. We must improve communication between people, between agencies, with our customers, and with the people involved in the incident. We must clarify which agencies have the lead role in particular circumstances.

4. We must identify the thresholds above which people feel safe and then communicate the true level of risk.

• *We must advocate federal support for public health infrastructure.*

6. We need a national, not just military, test bed where entrepreneurs can test their equipment against established standards.

7. We must improve our laboratory base at the county, state, and federal levels in order to identify and verify pathogens and chemicals of concern.

8. We must have medical intelligence, including disease and medical surveillance, to monitor diseases, injuries, and complications across the country so that we can intervene if necessary.

9. We must find a way to share public health information without compromising or impeding forensic investigations.

Analysis

The third panel considered the organizational and resource requirements for creating an effective structure to secure the homeland and to combat terrorism at home. The concept of homeland security requires an interagency definition; likewise, the legal boundaries and institutional organization within and among agencies with homeland security responsibilities must be developed. Especially interesting to the panel and audience was the evolving relationship between DOD and the Department of Justice, an interface that becomes much more significant as the lines between war and crime—at least in the case of terrorists—continue to dissolve. General Parker discussed the importance of encouraging increased cooperation to find homeland security solutions. Senator Hart argued that while some conveniences must be sacrificed to improve security, essential liberties must remain protected.

Admiral Loy discussed the need to recognize the threats and anticipate our vulnerabilities before addressing protection, response, and consequence management. He stated that homeland security involves prioritizing difficult tasks and improving risk-based decision-making skills, as well as developing an in-depth understanding of each aspect of defense. The panelists discussed the various approaches for integration that may maximize homeland security.

There was agreement on the need for better intelligence, especially human intelligence, to help preempt terrorist attacks; the need for better interagency coordination; and recognition of the central role of special forces in the new security environment. In order to improve consequence management, General Parker pointed out the importance of clarifying which agencies have the lead role in particular circumstances.

According to Senator Hart, the National Guard is the appropriate entity to protect the homeland; therefore it should be reequipped and reorganized for this mission. Admiral Loy suggested that the Coast Guard, as both a military service and a federal law enforcement agency, could help coordinate the various efforts of federal, state and local civil authorities to create a bridge between the DOD and the civil interagency community.

While developing a homeland security infrastructure, it is useful to examine the conclusions of the U.S. Commission on National Security/21st Century, which advocated several measures, including the creation of a homeland security agency. Unfortunately, according to Senator Hart, "virtually none" of the recommendations were implemented before the attacks. Echoing a recurring conference theme, Mr. Hart asserted that the new security situation necessitates a thorough review of national security-related laws, structures, institutions, and rules of engagement and conduct, similar to the review undertaken as prelude to the passage of the National Security Act of 1947.

The panel charter stated that homeland security includes not only counterterrorism measures, but also the responsibility to deter and defend against other threats to population and infrastructure and to cope with the immediate and longer-term consequences of terrorist acts. Ms. Van Cleave, special assistant to the Secretary of the Army in his role as the OSD executive agent for homeland security, described the organizational changes under consideration in DOD; similarly emphasized that homeland defense cannot be accomplished at the expense of warfighting capabilities.

In addition to discussing overarching homeland security themes and issues, the panelists also provided insights into their institutions' ongoing debates. Ms. Van Cleave and discussed how the QDR provides a useful framework for thinking about the military role in homeland security. It identifies the military role as one of prevention, support, and response. While broad parameters of the military role are still in development, the mission must include active defense, consequence management, and emergency preparedness to ensure continuity of government. Admiral Loy discussed the challenge of balancing the paradoxical requirements of loosening security at ports to encourage more trade while tightening security. General Parker emphasized the challenges in protecting Americans from bioterrorism.

Transcript

SPEAKER: Ladies and gentlemen, please welcome Dr. Jacquelyn Davis, Executive Vice President, Institute for Foreign Policy Analysis.

DR. DAVIS: Good afternoon. It goes without saying the unprovoked attacks against the Trade Towers in New York and the Pentagon here in Washington brought home to most Americans the urgency of devising a strategy and for procuring capabilities for dealing with new and prospective threats to the U.S. homeland. Since September 11th, the President has directed the establishment of a Homeland Security Office in the White House. And in the Pentagon, Secretary Rumsfeld is considering the creation of a new organization to include perhaps an Undersecretary of Defense for Homeland security and Counterterrorism. However, as the events of September 11th and the anthrax dissemination have demonstrated, homeland security and counterterrorism efforts will and are requiring an interagency, a national, and even an international response based upon a wide array of capabilities and approaches.

Today, we have assembled a panel of experts to discuss the conceptual, organizational, and resource issues associated with homeland security and counterterrorism and, in particular, post-September 11th planning. Obviously, the panel members here today are not new to these issues. For the most part, they have spent considerable time and applied their respective expertise to counterterrorism and defense of the United States and its overseas interests for quite some time. As the panel members now come in, I would like to briefly introduce them to you.

Our first panelist is former Senator from Colorado, Gary Hart. Senator Hart, as you may recall, was the cochairman of the highly regarded U.S. Commission on National Security for the 21st Century. And this Commission and the subsequent report spend considerable time debating unconventional warfare issues and recommendations for reorganizing the national security apparatus of the United States. Just by way of a personal note, Senator Hart, I don't know if you recall, we first met 20 years ago, in 1981, in London when you graciously agreed to speak at one of the first conferences that IFPA organized. And you were accompanied by then Senator Bill Cohen and Senator Sam Nunn. So, welcome back, Senator Hart.

Our second panelist today will be Ms. Michelle Van Cleave. Many of you will recall that Michelle was nominated to be the Assistant Secretary of Defense for Special Operations/Low Intensity Conflict. However, in light of the reorganization that is ongoing now in the Pentagon, she is serving as Senior Adviser to Tommy White in his capacity as Executive Agent for Homeland Security. And, I think she's going to tell us in her remarks today something about this reorganization and perhaps she will allude to the office which she may assume in coming days, weeks, months.

Dr. Davis

Our next panelist is Admiral James Loy, Commandant of the United States Coast Guard, who, by the way, was here and heard some of the remarks of the previous panel, and I think might be prepared to respond to some of the comments that were raised. But during his impressive service to our country, Admiral Loy, among other things, has spent the last several years working on a reorganization of the Coast Guard to meet 21st Century challenges. I wanted to mention also that it is with Admiral Loy that IFPA will be organizing its next grand conference endeavor in March of the next year, 2002, in Cambridge, Massachusetts. We are going to organize with Coast Guard sponsorship and also the sponsorship of the Defense Threat Reduction Agency a major conference on security, so we invite you all and hope to see you in Boston for that meeting.

Our final speaker today is Major General John Parker who is Commanding General of the U.S. Army's Medical Research and Materiel Command at Fort Detrick. And he is also Commanding General of Fort Detrick, by the way. General Parker has served in numerous headquarters and combat service support assignments and is very well positioned to discuss the challenges posed by bio-terrorism, including the recent challenges we have faced as a nation confronting the anthrax threat. With that, I would like to turn the panel to Senator Hart to begin the presentations. Senator Hart?

SENATOR HART: Dr. Davis, the Fletcher School, General Shinseki and the Army and all the sponsors of this forum, let me express my thanks and appreciation for being invited to be with you and to be on such a distinguished panel. I would like to divide up my few minutes here in the following ways. One, give you about two minutes background on the U.S. Commission on National Security for the 21st Century, summarize our conclusions and then give you, perhaps, some personal reactions to the experience of having served on the commission and, like all of us in this country, experienced the September treachery.

The Commission was created in the fall of 1998 by former President Clinton, former Speaker of the House Newt Gingrich and the Secretary of

Defense, Bill Cohen. There were 14 members of the Commission. We were given a mandate to report to the next, then unknown, President of the United States, no later than February 15, 2001. Our membership consisted of seven Democrats, seven Republicans, four former members of the Congress—two from the Senate, two from the House, including my Co-Chair, Warren Rudman from New Hampshire—three former flag officers from three different services, including General Charles Boyd, Retired Air Force General, who was our superior Staff Director. And in the course of preparing our report, which was meant to be the most comprehensive review of U.S. national security looking forward, since the combination of committees and commissions that operated in

Senator Hart

this country in the period of 1946-47. And we took our mandate and our responsibilities that seriously, that this was not just another federal commission, not just another commission on national security, but that we were given two and a half years to think about the next quarter-century, which was the arbitrary limit we set on our perspective views.

What we tried to do was, first, describe the world that we thought we, in the United States, were going to be living in. And we spent about a year thinking about that with the help of dozens and hundreds of experts across virtually every kind of field that you could imagine. That was our first report, "New World Coming," and I'll come back to that momentarily. That was September 15, 1999. Second report was "Seeking a National Strategy". This report came out in April of 2000. These, as you can see, are very small documents, but they were backed up with considerable supporting documentation. The third and final report, "Roadmap for National Security", was delivered to the President January 31, 2001. For those of you concerned about these things, as we like to say, ahead of time and under budget. We turned money back to the Department of Defense.

This report contains 50 specific recommendations, which I will summarize momentarily. The remarkable thing about this Commission, whose ideology spanned Former Speaker Gingrich, perhaps, on one end and Former Ambassador Andrew Young on the other, all 50 of these recommendations in five separate categories were unanimously agreed to. There were no dissenting votes and no separate or dissenting opinions. Present company excepted, the 13 other members of this Commission are about as distinguished Americans as you will find in this country, and they worked extremely hard. We estimated that among us we had 250 or 300 person years of public service, particularly if not in the uniformed service then in service having to do with the national security of foreign policy.

Our first recommendation, or our first conclusion, if you will, or finding, that has since September drawn the most attention was our first conclusion in the first report, "America will become increasingly vulnerable to hostile attack on our homeland and our military superiority will not entirely protect us Americans will likely die on American soil, possibly in large numbers." Now, it has been observed, and rightly so, that we had a horizon of 25 years. So, that was perhaps you can say, not that extraordinary a recommendation. But it did occur two years before the September treachery and for some of us, it was sooner rather than later. We did not reach consensus that that this would happen within one or two years, but most of us felt it would happen soon. I gave a speech—for myself, I gave a speech in Montreal on September the 5th. The newspaper headlines the next day were, "Hart predicts terrorist attacks on America." That day, the 6th. I met with the National Security Adviser, Dr. Rice, and urged the Administration to move as quickly as it could on creating a homeland security capability. Beyond that, as I've said, we made 50 specific recommendations, much too detailed to go into here.

The reports, although our Commission went out of existence in July of this year, the report—we got our Website back up. And, by the way, all these reports were on the Website contemporaneously and virtually all of our deliberations were public. The Website is back up, in case you want to get these. It's www.NSSG.gov. The National Security Study Group is the NSSG. I would encourage you—as I say, these are a dozen to 16 pages and then this is 143 pages with a summary of about 25 pages. And I would encourage all of you to read it, given particularly your official responsibilities. For virtually all of what we've recommended has not been done yet and should be the subject of a considerable national debate.

We did call for the creation of a national homeland security agency, and I'll momentarily come back to that. We did recommend in the national security interest recapitalization of America's strengths in science and education, noting the decline of our scientific base systematically over the past two or three decades. Both our researchers in math and all the sciences—chemistry, physics—but also our teacher core in all of these areas, and of course the precedent for this was the National Defense Education Act of the 1950s. That remains to be done. We called for institutional redesign. We found the State Department to be a dysfunctional institution. And we called for some specific steps for the State Department to reorganize itself to carry out, as General

McCaffrey said a few minutes ago, the absolutely crucial mission of diploma-cy. Obviously, the Defense Department also—gave some very specific recom-mendations for that, for the National Security Council, for space policy and the intelligence community. We called for, remarkable for a Commission with four former members of Congress, reform of the Congress. It wouldn't do any good for the Executive Branch to change itself if the Congress doesn't follow suit. And, as many of you know, national security responsibility is spread so widely across so many committees and both Houses of Congress, in the 24 or so subcommittees it's also dysfunctional.

So, Congress cannot merely point its finger at the Executive Branch and say, "Move yourself into the 21st Century," because they're going to have to do the same thing. Fifth and finally, we called for massive improvements in the human requirements for national security. In a word we found the best people in America are not entering public service, and that's not a social ill, that's a national security ill. We must make government service, not career necessari-ly, not the military necessarily, but some forms of national service across the board honorable in our society once again. And to do that we can't talk about the government as our problem or the government as our enemy. We're going to have to challenge young people to think about a few years of their lives, if not uniform then in some form of public service in the Diplomatic Corps, Peace Corps or whatever. It's absolutely critical to get talent in this country back into the public arena.

That's the Commission. And I want to now, in two or three minutes, give my own personal views that I very clearly want to distinguish from the Commission so they are not responsible. I think we're living with at least five and probably 50 new realities, and let me tell you what I think those five are. We no longer live within secure borders. We were used to that since virtually 1812. Somebody did point out recently that Pancho Villa crossed over into New Mexico in the early part of this century, I think. Leave that aside. Americans have not lost their lives to foreign attacks since 1812 up until September. Civilians are now targets. Traditional rules of war no longer apply. The distinction between war and crime has disappeared. If six or 60 people had died in New York we would have considered it a crime. 6,000 is war. Where in between was the threshold crossed? And, finally, conflict in the 21st Century, or at least the early part of that century, is as much cultural, indeed more cultural, than it is ideological. And that's important because we lived in the 20th century in an age of ideology.

What are the implications of these realities? Convenience is going to have to be sacrificed in the national security interest, but not liberty. And it's going to take an awful lot of hard thinking by people in this room and elsewhere to distinguish between our constitutional liberties and our conveniences. Bag searches in public places are one thing, and into sports events are another and are the same. But we get into the area of wiretap surveillance and so on, we're getting very close to constitutional liberties. Civil defense, or however you want to describe it now, what used to be called civil defense, is central to national security. Rules of engagement and conduct must be reviewed within the context of American principles and values. And, clearly, what I'm—that's a euphemism for reconsideration of policies such as assassinations and so on. But, we're going to have to—if war and crime have merged, we're going to have to think about the ways we combat both. The distinction between law enforcement, domestic security, the police function, and warfighting, the military function, is fading and could well disappear. And finally, reducing cultural friction, as General McCaffrey and others have said, is going to be crucial to this security effort. That's the role of diplomacy.

Quickly, five or six new ways of thinking. We're going to have to adopt a doctrine of preemption based on superior intelligence. We can't simply sit back and wait to be attacked. President Clinton tried that with the missile attacks two or three years ago unsuccessfully, but that's why I say intelligence has to be superior. Make—we're going to have to make the roles and the missions of the Special Forces perhaps more central to doctrine and planning, instead of a collateral or peripheral mission. We're going to have to give human intelligence a special status, almost an elite. There's going to have to be a human intelligence capability in our intelligence structure and community that's roughly, if you will, a parallel for lack of a better, more thought-out thinking, something like the Delta of special forces. But, it's an intelligence capability.

We're going to have to restore the constitutional role of the militia. Could not agree more with General McCaffrey, the National Guard is the constitutional entity to protect the homeland. Doesn't mean DOD and the standing permanent professional military doesn't have a role. It just means that we have a constitutional army on our soil, may or may not be trained and equipped for this mission, but it ought to be. It must be. General McCaffrey gave some ideas for doing that. We must never sacrifice constitutional principles. I think we need to review all Cold War laws, structures, and institutions for their applicability to the 21st Century, the same way we did when we passed the National Security Act of 1947. And, as you know, the centerpiece of making war combines the government, the Army, and the people. And, unlike the Cold War where the people more and more were separated from policy making, we must engage the people of this country in the structuring of the new security order. Thank you all very much. (Applause)

MS. VAN CLEAVE: Well, as many people have noted throughout this conference, in the aftermath of September 11th there has been an enormous awakening to the need for homeland security throughout the country and certainly within the Department of Defense. With the Pentagon still on fire in the days after that attack, the people who work there, including I suspect many

people here in this audience, stayed
on the job. They were concerned less
that the terrorists might return to fin
ish the job that they had started, but
more that their families might be at
risk at home. And this, I think, is a
fear and a concern that they shared
with all Americans.

And, so the generals and the
clerks, the senior leadership and the
staff sergeants turned to two fronts:
Protecting America at home and planning a war against the terrorists
abroad. Calls on military resources in
the aftermath of that attack have been
many and varied and they continue
today. Many crisis management decisions had to be made in a short period
of time and have been unprecedented
in the scope and kinds of questions
asked, such as determining the need
to fly combat air patrols in various

Ms. Van Cleave

urban areas throughout the United States, or what might be the most vulnerable points that we would need to be concerned about protecting; or wondering
about what information is available publicly about the critical nodes that might
give rise to an interest from terrorists, and should this information be protected? What about airport security and border patrols and other requests for the
use of National Guard resources in many and diverse ways, stressing those
resources in ways that they may have not been configured to be used? These
requests still come in where we are looking to having to provide extra protection of airports during the holidays or for special events, such as the upcoming
Olympics, or in response to specific threat concerns. There have been many
demands on DOD resources that the Department has stepped up to try to
answer, and many difficult questions calling groups of people together to think
in ways they haven't thought before, such as the red teaming exercises to try to
think creatively about what are the next set of risks that we might be facing.

Continuity of government has been another concern. Many have noted
the possibility that the aircraft that was downed in Pennsylvania by the hero-
ic acts of the passengers may have been headed for the Capitol or the White
House. And the aircraft that came into the Pentagon, if it had traveled just a
little further, would have gone right through into the National Military
Command Center and impacted where the senior leadership was meeting to
deal with the crisis.

One could regard this dimension of the attack as a decapitation effort, rais-
ing again questions about the need to have clear capabilities and plans for the
endurance of the government.

So, for the future, stepping back from the handling of this immediate crisis, we're left with many, many critically important questions for policy and
strategy for the country and the Department of Defense. I'm certain that many
speakers at this Conference have cited the Quadrennial Defense Review language with respect to homeland defense being the highest priority of the U.S.
military to defend the nation from all enemies. The QDR sets out very specific objectives: to maintain sufficient military forces to protect the domestic population, its territory, and its critical defense-related infrastructure against
attacks emanating from outside U.S. borders, and to have the abilities to support U.S. civil authorities as directed in managing the consequences of an
attack. Finally, still quoting from the QDR, "The U.S. military will be prepared
to respond in a decisive manner to acts of terrorism committed on U.S. territory or on the territory of an ally."

This is a very broad set of essential objectives. Within the Office of the
Secretary of Defense, capabilities, missions, programs, activities that impact
these mission objectives are dispersed across many organizations within the
Secretary's office. We recognized this before September 11th and have established within the Office of ASD SOLIC a division to support territorial security, which had just begun to establish the necessary resources and capabilities
when the attack occurred. Post the attack it was very clear that homeland security required higher level attention within DOD. Accordingly, the Secretary of
Defense created an Executive Agent, Secretary Tom White, to handle the
immediate operational requirements, day to day taskings and interagency
coordination for homeland security purposes. That executive agent was established as a bridge to a more permanent entity within the Office of the Secretary
of Defense. And, I have received the task from the Secretary of the Army in his
capacity as Executive Agent to provide the conceptual foundations to consolidate different aspects, missions, programs within OSD under a new entity that
would be responsible for homeland security. The final form of that organization will be decided by the Secretary of Defense, and I suspect the Congress
will have something to say about that, too.

Secretary White has said very clearly that, in his view, we need to have a
new Undersecretary for homeland security, and that is certainly the leading
option that we're looking at right now. But many offices, as I've mentioned,
within OSD and the services as well, presently have responsibilities impacting
homeland security. For example, the Secretary of the Army is also executive
agent for the direction of military support to civil authorities, but policy
responsibility for MSCA resides within the Office of the Undersecretary for
Policy. The ASD SOLIC is currently assigned responsibility for territorial security and counterterrorism and counterdrug activities. Policy also has responsi-

bility for crisis management and continuity of operations and continuity of government. There are responsibilities outside of the policy realm as well. For example, Health Affairs clearly has important lead responsibilities, as does Guard and Reserve Affairs, both of which are within the Office of the Undersecretary for Personnel and Readiness. The ASDC3I has many responsibilities in critical infrastructure protection and information assurance and security and counterintelligence that one might find appropriate to bring under a new entity for homeland security, and even acquisition. The Undersecretary for AT&L (Acquisition, Technology, and Logistics) also has responsibilities in the technology development for homeland security, including questions of how you marry up and rationalize those requirements with other battlefield requirements. So, the list goes on and on and on. Indeed, at one level everything that we do to protect and defend the United States and our interests can be seen as contributing to the defense of the homeland, including going after the terrorists and their sponsors where we find them.

Consequently, what we mean by homeland defense and homeland security needs to be bounded so that these responsibilities and assignments are clear. There are obviously many ways of approaching doing this, so I would like to interject a commercial break and say to those of you who have ideas and recommendations and insights in some different aspects of this, that I am in the market for such good ideas and I hope that you will bring them to my attention as we proceed with this project.

One way of looking at homeland security is to look at the included missions within that subject heading. I would suggest that there are at least three broad areas that one could consider to be within homeland security. First, the area of active defense, which includes those activities that the Department of Defense can be directly responsible for in terms of air defense or defending the borders or missile defense or perhaps computer network defense. These things may well fit into a homeland security definition. Then there are the support responsibilities that DOD has to support civilian agencies such as support for consequence management in the event of a WMD incident. And, finally, there are all the things that we do in the category of national security and emergency preparedness, continuity of government, continuity of operations activities. In each of these areas the drawing board is certainly not blank, but we can and will do better for the future.

For example, in the area of active defense, while parts of active defense are currently assigned, such as computer network defense, some of these things may be imperfectly developed. But what is really new is the need for conventional homeland defense, including the questions about how much is enough against the terrorist threats that we will face. Homeland defense planning may also require some kind of a theater engagement plan that arrays defense resources within the United States, and an ops plan that integrates homeland defense operations with theater operations to ensure that homeland defense is not purchased at the expense of winning the war. There are major questions involving the Guard and the Reserve, to be sure, and some have suggested that there may be a need for a new warfighting CINC to take on some or all of these active defense missions. And, therefore, the reorganization within the Office of the Secretary of Defense is proceeding hand in glove with the review of the Unified Command Plan.

Within the area of military support to civil authorities and the supporting role of the Department of Defense, these questions are many and they are deep and they will—we will be looking largely to the lead coming out of Governor Ridge's office and the need throughout the government to pull all our resources together to have a strategy for homeland security that everyone can support. But, for the future, whatever organization may be chosen, the important starting point is to think clearly about what needs to be accomplished to lay out a path to accomplish these things and to get the work done.

And yet as we all know, it is not possible to add enough layers of security to protect against all threats. The real protection against terrorists is to go on the offensive. Our strategic purpose must be to create conditions that make it impossible for terrorists to succeed. That will require a full range of tools to include military capabilities, aimed at disrupting the terrorists cells, support, communications, logistics and safe harbor. The terrorists rely upon, as their strength, their amorphous nature, their diverse cell populations, their use of Internet communications for continuity and connectivity, their lack of a fixed location, their mobility across international borders. These things can be turned into vulnerabilities. But, as Senator Hart has observed, as a first-order priority we need to develop the intelligence capabilities vital to support military operations against the terrorists.

Many people have observed that U.S. special operations capabilities will prove central to this war effort. The strategic use of SOF assets is a policy decision that must be predicated on sound intelligence. And the quality of our intelligence is equally important to the quality of the forces, the men and equipment, which are employed in an operation. Both are essential to our success. So, we have a voracious need for high-quality intelligence in this endeavor.

I remember reading or hearing that not long after September 11th some news organization—I think it was CNN—received an invitation to posit some questions to Osama bin Laden for him to answer. And I believe they had come up with a list of questions that were very thoughtful, designed to provide some insight into his strategic purpose and to elicit an admission of culpability. But I recall hearing a commentator on the radio list the questions that he would ask if given a chance. His questions to bin Laden included, "Where are you, exactly? And, how long will you be there? And, how many of your guys are with you?" Now, all that would be useful information, the kind of very particularized intelligence that we need.

I know that everybody has personal stories coming out of September 11th and I would like to close by sharing one of mine. Like many people, I was on the phone with my mom, who was back home in California. She was checking to make sure that I was all right. I was a little close to the action for her comfort level. And my sister is a flight attendant with American Airlines. She, in September, was flying the Los Angeles to Boston route. She had been flying the day before, but she wasn't flying on Tuesday of that week. And so both of her daughters were safe and sound, but my mother was on the phone and she was very upset and she was close to tears. And I kept reassuring her. I said, "Mom, you know, we're fine. Everything's fine. It's all going to be fine. Don't worry." She said, "That's not why I'm crying. I'm not upset about you and your sister. I am concerned about my grandson. My eight-year-old grandson," she said, "will now grow up in a world in which he has to be afraid. So much has changed now, and he will not live with the kind of carefree sense of security that we have always had. He has to now live in a state of fear." And, I say to myself and I say to you, "That is unacceptable." It is unacceptable that children in America should have to live with such fear. Or that any of us should.

As Secretary Rumsfeld has said many times, it is clear that our task is much broader than simply defeating the Taliban or al-Qaeda. It is to root out global terrorist networks and the governments that sponsor them, not just in Afghanistan but wherever they are, to ensure that they cannot threaten the American people or our way of life. Our homeland will be secure when we win that war. Thank you.

ADMIRAL LOY: Good afternoon to you all. I think you're out there. These lights are tough up here. I don't know whether anybody else in the panel is wondering, but I do think there's an audience out there. We have heard some wonderful strategic issues on the table and offered for our consideration by both Senator Hart and by Ms. Van Cleave. I have been asked by the Fletcher School to talk to you a bit about what I imagine the role of my service to be in this homeland security challenge that we now face. And so I'm going to try, at least, to bring that strategic set of issues down a notch or two to some practical realities, if I can. As a nation that depends so heavily on the oceans and sealanes as avenues of our prosperity, I think we have concluded, and certainly we have within the Coast Guard's deliberations, that whatever action we need to take against terrorism must protect our ports and waterways and the ships that use them. These ships and ports are even more valuable to our commerce with the world than airlines and trade centers, I would offer. And, I would further offer, perhaps even more vulnerable.

Let me just offer a couple facts. Almost a trillion dollars of our GDP is provided by way of the maritime industry. 95% of the trade that comes and goes to America comes and goes by ships. We have some 98,000 miles of coastline to worry about between those ports and harbors; over three and a half million square miles of exclusive economic zone to be dealt with as if it were truly our territorial seas; some 51,000 port calls from some 7,500 ships on an annual basis; six and a half million passengers on cruise ships; 200,000 sailors on those commercial ships that come to our ports; a billion tons of petroleum delivered to this nation on an annual basis; 16,000 containers per day yielding over six million a year with significant questions as to the inspection capability of our nation to deal with them. Valuable and vulnerable. Not a bad combination if you happen to be on the target team for the bad guys.

But how do we prevent another attack? Is that possible? And what can this particular service, the Coast Guard, do to protect the vulnerability of our maritime interests? More importantly, and perhaps an extrapolation of that line, is how do we find ourselves as a nation to get out of the response business, which we literally have been in since the 11th of September, and into the prevention business, a much more reasonable thing, for us to reestablish that comfort zone that Ms. Van Cleave spoke about. I think it's about prioritizing very difficult lists and initially it's about getting very, very good at risk-based decision making, and many of us in our business need to be about doing both of those things. Preventing another attack requires an understanding of the maritime dimension of homeland security.

We simply can't afford to bring the maritime dimension of our economy to a stop. And, if you think for a moment, that's what we did to the commercial aviation business on the 11th of September. When those 480 planes were directed to the ground by Secretary Mineta, it took us days and, perhaps, weeks to restore a credible aviation economy and system back to our nation. To do the same thing in the wake of four or five or six ports of our nation being brought to their knees would be speaking—we would be speaking about weeks and months, if not years, to restore that kind of fabric, which is the fundamental foundation block for the prosperity of our nation. The biggest challenge facing our marine transportation system today is how to ensure that legitimate cargo, therefore, is not unnecessarily delayed as we and other nations introduce enhanced security measures against some very real and potent threats. Sustained prosperity clearly depends upon our accommodating this global trade that is predicted to double, if not triple, over the next 20 years. Most of that trade will come and go through our seaports. So, government needs to be attentive to finding ways to minimize the disruptions and delays caused by federal inspections and other border security kinds of activities. More stuff has to move faster so ports need to become more open. Hold that thought.

Ensuring maritime security, on the other hand, suggests a requirement to tighten down those very ports that we were just so eager to open. Government has an obligation to keep illegal migrants and drugs and weapons and other contraband from entering and leaving through those same ports whose throughput we want to maximize, literally for the interests of prosperity for

our nation. This is precisely the
dichotomy that was presented to us
by the Hart-Rudman Commission in
the first phase of their report. Well,
how in the world do we protect our
nation's maritime security in such a
dynamic environment against such
elusive threats? This is a question
that we had discussed a lot, but rather
academically until two months ago.
And it has now become uniquely and
vitally important to us as a service
and as a nation to get the answer to
that question right. We need a systematic approach of complementary
security measures to put together an
effective offense and defense on this
multilevel chessboard of maritime
security.

Admiral Loy

Of course we need to think more
seriously than ever about how to prevent, how to respond and how to
manage the consequences of asymmetric attacks. But I would offer to you that
this notion of prevention, response, and consequence management, which was
very prevalent in our nation and all of the services and all of the agencies, was
not where the failure occurred on the 11th of September. I believe the failure
occurred in some piece in advance of prevention that I have at least termed
"awareness." We simply were not as aware as we could, would, or should have
been with respect to the domain in which we work. Awareness involves recognizing the threats well in advance and anticipating our vulnerabilities. And,
in maritime port security, it's about ships, people, and cargo. It has to do with
having access to detailed intelligence about our adversaries, and sharing that
information more effectively among federal agencies and with our domestic
and international partners in both the private and public sectors. Not talking
about it, which we have done a lot over the years, but actually doing it.
Without better awareness, we will be forced to take more stringent actions
with regard to prevention and response that will close down our economy and
threaten literally our economic security.

Well, maritime domain awareness is a concept that serves to reconcile
these competing interests of security and prosperity in our ports and waterways. Maritime domain awareness covers all of the information requirements
of everyone with any responsibility for homeland security in the maritime
domain. Applied to the government interest of getting more cargo through

customs and Coast Guard inspectors in less time with greater security. I think its key elements would be these: An integrated, accessible database of information; point-of-origin inspections overseas in those foreign ports by U.S. or by trusted inspectors in sanitized facilities; in-transit transparency to what is mostly a focus of the cargo and containers coming in our direction; one-stop coordinated inspections here in the United States; high-technology centers and readers and gamma ray scanners; solid, risk-based decision making forums charged with taking on and actually solving problems with accountability at the other end of the day. Thus armed, I believe we can take a risk management approach to decide which vessels need to be boarded on the high seas, at the sea buoy, or at the pier, based on the greatest threats represented to us.

We must push the maritime borders offshore, out from the coastline, by sharing information on international arrivals and departures within the United States and among our partners around the world. And that will help prevent future attacks. We could even incentivize the good guys by offering some kind of quick-pass handling to those fully compliant with the security profile that we insist upon. It will also help by telling us simply what's going on daily in our ports and waters and, yes, even in the exclusive economic zone. Events that very well could have escaped our attention before, but now may be vital to our understanding the impending threats against us. International and domestic cooperation, both civil and military, is essential in this regard because we can't hope to ensure our security by working alone or by waiting until the threats have already crossed the thresholds of our ports.

So, I will introduce at the International Maritime Organization's Bi-Annual Assembly next week resolutions and calls for accelerated activity on their part to help us establish international standards for the well-being of those ports over there. I think awareness is the key to preventing the potential threats from being realized and becoming a consequence to manage. Awareness must be an all-hands evolution, including returning the Coast Guard to important national security missions in the deep water environment that, because of our multimission character, we were able to depart from immediately on the 11th of September to go to where the nation needed us most, which was within the ports and harbors of our country.

So, what is the role of the Coast Guard in homeland security? The Coast Guard is committed to improving awareness of our maritime vulnerabilities and threats, using some of the means that I've tried to describe to you. With regard to the other elements of a maritime security strategy, prevention, response, and consequence management, the Coast Guard also stands ready there, as well. As both a military service and a federal law enforcement agency, I think we are uniquely positioned among federal agencies to fight an enemy that crosses boundaries with seeming impunity. Threats can pose as legitimate trading vessels very easily among a very large volume of commercial, and even recreational, traffic. Somebody has to engage these vessels one at a time up close and personal. Somebody has to distinguish the suspicious from the obviously innocent.

To separate the guilty from the merely suspicious, somebody usually has to get along side, put a boarding team aboard, even if the suspect refuses to stop. Somebody has to size up each case and dispose of it based often on a very complex humanitarian, diplomatic, military, geopolitical, environmental, and legal issue, which often are at stake. Somebody has to coordinate proposed enforcement actions with other government departments, flag states, law enforcement agencies, and anyone else who seems to come out of the woodwork with a seemingly legitimate voice in the matter of the day. And, as Senator Hart has mentioned, it must all be done according to the rule of law in our country. And for 211 years that someone in our country has been the U.S. Coast Guard. The Coast Guard offers scaleable command and control frameworks, suitable for preventing or responding to nearly any military or civil domestic emergency. We do it all the time. Our captains of the port have broad and strong legal authority to secure and manage any situation that arises in our ports or on our waterways. This authority gives them the legal basis for ordering or approving just about any movement of shipping within any of our ports. And our port security units give enforcement teeth to that legal authority.

To that foundation, we offer experience in disaster relief and pollution response, experience that has made us the most proficient agency in conducting things through the incident command structure. And that incident command structure, which has been now adopted by FEMA as their standard, I believe is the most effective way for coordinating interagency responses to domestic emergencies. And if one of those emergencies should require DOD involvement, our status as one of the nation's five armed services links us to the others in a joint warfare environment. So, the sum of these elements—legal authority, coastal assets, command structure for military and civil agencies, command and control systems—offers a bridge among the various players who must get involved within the civil interagency community and the Department of Defense.

Well, since September 11th we have had five goals emerge as to what we are trying to do—what we are trying to do on our ports and waterways: Controlling the movement of shipping in our ports; increasing our presence within those ports for both the value that it represents for deterrents and for potential response capability. We have inventories and critical infrastructure and we have reached out to others who can help us: the Office of Homeland Security, the Joint Forces Command, the Navy, state and local governments, other federal agencies, and, certainly, the private sector. We've conducted over 50 different sessions with many of our private-sector colleagues that we work with all the time in our ports and waterways. And the challenge we left with each and every one of them was to understand this is an all-hands evolution and they each must make their contribution to the higher port security profile of our nation.

Immediately after the attacks on September the 11th, the unique multimission structure of our service allowed us to radically increase dramatically the security posture using active duty, reserves, civilian and auxiliary personnel, as well as existing shore units, ships, boats, and aircraft. We began placing sea marshals on arriving commercial vessels to control the movement of shipping in some ports, which we hope to do so on a broader basis very soon, budgets allowing. We established a 96-hour advance requirement for notice of arrival for foreign flag vessels entering U.S. ports. It used to be 24. Coast Guard men and women everywhere have significantly increased the security of the nation's ports and waterways, protected people and property, and assisted in rescue and recovery efforts. We've increased our presence within the ports while doing our very best to keep commerce flowing smoothly. We've begun to take an inventory of critical infrastructure needs of those ports, and we have gone to each of those critical infrastructure piece owners and challenged them to rise to the occasion of being responsible for the security of that particular piece.

It is crystal clear that never will the Coast Guard have all the adequate resources necessary to guard every piece of that infrastructure. It must be an all-hands evolution. Our broad outreach to federal, state, and local government partners, as well as members of the maritime industry, is leading to a mutual understanding of ways and means to improve the security of our ports and waterways. Although the Coast Guard is primarily responsible for the security of our ports, as I said before, we can't do it alone. Civil and military authorities will act together to protect those ports and waterways. Private industry must also take a lion's share of responsibility for protecting what is vital to them and to us. The Coast Guard is helping where we can and we will also be there to ensure that the industries achieve a layered approach to security, including adequate facility, vessel, and port security plans and the exercises that will demonstrate their adequacy. The role of the Coast Guard in homeland security is to help provide the maritime security piece to the comprehensive puzzle.

We aim to be effective, we hope, so as to remove maritime security from the host of issues that Governor Ridge is concerned about. We can be most effective in the maritime domain by helping to coordinate the efforts of various levels of federal, state, and local civil authorities, as well as of the industries of the private sector. We already perform on a smaller scale the necessary function that is vital, I believe, to the overall success of the Office of Homeland Security. Some people see this function as an adjunct mission, another new task added to a growing constellation of tasks for the Coast Guard, but as I suggested to Senator Hart before we came out, this clearly has become our north star. This clearly has become the most important mission that the Coast Guard offers to America today.

The mission of maritime security may be more urgent today than it was two months ago, but it is no less important than it was 211 years ago. Since our founding in 1790, our primary purpose to this nation has been to provide maritime security to our homeland by guarding its coasts. We plan to continue to do that. Thank you very much. (Applause)

GENERAL PARKER: Dr. Pfaltzgraff, the Fletcher School, General Shinseki, General Peak, I'm very honored to be here this afternoon. Our national power is its people, and we need to think about that for a minute because without the people that we have mentored and educated in this land, we would be nowhere today. I'm here and I've been asked to talk about countering bio-terrorism. I have 21 points and I'll deliver them in 15 minutes or less. The battlefield has been redefined. In military terms we used to say, "detect to avoid, detect to identify the threat, detect to protect." And we were thinking of working in some far-off land with a face-to-face enemy and now, all of a sudden, the battlefield is the continental United States. Only our people can solve the issues at hand. No device, no computer, it's our people. We must raise them up.

In my experiences with the recent anthrax contingency that occurred here in Washington, D.C., I learned one thing above all else. It boils down to one person who wants to know, "Am I contaminated? Am I going to get ill? What should I do?" One person. Everybody wants to know if they're personally at risk when something happens. How do we answer that question? We have the technology today to develop sensors for just about everything. If someone comes to me and says, "We need a sensor to detect banana peels in the room today", we can go somewhere in our great system and we'll find a scientist that knows how to take banana oil and get its structure and create a microchip and put a little chip on you to detect the odor of banana oil in this room at some level where your nose won't even detect it. We have that capacity. Now, if we go and we build detectors and we have little buttons on our shirt and we say, "We can detect anything," and someone gets a little detection on there, they're going to come to someone and say, "My detector says I've been exposed to "X." And, that's where the mystery begins because we better know an awful lot about "X." We better know what it is, what its physiology is, what its human effect is, what the therapy for "X" is, at what level do we provide therapy for an exposure to "X." There's a lot of work to be done and I think this nation can do it, but we have to think almost at the individual level.

Decontamination took on new meaning. Decontamination of people, places, things, papers, file drawers, your favorite pencil, they all became important in the decontamination process. Have we done enough research on a way of decontamination that is done quickly leaving no residual so that people can leave a building, have it decontaminated, and immediately return? I think there are few senators that would pray for that today. What are our research priorities? I'll tell you, since September 11th there's been a sea change in cooperation across this country. Academic institutions, foundations, small study groups, and small manufacturing industry want to come together to find the solution of how to protect and defend against bio-terrorism. For years, the Department of Defense set the standard working the issues of biological exposure, chemical exposure, and nuclear exposure. Ladies and gentlemen, the Department of Defense worked for 50 years to develop the knowledge base that we have today so that we can bounce off and provide answers to some of the questions that are being posed to us today. We must now take advantage of this great sea change and engage and enlarge our capabilities of research across this nation so that we can monumentally change that fountain of knowledge to solve these difficult problems. We must think out of the box.

I defend the Food and Drug Administration. It's an important part of our life to be able to turn and look at a label and say, "It is FDA approved." It gives us a sense of well-being, that it's tested, it's efficacious, and it's safe. But, in a crisis contingency, should we have some auxiliary contingency codes of federal regulations that allow the Federal Food and Drug Administration to bless certain products that have 50 percent efficacy rather than 100 percent efficacy when we know that the alternative is death? These are the types of things that we must wrestle in the future as we think about countering bio-terrorism. What are the standards of contamination? Do we worry about one spore on the table? Do we worry about 100 spores in the rug? When do we worry? We need to develop some standards of what is safe and what isn't. I don't think we can guarantee no spores ever in the Hart Building forever and ever and ever. One tiny little spore is going to find some niche and survive. Now, is that a danger? Well, to some people it is. In reality, I don't think it is. I think there are thresholds that we need to identify where people are safe.

As we walk through our world today, people are shaking hands, hugging, coughing, sneezing, and the bacteria and the viruses are invisible to us, but we seem to survive in a sea of pathogens that just would love to set up housekeeping in our rich environments of our physiological fluids. We seem to survive until one of those gets out of balance and we need to know when that balance is changed. Learning as we go. Is that bad? No. We need to learn how to do that better. We can't ever know everything all the time. We must accept that a new crisis or a new event may be new to our minds and to our population, and our population must accept the fact that we will bring the brilliance of our people to that event, and we will learn as we go thinking every single step of the way that people are important. We will save lives and we will contain the incident. And we will learn so that the next time we will lose less lives than we lost before.

We in the military probably have quite a library of scenarios. We live and we think scenarios and how we would—what type of a battle plan we would have, what kind of a logistics plan, what kind of a medical plan would we have for that scenario. If we think of the vast future ahead of us, I don't think we can have a complete library of every possible scenario that could happen to this nation. We must depend on a few basic principles. The Army calls them Commander's Intent. The intent is easy. Discover the incident, contain it, treat those who need to be treated and get to the perpetrators as rapidly as possible so that that event never occurs again.

During this crisis, if I have had one phone call from someone who has the ultimate product, I have had at least a hundred. I was worried about getting down here today. I was on the Hill testifying. And when I finished, someone else came up and they handed me a whole bundle of stuff

General Parker

with a letter from Senator Helms. I think it has 50 letters in it from people that have something that is important for the events of the current day that they want us to buy or to support. What we need is a national testbed. Not just a military testbed, a national testbed where entrepreneurs can bring their equipment to that national test bed and have it tested against a criterion. I think we need to move rapidly in that particular direction, and it has to be well funded and it has to be well supported with manpower because, just like the thousand drugs waiting for clinical trials to cure cancer, I bet you there are 10,000 great products out there that are waiting to be tested and the capital investment is not there for the entrepreneur to get it tested.

The other thing that I've learned desperately is that no matter what we do, communication is critical, communication between people, communication between the agencies, communication with our customers and with the people that are involved in the incident. We must do better with communication. I've been in the United States Army for 38 years. I've been in a lot of scenarios, be they real or be they exercises. And, in the after action report of almost every single one of those scenarios or exercises, it's been, "We could have communicated better." We need to think about communication. We need to put dollars to it, put manpower to it, and we need to learn to do it better. We've struggled with public health versus forensic investigation. When is material so important to a forensic investigation or to a prosecution where it cannot be shared openly where it may have a public health consequence? We don't know when it has a public health consequence.

How can we share information and still allow the proper authorities to capture and prosecute intelligently those who have perpetrated against us. I will go back to the coordination of the agencies. We live in a competitive society. We compete individually and that carries into our workplace and carries into the pride, carries into our agencies, and our agencies compete. We need to take a look at that because we want coordination, not competition. How can we award and reward for people getting equal credit for working solidly in their lane toward a success of a mission? We do need to identify lead roles. Senator Cleland said it greatly about two weeks ago. He said, "You know, we make rules. The President makes rules. Other people create policy, other people create regulations, and sometimes they do this." Not meaning to do that, but we've got to diffuse the confusion of who has what lead role when.

The laboratory base. This goes back to public health. Counties, states, and the federal government need better laboratories to be able to identify and verify pathogens and chemicals that are supporting the terrorist events. We need to support that by giving good education and training to those people who want to set up a good laboratory. We in the DOD have developed reagents that identify these pathogens that create havoc on the threat list. I had a reagent meeting just last week. The Department of Defense can stand proud in the fact that they have developed over 100 reagents for developing pathogens. Some overlap. That's good. You want overlap so that you can verify. We now need to take that defense technology objective and expand it, enlarge it, and allow the American public and the universities across America to participate to get the right answer.

Our public health infrastructure must be supportive. In various cities across the country they have very good public health systems. And then as you travel away from some of our biggest cities, it just dives off like a cliff. We must support federal support for public health infrastructure.

We must have medical intelligence, and medical intelligence translates into disease and medical surveillance. We must get beyond the privacy gaps of the medical record. We must be able to interrogate all of the medical records in the United States, not looking at a person's name, not looking at a social security number, so that on a minute-to-minute basis we know what diseases, injuries and complications are happening across the country so that we can intervene. Funding is always a problem. And I think I heard it mentioned by the eloquent speakers before me that it's going to be a priority issue. God bless those who have to set the priorities. Education and training: Critical. If we're really going to go into the 21st century and counter bio-terrorism, we need smart people. We need them to be trained in what's out there. And I'm not just talking doctors and health care workers and nurses. I'm saying that the general public must have a knowledge base of what is in their environment, how to act with it and how to take care of it if it becomes personal.

We must launch a campaign across this nation to understand why the American public wants no risk. Zero risk. That's what the American public wants. Can we afford zero risk in this nation? Getting to zero risk is an isotonic curve in which there may be not enough dollars in the future to get there. At what level of risk will a human being feel safe? Every single day we have people on motorcycles. Every single day we have people on motorcycles without helmets. Every single day a thousand more children learn how to smoke. Every single day 50 people die on the highways because of drunk driving. There must be a level of risk that the American public will accept because those statistics prove it. Now, will they accept more than zero risk in a biological event?

Avoiding panic. A terrible onus on someone that has to speak into a microphone in front of cameras when an incident is just unraveling. What do you say? Do you want to tell everybody that it's the worst thing that's ever happened to the United States? Or do you want to speak to certain facts that you know about and give the sense that the people of this great nation will learn through this and have the right answers? I think it takes strength not to create panic up front.

I'm going to close with a very important personal relationship that I've had with the Executive Branch, with the Legislative Branch, the Department of Defense, and other agencies. Ladies and gentlemen, you can be very, very proud that you have great leadership. This is a lucky nation. And it will continue to be a great nation because of that leadership. Thank you very much. (Applause)

DR. PFALTZGRAFF: We will now proceed to our discussion period. We are going to extend this session by 15 minutes so we will have a bit of extra time. We'll go to 5:45. Before I do that, however, I simply want to express thanks to each of the panel members for what they've said so far, for having the statement from Senator Hart about the NSSG study with its prescient recommendations; to Michelle Van Cleave for what she had to say about the new organizational initiatives being taken in the Department of Defense with respect to homeland security; to Admiral Loy for what he has told us about the very important role of the Coast Guard and especially its role in port and harbor security; and finally, to Major General Parker for all that he has said to us about countering bio-chemical terrorism and issues of decontamination. We now turn to the audience for comments and discussion. Who would like to pose the first question? I think we'll raise the lights, hopefully, and shed additional light on the issues that we're dealing with. Who would like to be first? I see a hand in the back of the room, there. I was about to begin to ask my questions because I have a lot of questions if no one else does. But go ahead. Please get the microphone and identify yourself.

AUDIENCE MEMBER: Dick Field, *Defense Technology*. A question for Admiral Loy. Do you think increasing the number of U.S. flag vessels would make your job in keeping our ports safe help?

ADMIRAL LOY: Well, I think the easy answer to the question is probably yes, but there is a marketplace reality that you have to grapple with as the real answer to your question. The essence goes back to the—to what I mentioned earlier in my remarks. It's about vessels, people, and cargo and to the degree we gain comfort with an adequate review of who's on board, what's on board, and the vessel itself that will heighten our Captain of the Port's comfort zone that that vessel is among those that he has to spend less attention to than to others. So, I think the flag is important. There's no doubt about that. But at the other end of the day it's all three factors that have to play into a risk-based decision making process that they'll have to consider.

DR. PFALTZGRAFF: Anyone else want to comment? Let's now move on to the next question. Let's try to take one from this side of the room, if we can. If there's someone over here who would like to pose a question? Please wait for the microphone.

AUDIENCE MEMBER: Thank you. I'm Lee Ewing from *Homeland Security and Defense New Publication*. I'd like to ask Admiral Loy, considering all the discussion recently in Congress and elsewhere about who should handle airport security, whether it should be federal or private contractors, what do you think about the idea of the Coast Guard having a role in that?

ADMIRAL LOY: We work on the water. I use three "M" words to talk about my service. It's "military," it's "multi-mission," and it's "maritime." And the maritime point is, I think, the telling point with respect to that. So, I think there is and has been an absolutely excellent discussion both on the Hill and in the Administration with respect to getting that right. There had been, unfortunately, a little bit of finger pointing in one direction or the other, but the reality is the cards you face up on the table are the Administration and the Congress are working that very, very hard, and I'm confident they'll get the right answer.

DR. PFALTZGRAFF: Are there any other comments on this very important issue of who should control airport security? Does anyone want to venture into that arena? With all the minefields that may lie there. Anyone else? I take it that no one would like to do that at this point. Let's go to our next question, then. Who would like to be next. Please?

AUDIENCE MEMBER: A question for Senator Hart. Sir, Bob McClure, Army Fellow at the Council for Foreign Relations. With the Office of

Homeland Security, do you fear perhaps a fault line developing between the actions we're going to take in a war on terrorism that will be the war overseas and the war in the homeland, and, given the responsibilities between the Department of Defense and the Homeland Security Office, do you see a fault line developing there that perhaps we can avoid?

SENATOR HART: I really don't. I see more seams and gaps, and I think the Commission did as well, between the approach presently being adopted by the Administration domestically than I do between the domestic effort and the international effort. One of the reasons why I'm optimistic about a coordination, international and domestic, is the historic 20th Century relationship between the standing Army, the professional military, and the National Guard and Reserve. The National Guard—the National Guard was the militia under the Constitution. In the late 19th Century it became the National Guard. In the 20th Century it became a follow-on expeditionary force to the regulars. And, that's the way the Guard has come to think of itself as they would say as their primary mission. What I believe, and I think others in our Commission believed, was that they have a new primary mission and that is homeland defense, which brings it full circle to 214 years ago, which is what the Founders intended.

The question is, are they properly trained and equipped? Probably not right now, but they can be. There is nothing institutionally that prevents them from doing that, and it solves a constitutional problem, it solves a statutory problem—the controversial Posse Comitatus Act—and it solves a practical problem, they are forward deployed. They are a forward deployed force and they are citizen-soldiers. So that's the reason we advocate the role of the Guard. But given the century of cooperation between the Guard/Reserve and the regulars, I think that helps prevent some of the gaps that you're talking about. Now, you may have a more precise problem in mind than I've touched on, but I think what we're concerned about are the gaps and seams on the three uniformed border patrols, Coast Guard, Customs, and Border Patrol. Those, it seems to me, need to be brought closer together, not losing their identities by any means, with their historic missions. But coordinated or commanded, if you will, by a cabinet officer rather than a council. That's a long discussion.

DR. PFALTZGRAFF: Would anyone else on the panel, especially Admiral Loy, want to comment on this question?

ADMIRAL LOY: Anyone else on the panel, especially—(laughter). Senator Hart and I have chatted about this before we came out. I think clearly there are potentially some organizational implications to the challenges that face the nation in this crisis. There's no doubt about that. But I would also hasten to add two very sort of Management 101 cautions. And the first one would be, I hope we get around to understanding that form must follow function, and our imperative is to get the functionality right and allow the form stuff to follow whenever it is appropriate for that to occur. The second point is that in the middle of a crisis it's probably about the worst time you can go through, the reorganization upheaval associated with [it] must be part of that process to gain the organizational integrity that I think Senator Hart and his colleagues had very much in mind with an Office of Homeland Security integrated well, put together well, and, you know, with that being accomplished in the middle of a crisis. So I think the notion at the moment is to sort through the crisis carefully and to give certainly the Executive Order direction that has been generated by the President, enacted now by Governor Ridge, an opportunity to do the right thing and be watchful with respect to that as it plays out and have voices at the other end of the day that could—to bring the right things back onto the table when it would be appropriate to do that.

DR. PFALTZGRAFF: Who would like to—yes? Next question. Right down here.

AUDIENCE MEMBER: Hi. Ed Winn with Raytheon. A question to Ms. Van Cleave and also to Senator Hart. It relates to terrorists. A terrorist internationally is a SOLIC (Special Operations and Low Intensity Conflict) problem. A terrorist in Kentucky is an FBI problem. Some of us were joking that the right thing for bin Laden to do was to give himself up to the United States and fall under the U.S. Rules of Evidence. There's a policy issue in terms of the coordination between the Department of Defense in terms of how do you suppress a terrorist actively, potentially overseas, versus how do you do the same thing in the United States? With these people going back and forth, they're actually working in two domains. Probably within a week they'll be in both domains, and that's probably how they'll work the hiding. So, could you comment a little bit maybe, both of you, on number one, the coordination between Defense and let's say Special Operations and FBI? And, then, Senator, from a standpoint of Rules of Evidence, how you see how we handle bringing terrorists to justice and still follow rule of law? Thank you.

DR. PFALTZGRAFF: Who would like to begin with that question? Senator Hart?

SENATOR HART: Go ahead, please.

MS. VAN CLEAVE: No, you go ahead.

SENATOR HART: I can hardly wait to hear what you have to say.

MS. VAN CLEAVE: This is difficult to address. Clearly, the need for defense and law enforcement coordination is not a new problem that has arisen in the wake of September 11. Delineating the appropriate lines of authority between the FBI and other national security agencies have been questions that have been with us for quite a long time. And working through the proper relationships between those organizations has, in fact, been done in many areas. For example, in appropriate ways, there is a sharing of information and operational understanding, although it is admittedly far from perfect. I think that it is fair to say that that essential cooperation has been enhanced in the aftermath of this crisis.

If you're asking specifically, how do you divide up responsibilities between law enforcement on the one hand, and defense on the other, given the porosity of our borders and the fact that we have threats now that go across our borders, I may not be able to give you a good answer. Indeed, that question is central to national security strategy in many different respects today.

Dealing with specific terrorists who present physical threats is a part of that challenge. Another part might be the cyber threats that we're seeing and the difficulty in discerning whether we're facing a foreign adversary or whether we're facing a domestic criminal activity. Those things are very ambiguous and they're very, very difficult to characterize. I guess that the best thing that we can say is that we're bringing technology to bear to try to find ways to discriminate between origins of the attack, and then the appropriate roles and missions for the different government agencies have to flow from that. But whatever we do in the national security context, I think we need to be mindful of the inherent civil liberties concerns. The distinction between dealing with a domestic U.S. person or a foreign person in any particular context can make an extraordinary difference under our Constitution, and the obligations of government to the individual. I think that we're very sensitive to the need to be attentive to that distinction in many different areas of national security policy.

SENATOR HART: One of the reasons I emphasize the blurring of the distinction between war and crime and the police and the military function commonality is that we're in a new era. I mean, we are treading on new ground here. And we will spend the next five to 25 years or more trying to strike, not just the risk balance, which I think is a very important factor for our society, but the liberty/security balance. And, there's no true north in a system like ours, a mass democracy with Constitutional, guaranteed freedoms and a judicial structure. And it is—and I think we've seen this week or even yesterday the first indication of this amorphous gray area when the President assigned Mr. bin Laden to a new—to a military court, which as I heard on NPR today, can be conducted on a ship offshore. Now, that's going to be an interesting—maybe one of the Admiral's ships. I don't know.

ADMIRAL LOY: We'll order that. (Laughter)

SPEAKER: And if you get lost we won't mind. And, I think, although I didn't get to read the story precisely, I think there are rules—there are going to be rules of evidence to go along with that court. Maybe not. If not, if they don't adopt courts of military justice rules or whatever are standard there, then you could have a whole new field of the law, which I think also is going to happen. I'm going to lecture next summer—spring—at Yale Law School and it's amazing. The law school is now offering courses in terrorism, courses in the areas of law that didn't even exist a year ago. It's amazing. And so, society is trying to adapt to this new era.

DR. PFALTZGRAFF: We have time for one more question. And, since I do not see a hand, I'm going to ask the final—oh, there is a question. OK. Then I will not ask my question. Right here, ask yours.

AUDIENCE MEMBER: I'm Pete Schifferly. I'm with the U.S. Army from Fort Leavenworth, Kansas, heartland. General Parker, you made a comment that said that we needed bright minds. You also, I think, began your presentation by saying it was people. And, for I believe this is really for Senator Hart, if you want a militia, you want a conscription. And so my question is, if we're focusing national power and national power is the people, when do we start conscription?

GENERAL PARKER: Did he aim it at me or you? [Looking at Senator Hart] (Laughter) Well, I think if you look back in history, there are a lot of good things that came out of conscription. I think it was the early opportunity for youth to understand what the nation was all about. It was the basic entry point where people started to understand that people are different, they come from different parts of the country, they look different; but their hearts and souls are the same. It created that mandatory mixing bowl that was very important for a society. It had the benefits of when that youngster left that service, and history would say "only males," when in the 21st Century that will change, I believe. I think it has to be debated. It has to be looked at very carefully. And I think history will say that it gave a lot of youth a second chance in life. It gave a lot of youth a purpose. It gave a lot of youth a reason to look back and say, "I served." So there are a lot of positives for conscripted service. It doesn't all have to be in uniform. There are all sorts of sectors of this great government where people could serve and learn the same cultural benefits. So I, for one, will be for it. And I think it would be a great debate.

DR. PFALTZGRAFF: Are there any other comments on this very important question? Senator Hart?

SENATOR HART: Well, we've had a militia for 214 years without—except in time of war—conscription. When there was conscription enlistments in the National Guard and reserves obviously went up because a lot of people didn't want to go to Vietnam. I think you can maintain—it would be an interesting thing to watch—that we can maintain strength levels in the Guard and reserve without conscription. If not, then we'll have to reconsider that, obviously, given the national emergency. But having been on campuses in the last two months, it is amazing to me how young people in this country are reevaluating—are reconsidering their values. Young people, bright young people, said to me, "You know, before September it was Goldman Sachs or Arthur Andersen or I didn't know what. But for the first time in my life, I'm thinking about going into the government." Well, we haven't heard that for 25 years. I mean, my generation heard it in the early '60s and it conditioned us heavily.

But, we need—our political leaders now need—to take up this new patriotism, if you will. Kids were asking me, "What does patriotism mean? What does it mean to be a patriot?" And they weren't being facetious and really didn't understand the concept. Was it just waving a flag or wearing a pin? They thought it was more, but they needed someone to tell them what it meant. So, they were hoping that the State Department would recruit, the military services would recruit, the CIA is very popular. So I don't think we need conscription right now, but obviously we've got to think about that. I have been, in my public life, a long term advocate of a national service program. I very much support the legislation John McCain is putting forward now, which is very close to legislation I introduced 20 years ago.

With a military/nonmilitary option, probably not mandatory for the time being at least, because we've got all kinds of cost and administration problems, but I think now is the time to give young people a chance to serve their country in some capacity. Maybe not the rest of their lives, but for a little while. And I—by the way, just finally and off the point, this idea of the testbed is fascinating, General, because as a civilian, as a out-of-office citizen, I've been inundated with phone calls, emails, faxes, proposals, people saying, "How can you get me to Governor Ridge?" Well, obviously, we can't get to Governor Ridge. But there are a huge number of Americans out there who think they can do something for homeland security. It may be a technology, it may be an idea, a concept, or it may be a way of screening people coming into the country, but the Administration would be well served if you do set up a clearing house and just walked people through on a 15-minute basis and said, "Tell me your story. Leave your documents behind." And, I must say, there are a few of us, General, on the banana detector that would like to know if you could devise one that would work with the *National Enquirer*. (Laughter) (Applause)

DR. PFALTZGRAFF: Well, ladies and gentlemen, on that concluding note . . .

ADMIRAL LOY: I hate to follow that one. . . .

DR. PFALTZGRAFF: OK. All right. We can stay as long as you wish.

ADMIRAL LOY: But I do have at least a thought with respect to the national service question, and I couldn't agree more on a personal level with Senator Hart as to the notion of national service and its value to all the citizens of our country, who many of us have encountered just looking for an opportunity to contribute. How do I find a way to make a contribution? I can't tell you how many times my email circuit is lighting up with retired Coast Guard folks who are looking for a way to make a contribution. I think it is a concern that we have what I'll call a widening gap between those who find themselves in uniform and those that do not, whether those are professional folks, especially, you know—I ask the question every time there's a bi-year election. OK what's the freshman class look like? How many of them have ever served their country in uniform? And, sadly, those numbers are deteriorating. And it's the same with judges, and it's the same with fill-in-the-blank.

So I think the notion of a widening gap between those who serve and those who don't, whether it's serve at-large, that is, military, or as the Senator suggests, a public service of some kind, federal service of some kind, Peace Corps, Americorp, call it what you will. I find today Americans are looking for a way to contribute to the national well-being, and we should be finding ways to help them do that. I also do believe that there are very real competency implications to this at the long end. Someone asked the original question about are we going to have competent people dealing with the sophisticated hardware that your Army, Navy, Air Force, Marine Corps, and Coast Guard are using these days, and to whatever degree you take that widening gap to some unknown end, you truly do have an opportunity to put the challenge on the Services to make up the difference, so to speak, when at the other end of the day a national-service notion would perhaps have less of a challenge placed on the Services and more of an opportunity to contribute at a sophisticated level available to an awful lot more Americans.

DR. PFALTZGRAFF: Let me express thanks to the members of the panel and to you, the audience, for what has been an outstanding contribution to this conference. We will, of course, be building upon the themes that have been discussed today and especially in this last panel in the sessions that follow tomorrow. Let me now adjourn this session and invite everybody to the atrium where we have refreshments, where we have a reception, and then, of course, the dinner beginning at seven p.m. which will also be held in the atrium with, of course, the address by Secretary Wolfowitz. So, again, we look forward to seeing you shortly. Thank you very much.

KEYNOTE ADDRESS

OPPORTUNITIES AND CHALLENGES FOR AMERICAN POWER

The Honorable Paul Wolfowitz, Deputy Secretary of Defense

Summary

• *September 11, 2001, was as much a turning point in American history as December 7, 1941. The attack on Pearl Harbor inspired the United States to take a more active role in the world. The terrorist attacks on New York City and the Pentagon are the wake-up call for this generation.*

• *The strategic response of the United States should not be planned around one or two well-defined threats. We must develop plans that allow for complexity and uncertainty, provide a range of options, and can be adapted quickly and effectively.*

1. The United States needs to focus both on the war of the present and on wars of the future. There is a danger of focusing exclusively on the new challenges posed by terrorism.

2. An evolution in threats has caused a revolution in how we think about defense. Adapting to surprise quickly and effectively must be a central element of defense planning.

3. To deal with surprise and uncertainty, we must shift our planning from a threat-based model to a capabilities-based model that accounts for an adversary's existing and potential capabilities and compares them with our own.

• *The six top transformational goals of the Quadrennial Defense Review will guide our efforts to build a 21st century military. The capabilities that looked so expensive in peace seem relatively cheap in light of the challenges we face today.*

1. Protect the U.S. homeland and bases overseas, particularly against the threat of WMD, by developing passive defenses, such as medical countermeasures and biological surveillance systems, as well as active defenses against ballistic missiles.

2. Project and sustain power, even in anti-access environments, by reducing the military's dependence on logistical support and by exploiting technologies such as long-range aircraft and stealthy platforms.

3. Deny our enemies sanctuary, particularly by exploiting the asymmetric advantages of long-range precision strike capabilities, intelligence, and undersea warfare.

4. Enhance offensive and defensive information network measures.

5. Leverage information technology to enhance joint operational capabilities.

6. Maintain unhindered access to space and protect the infrastructure that supports critical space capabilities.

• *Our recent successes can be attributed to leveraging the capabilities of friendly forces on the ground, exploiting our asymmetric advantages, attacking the weaknesses of our enemy, taking risks, thinking boldly, and adapting to circumstances.*

1. Today, our greatest asymmetric advantage is the unlimited power of a free democratic people whose government is based on universal ideals. We should support the successes in the Muslim world and encourage freedom and self-governance.

2. The Taliban, by contrast, ruled by terror and weakened their country through barbarism. Every state that sponsors terrorism also terrorizes its own people. People who suffer under their own government can become our allies in the war on terrorism.

3. Our mission in the war on terrorism is not only to eliminate the terrorists, but also to enlarge the circle of freedom to include people of Muslim nations who are still seeking the benefits of a free and prosperous society.

Analysis

In his keynote address, Deputy Secretary of Defense, Dr. Paul Wolfowitz, stated that September 11—like December 7, 1941—was a turning point for America and the world, and that gave the American people a new perspective on what is affordable for national defense. Yet he cautioned against focusing exclusively on the terrorist threat; we must also plan for complexity and uncertainty. Adapting to surprise must be a central tenet of U.S. defense planning. Force planning must also concentrate on developing certain capabilities rather than countering specific threats. The flexible future force must exploit America's asymmetrical advantages, such as precision strike and undersea warfare.

Dr. Wolfowitz asserted that military transformation goals, such as protecting the homeland and bases overseas, sustaining power projection capabilities in anti-access environments, and denying the enemy sanctuary, must be realized during the current war against terrorism. To guard against future uncertainties, additional objectives must also be achieved, including developing offensive and defensive information and space capabilities that will safeguard our computer networks, enable joint interoperability, and ensure unhindered access to space.

Dr. Wolfowitz discussed the effectiveness of U.S. forces in leveraging several capabilities in the current war on terrorism, including collaborating with friendly forces on the ground. He also reminded the audience that the United States has recently come to the aid of Muslim people in Kuwait, Somalia, Bosnia, Kosovo, and Afghanistan. He suggested that the United States should continue to support moderate Muslim regimes and citizens repressed by state sponsors of terrorism, as they can become our allies in the war on terrorism.

Transcript

DR. PFALTZGRAFF. Welcome to this gala occasion, and of course we thank the U.S. Army strings for this wonderful concert. I kept thinking about the years that I took violin lessons and never could master the instrument as they have. It's great to have them with us. I would like in welcoming you this evening to turn the podium to Secretary of the Army Thomas White, who will introduce our speaker, our keynote speaker.

SECRETARY WHITE. I almost expect to be opening the envelope and saying the winner is Paul Wolfowitz. My goodness. (Laughter) Thank you, Bob, for this very warm introduction, and thanks for moderating this very important conference, now in its 31st year. Defense ministers, administration officials, ambassadors, flag officers, scholars, distinguished guests domestic and foreign, ladies and gentlemen, thank you so much for such a wonderful turnout and thanks for joining us as we focus on the security challenges confronting America at home and abroad. Thanks also, to our cosponsors, the Institute for Foreign Policy Analysis, the Fletcher School of Law and Diplomacy, Tufts University, and the Office of the Secretary of Defense for Net Assessment. Given current events, this is certainly a very timely and relevant forum, and we are truly grateful for the enthusiastic support and participation we have gotten for this year's conference.

I'm honored tonight to introduce our keynote speaker, Deputy Secretary of Defense Paul Wolfowitz, a man who really needs no introduction amongst those gathered here, but then I will carry on for just a minute as if he did. As most of you know, Secretary Wolfowitz is now in his third tour of duty in the Pentagon. Now, experience is certainly [a] valuable and desired attribute in our senior leadership, particularly in this conference. Surely, Paul, this time you're going to get it right. At the same time, I must admit it's reassuring to have a Deputy Secretary of Defense with his experience, his intellect, and vision during this time of war and change. We are lucky that when faced with the choice of serving this nation or pursuing some other avenue, he invoked the indisputable logic of that great New York Yankee and sometimes philosopher Yogi Berra [who] observed, "When you come to the fork in the road, take it." It's our good fortune that he took the fork in the road that led to the

Department of Defense. There is no greater need for his experience and skills than right now.

Today America is a nation awakened to danger. It is a world threatened by the evil of terrorism. But America did not become what it is by submitting to our adversaries. We will win this war. A far-flung war we will absolutely do. (Applause) And as we all know, it's a far-flung war against al Qaeda and other international terrorist networks, not just the Taliban in Afghanistan. As the President said, we did not ask for this mission, yet there is honor in history's call. The threat posed by terrorism cannot be ignored or appeased, as we all know. Even as we meet, the terrorists no doubt are planning more attacks and more murder, despite the positive developments that we've all witnessed unfolding in Afghanistan.

So it is our task, the task of this generation, to act decisively in response to aggression and terror. History will record our response and judge or justify every action that we take. We have risen to this responsibility, we act to defend ourselves and deliver our children from a future of fear. As we go forward Secretary Paul Wolfowitz will help guide our great nation to certain victory, of this I have no doubt. Yet Secretary Wolfowitz has the vision and foresight to look beyond the current war against terrorism to prepare for the next war and the war after that. As proven during our rigorous QDR debates over the summer, he is a vigorous proponent for transformational change in our armed forces. And he is fully committed to the Army's objective force, a force that will enable us to meet emerging challenges and remain relevant to the needs of the nation.

Thus, we are extremely fortunate that he is our keynote speaker tonight. I can think of no one better qualified to address the many challenges that confront us on the road ahead. Ladies and gentlemen, it's my great honor and distinct privilege to introduce a true patriot, an outstanding leader, our Deputy Secretary of Defense, the Honorable Paul Wolfowitz. (Applause.)

SECRETARY WOLFOWITZ: Thank you, thank you. Thank you. I did feel like you pulled my name from an envelope. I have to confess, I never have spoken in a place like this before. I've never been asked to make an entrance like that before. And I have to tell you, Tom, the acoustics back there are so bad that you could have said anything you like about me and I wouldn't have known it. (Laughter) But I'll assume it was a warm introduction. I'll thank you for it.

I've always wondered, this is a magnificent building, but always wondered what Ronald Reagan, that great apostle of small government, would think about having his name on this building. (Applause.) It's a great pleasure to be here. I know there are many very distinguished guests in this audience, so I won't get myself in trouble by singling out any of you, and I think all of you are distinguished. This is an impressive conference and my compliments to Bob Pfaltzgraff and the Army and everyone who put this together, and I gather you've been doing it for 31 years. I hope you have another 31.

Secretary Wolfowitz

I think, but I didn't hear him, that Tom mentioned that this is my third tour at the Pentagon and since I was coming back to familiar turf, I thought that things might be easy. A lot of you probably know that that great catcher, Yogi Berra, was also the author of some of the most profound observations in the American language. One of which was "this is deja vu all over again" and I thought maybe that's what my third tour at the Pentagon be would be like. But I was quickly disabused of that when Secretary Rumsfeld swore me in and said "Paul, we're going to keep bringing you back until you get it right." I must say it is fantastic to have a Secretary of Defense who has been there before. I can't imagine a better person to be our Secretary of Defense at a critical time like this. And we are getting it right, I guarantee you. I also can't imagine a better Commander in Chief. Those of us who know him were not surprised by his fierce determination and his genuine humility and all the qualities that make a great leader a great leader that the whole world is now coming to see.

I face a challenge this evening. Extensive scientific research has demonstrated that after dinner, the average human brain has difficulty remembering two thoughts at once, just as Washington has difficulty handling two crises at one time. But since this audience is definitely above average, I'll challenge you this evening to think about two ideas: wars of the future and the war of the present. And we as a nation must address both at the same time.

The attacks that came so suddenly and brutally on a date that is now etched in our national consciousness were targeted not only against our citizens and our buildings, the attacks of September 11th were targeted against everything that defines America, targeted by oppressors who seek to impose on their own people an almost medieval regime of terror. These terrorists, as President Bush told the nation, kill not merely to end lives, but to disrupt and end a way of life. With every atrocity, he said, they hope that America grows fearful, retreating from the world and forsaking our friends. Until two months ago, the date most synonymous with surprise, was December 7th. As we mark the 60th anniversary of Pearl Harbor next month, we may also recall that

Japan's attack drove us not to fear, but to action, not into isolation, but to accepting a greater role in the world, not to forsake our friends, but to form with them the most powerful alliance against evil in history.

December 7th was a turning point for the world, and September 11th should be no less a turning point. On 9/11, our generation received one of history's great wake-up calls. Like the greatest generation, we must answer that call. And as we do, we have a chance to make sure that the world that emerges will be better for our efforts. Maybe we shouldn't have been surprised on September 11. Yet throughout history, people have been surprised not only by the timing of attacks, but by their character. All too often, people focus on one threat or one possibility, to the exclusion of all others—suffering from what one scholar of Pearl Harbor called a poverty of expectations, a routine obsession with a few dangers that may be familiar, rather than likely. Often people say that the solution to the problem of surprise is better intelligence. But the solution is not just better intelligence. We always need better intelligence, but we must also learn not to depend too much on intelligence; not to assume that other people operate on assumptions that mirror our own about what is impossible, what is irrational, or both.

The answer is not building our war plans on one or two well-defined familiar threats. We must have plans that make allowances for complexity and uncertainty and the unexpected, plans that give us a range of options and the flexibility to respond to surprise. Reportedly once at a dinner with Mark Twain, a fellow diner was eager to impress the famous author. He asked Twain to pass the sugar and then he said, "Mr. Twain, don't you think it's unusual that sugar is the only word in our language in which SU had a *sh* sound?" And Twain replied, "Are you sure about that?" Now as we absorb the implications of the surprise that that struck us on September 11, there is a danger that those previously unfamiliar events will become the new definition of the familiar and the expected.

As we develop a successful strategy for this first war of the 21st century, we might be tempted to conclude that we have covered all the eventualities that we must now be concerned about. One thing we can be sure of—adapting to surprise, adapting quickly and effectively, must be a central element of defense planning. And that is hard to do. We were spoiled by the seeming certainties of the Cold War. Then we perceived a predictable, albeit growing, threat, a threat that we could make precise predictions about. We knew the schedule on it, which enemy divisions planned to mobilize. We matched our armies to meet our adversary on a very precise schedule on the battlefields of Europe. We measured our ballistic missile capabilities so they would be sufficient to strike the right balance. We knew the threat. We planned for it. We matched it. But that's not where we are today.

There has been a revolution in threats that calls for a revolution in how we think about defense. Surprise and uncertainty provide the context in which we must think about future war, and these two concepts were at the heart of the major defense review that we undertook at the President's direction earlier this year. That review spans some nine months, and it involved an unprecedented degree of debate and discussion among the department's most senior leaders. Out of that intense debate, we reached agreement on the urgent need for real change.

To deal with surprise and uncertainty, we agreed that we needed to shift our planning from the threat-based model that has guided thinking in the past to a capabilities-based model for the future. We don't know who may threaten us or when or where, but we do have some sense of what may threaten us and how. Capabilities-based planning requires taking account of an adversary's existing and potential capabilities and assessing them against our own. It requires thinking about asymmetric threats, a term that is now part of our lexicon, referring to the tactics and weapons our adversaries will choose to circumvent our well-known and enormous military strengths and to attack us where we are vulnerable. Such threats include forms of warfare that most civilized nations long ago renounced: chemical and biological weapons and the intentional killing of civilians through terrorism.

But we must also exploit our own asymmetric advantages, capabilities such as precision strike, intelligence, and undersea warfare. Our challenge is to deny our adversaries the benefits of asymmetric threats and capitalize on our own asymmetric advantages. Our review also reached agreement on the six top transformational goals that should guide our efforts to build a 21st century military. Very briefly, these six goals are, first, to protect the U.S. homeland and our bases of operations overseas, particularly against the threat of weapons of mass destruction. Second, to project and sustain power in what we call antiaccess environments, or those environments in which adversaries seek to hinder our presence. Third, to deny our enemies sanctuary, particularly through long-range precision strike capabilities. Fourth, to protect our own information networks from attack and to attack those of our adversaries. Fifth, to leverage information technology to enhance joint operational capabilities. And finally, sixth, to maintain unhindered access to space and protect the infrastructure that supports our critical space capabilities.

As you think about those six goals, I think you can see that the first three capabilities are being immediately applied in the crisis that we face today. The last three are capabilities are not particularly stressed in the current crisis, but if we ignore them we might be creating the conditions for the Pearl Harbor of the next decade.

I think it's obvious today that the first goal, homeland defense, is an urgent priority and should have been one years ago. Providing for homeland defense must include not only passive defenses, such as medical countermeasures and biological surveillance systems, but the development of active defenses against ballistic and cruise missiles as well. We know that both terrorists and state supporters of terrorism are actively looking to build or buy nuclear and chemical, biological weapons. As the President described it, barbarism emboldened by technology. With such barbarians we should anticipate the likelihood of future nuclear, chemical, and biological attacks and build our homeland defenses accordingly.

Projecting and sustaining power in antiaccess environments, the second goal, is also a necessity in the current campaign. Although our access to Afghanistan has improved steadily and most recently spectacularly, we have been forced by circumstances to operate from very great distances, and this against an enemy whose active efforts to deny us access have met so far with very little success. It's only a shadow of what a more determined, more advanced enemy could do. And I might remind you, lest you think it's not a problem at all, I might remind you that clearly one of al Qaeda's principal targets from the beginning was Pakistan, and it was a near-miss and a mere thing that we got what we have there, and hopefully we will keep it. We need to reduce our dependence on a predictable or vulnerable base structure by exploiting a number of technologies that include long-range aircraft, unmanned aerial vehicles, and stealthy platforms as well as reducing the amount of logistical support needed by the ground forces.

Our third goal, denying our enemy sanctuary, is also important as our adversaries in Afghanistan try to evade attack by a variety of means. As we try to root out al Qaeda and remove the Taliban regime, it's readily apparent of how important it is to rob our enemies of places to hide and function, whether it be in caves, in cities, or on the run. The key element in doing that is our ability to conduct long-range precision strikes. That is a capability that should be approached not simply as an air component, or simply as a ground component, but as an integration of the two that will greatly enhance our ability to take out targets at great distances. We had an early experience of that during the Gulf War ten years ago, when our most effective means for finding Iraqi Scud missiles was putting very brave Special Forces people on the ground in western Iraq. But when they found the targets, which our pilots from 15,000 feet couldn't, when they found the targets we didn't have the kind of integration with our air capability to make their bravery as effective as it should have been. We have improved in the last 10 years, but we still have a ways to go.

In hindsight, it's clear that we should have been investing heavily over the past several years to address those three goals, homeland defense, projecting power in antiaccess environments, and denying our enemies sanctuary with long-range precision strike. But if anyone predicted when we presented our budget request on Capitol Hill last July that the Department of Defense would soon need billions of dollars to conduct combat operations in central Asia, moreover do so while some large fraction of our surveillance assets and combat air patrol aircraft were engaged over the United States, there would have been any number of skeptics on hand to say no way, you're just building the budget again. September 11th ought to give this country a new perspective on the issue of what is affordable. The economic losses alone from that attack have been measured in the hundreds of billions, if not trillions of dollars. And there is no way to put a price on the lives of the Americans who were lost.

The capabilities that looked so expensive in peace seem relatively cheap when you are confronted with the challenges we face today. But if today we focus on those first three goals alone, we are likely to neglect the last three transformation goals, which have not been heavily stressed in the present crisis, at least not so far. Again, those are conducting effective information operations, and I suppose when I say so far I have my fingers crossed that we won't see cyber terrorism before we are finished. Leveraging information technology to enhance interoperability and maintaining unhindered access to space. Yet these may all play major roles in wars of the future. If we neglect these areas, they could provide the Pearl Harbors of the next decade at costs that could exceed even the enormous sums that we have lost in the last two months.

Having talked about future wars and our need to expect the unexpected, about our transformational goals and the need to make the right investments for the future, I'd now like to share with you some observations about the current campaign. It is often said especially around the Pentagon that it's better to be lucky than to be smart. We certainly have been lucky in Afghanistan in the last few 11 days. But we've also been smart. Our recent successes can be attributed in considerable measure to exploiting our asymmetric advantages while going after the asymmetric weaknesses of our enemy. One of the U.S. military's great asymmetric advantages is that ability I've already mentioned to strike at long distance with great precision. But the real leverage from long-range strike comes not simply from destroying targets from the air, but from using that capability to leverage the capability of friendly forces on the ground. We have seen that in recent weeks, and that success has come not just from our remarkable ability to fly bombers from the base in Missouri, halfway around the world to strike targets with great precision. Successes also come from putting some extraordinarily brave men on the ground so they could direct that air power and make it truly effective.

I'd like to share with you a couple of situation reports from one of our men in northern Afghanistan. It will give you an appreciation for what I'm talking about. Some of the classified details I removed, and until a few days ago the whole report, the mere fact of it, I suppose, would have been classified. But the content of the message is now unclassified and I'm giving it to you verbatim. This from the 25th of October. Our Special Forces man reports, "I'm advising a man on how best to employ light infantry and horse cavalry in the attack against Taliban T55s, mortars, artillery, personnel carriers and machine guns, a tactic which I think became outdated with the invention of the Gattling gun. The Mujahideen have done this every day since we've been on the ground. They have attacked with ten rounds of AK47 ammunition per man, with snipers having less than 100 rounds, little water and less food. I've observed a sniper who walked 10 plus miles to get to the fight, who was proud to show me his artificial leg right from the knee down. We have witnessed the horse cavalry bounding overwatch from spur to spur, to attack Taliban's strong points. The last several kilometers under mortar, artillery and sniper fire. There is little medical care if injured. Only a donkey ride to the aid station, which is a dirt hut. I think the Muj are doing very well with what they have. They have killed over 125 Taliban while losing only 8. But we couldn't do what we are doing without the close air support. Everywhere I go, the civilians and Mujahaddin soldiers are always telling me they are glad the USA has come. They all speak of their hopes for a better Afghanistan once the Taliban are gone. Better go. My local commander is finishing his phone call with someone back in the United States." Yes, they were reporting by cell phones constantly. With that, one of our amazing Special Forces members went off on a cavalry charge with his Northern Alliance Commander.

This from the same man, November 10th, "Departed position from which I spoke to you last night. We left on horse and linked up with the remainder of the element. I had a meeting with commander. We then departed from our initial link-up location and rode into Mazar-e Sharif on begged, borrowed, and confiscated transportation. While it looked like a rag tag procession the morale into Mazar was triumphal. All locals loudly greeted us and thanked all Americans. Much waving, cheering, and clapping even from the women. U.S. Navy and Air Force did a great job. I'm very proud of these men who have performed exceptionally well under very extreme conditions. I personally witnessed heroism under fire by two U.S. noncommissioned officers, one Army, one Air Force, when we came under direct artillery fire last night, which was less than 50 meters from me. When I ordered them to call close air support, they did so immediately, without flinching, even though they were under fire. As you know, the U.S. element was nearly overrun four days ago and continued to call close air support and insured that the Mujahaddin forces did not suffer defeat. These two examples are typical of the performance of your soldiers and airmen. Truly uncommon valor has been a common virtue." That is the end of the quote. It's remarkable.

In Afghanistan, a country that we think of in somewhat medieval terms, our Special Forces have taken a page from the past, from the history of the horse cavalry, with soldiers armed with swords and rifles, maneuvering on horseback. But now they are using radios to direct close air support and bomber strikes, sometimes from halfway around the world. When reporters asked Secretary Rumsfeld about the reintroduction of horse cavalry in modern war, he told them it's all part of our transformation plan. (Laughter.) Indeed, it is. Taking risks; thinking boldly; adapting to circumstances; exploiting our advantages is what we're after.

Perhaps the greatest asymmetric advantage with which we've been blessed is the one that terrorists attacked on September 11th. That is the power of a free democratic people whose government is based on universal ideals. We govern by law and self-determination. The Taliban on the contrary rule by terror, one of their great weaknesses and apparently one of the reasons why they are collapsing so quickly. We have grown stronger as a nation since the attack. The Taliban has only weakened their country through their barbarism. Their collapse is making unmistakable what should have been clear to the whole world from the beginning. They are oppressors of the Afghan people they never had a chance to elect or choose.

Indeed, Afghans have been suffering at the hands of the Taliban's rule, as one Afghan said to a Canadian reporter, in the name of Islam, but at the barrel of a gun. As one of our country's foremost experts on the Middle East and Islam, Farad Adjami, has said, "The Taliban has become the Khmer Rouge of our time." Beyond Afghanistan one of our great assets in this large and broad campaign is that our enemies not only menace us, but they terrorize the vast numbers of people they claim to speak for. It should be no surprise that every state that sponsors terrorism also terrorizes it's own people. The people who suffer from the terror of their own rulers can become our best allies in getting their rulers out of the business of supporting terrorism. Our soldiers on the ground helping liberate Mazar-e Sharif reported the Afghan people greeting the arrival of their liberators with joy. Hopeful that this is the beginning of the end of their national nightmare and proving that barbarism cannot kill the human desire for freedom.

That is a truth that Ronald Reagan understood well. In 1982, during one of the darker moments of the Cold War, he told the British Parliament that even in the Communist world, as Reagan said, man's instinctive desire for freedom and self-determination surfaces again and again. How we conduct ourselves here and in the western democracies, he said, will determine whether this trend continues. History records that his insistence on promoting democracy and human rights throughout the world resulted in one of Reagan's most important legacies: the triumph of democracy in many previously totalitarian and authoritarian regimes on both sides of the cold war divide. It is not unreasonable to think and hope that similar legacies are yet to come.

As President Bush said to Naval Academy midshipmen last May, "Remember, America has always been committed to enlarging the circle of freedom." Our mission today is not only to root out and eliminate the terrorists, we must also enlarge the circle of human freedom to include that vast majority of Muslim people who are seeking to enjoy the benefits of living in a free and prosperous society, but do not yet do so. Turkey and Indonesia are two important models of nations who are becoming part of this world. And it is no accident that the prevailing practice of Islam in those two countries is vastly different from the fanaticism preached by bin Laden and the Taliban.

It's an infrequently noted fact that over the last ten years, on five different occasions, the United States has led armed coalitions on behalf of Muslim people. Not only in Kuwait but in northern Iraq and Somalia, Bosnia and Kosovo, the United States has come to the aid of Muslim victims of aggression or war-induced famine. And now we can add the Afghan people and other Muslim people to that list. It is a sound strategic principle to reinforce success. There are successes in the Muslim world, and it is very much in our country's interest to support them, even when they are fragile.

The tragedy of September 11th demonstrates that we have an enormous stake in encouraging the successful progress of those countries that are now pursuing freedom and self-governance as a model for the rest of the Muslim world. Showing other Muslims that there is an example to follow is critical to achieving future success.

Nations throughout the world see that our democratic and free society was blessed by other significant advantages: the power generated by the innovation of the individual as well as the power of the people united in one purpose. This freedom to build and create is what has drawn so many from around the globe to our shores. The collective will of the American people united in the war on terror will be the decisive factor in this war, just as it was during the Second World War. Still, along with the incredible moral resources of our nation, it's good to know that we do have one heck of a war machine. It includes men and women who, as the President has said, contribute not just to military might of this country, but to its meaning and conscience and soul.

I began by mentioning the attack on Pearl Harbor. Let me conclude by mentioning what Winston Churchill wrote in his diary on December 8, after he learned of the attack. It may not surprise you that he didn't waste a lot of sympathy on us. To the contrary, his words were words of joy. "I knew the United States was in the war," Churchill wrote, "up to the neck and into the death. So we had won after all. Silly people, and there were many not only in Germany but even here in England, discounted the force of the United States. Some said they were soft, others said they would never be united. The Americans would fool around at a distance. They would never come to grips. They could never stand bloodletting. Their democracy and their system of recurrent elections would paralyze their war effort. They would be just a vague blur on the horizon to friend or foe. Now these people said now we would see the weakness of this numerous but remote wealthy and talkative people." We haven't changed much in 60 years, have we? But Churchill said, "I have studied the American Civil War fought out to the last desperate inch. American blood flowed in my veins. I thought of a remark which our Foreign Minister Edward Gray had made to me more than 30 years before as the United States entered World War I. 'The United States,' he said, 'is like a gigantic boiler. Once the fire is lighted under it, there is no limit to the power it can generate.'"

Today, our greatest asymmetric advantage is that there is no limit to the power that we as a free people can generate. Consider what the people of this nation have been willing to sacrifice since our nation's birth and keep it. We instinctively know what we have here, as Abraham Lincoln said, is something that holds out a great promise to all the people of the world for all time to come.

Last week President Bush spoke about the courage and defiance of those passengers on Flight 93 over the skies of Pennsylvania. They rebelled against the terrorists giving their own lives to save lives on the ground. They were led by a brave young man named Todd Beamer whose last known words were the Lord's Prayer followed by "Let's roll." The President concluded his remarks by saying: "Our cause is just and our ultimate victory is assured. We will no doubt face new challenges, but we have our marching orders."

My fellow Americans, let's roll. In the Department of Defense, our direction is clear and we are rolling—in this war and in our mission to prepare our forces for the future, to protect the great promise that is the United States. May God bless America, may God bless the wonderful men and women who serve our country so nobly and so faithfully. And thank you. (Applause.)

ANNOUNCER: Ladies and gentlemen please welcome back your master of ceremonies, Dr. Pfaltzgraff.

DR. PFALTZGRAFF: On behalf of all of us, Paul, I want to thank you for this address which has been magnificent, it has been eloquent, it has been far reaching, comprehensive, and, of course, telling us a great deal about what is going on now and of course about the wars of the future. We thank you very much for being with us on this occasion and for giving this magnificent keynote address. (Applause.)

And now I have just a few administrative announcements. The first is that we will have refreshments, breakfast, continental breakfast at 7:30, if you wish it tomorrow morning. We will resume tomorrow morning at 8 a.m. in the amphitheater. We have the Chairman, Joint Chiefs of Staff, General Myers, as our opening speaker. So please be there well in advance of 8 a.m. We also have Governor Ridge will be with us at 11:45, speaking tomorrow.

Finally, I would like to remind you that we already have transcripts as well as video from all of today's sessions that will be on the conference website this evening. So, I wish you a very pleasant evening, what remains of it, and look forward to our meeting tomorrow morning at 8 a.m. Thank you very much. (Applause.)

MORNING ADDRESS

THE MILITARY INSTRUMENT OF POWER AS A CRITICAL
ENABLER FOR NATIONAL SECURITY

General Richard B. Myers, United States Air Force, Chairman, Joint Chiefs of Staff

Summary—Introduction by General Eric K. Shinseki, Chief of Staff, United States Army

• *The power of information and the confidence of the American people are central to the strength of our nation*

1. The military instrument of national power nurtures this confidence in our citizens, and in those of other countries, by providing stability for economic growth and development.

2. The military's ability to transition from unconventional to major conventional war when and if necessary is what makes us world class in the profession of arms and inspires the confidence of the American people.

• *Although the current conflict against international terrorism is not the large conflict for which we maintain major standing forces, it is essential for our forces to fight and decisively win this asymmetric war to prevent further attacks on the American homeland.*

Summary—Remarks by General Richard B. Myers, Chairman, Joint Chiefs of Staff

• We have the following immediate goals for this war on global terrorism:

  • Deny terrorists a base of operations in Afghanistan
  • Destroy the military capabilities of the Taliban and Al-Qaeda
  • Alleviate the suffering of the Afghan people
  • Convince other states to deny support to terrorist organizations

• *In this campaign, the U.S. government seeks to coordinate the use of all instruments of national power with the actions of our coalition partners*

1. The war on terrorism will be an extended campaign that will require patience and will challenge the resolve of the coalition. The United States will have to balance actions necessary to maintain the evolving coalition and those necessary to wage war successfully.

2. Gaps in technology between coalition members make coordination increasingly difficult. In the current strategic environment, our coalition partners need to increase their defense budgets to improve interoperability.

• *The war on terrorism requires significant coordination to focus the elements of national power. We are developing organizations and procedures that are proving effective and have implications for future joint warfighting capabilities.*

1. We are sharing information, people, and resources at unprecedented levels, and we must foster this increased cooperation.

2. The effective coordination of joint interagency task forces in Washington, DC, is being exported to the theater of operation.

3. However, there are areas for improvement. For example, information operations in the current campaign began too late and should have been integrated with all government agencies, the National Security Council, and coalition partners to present a timely and coherent message.

4. The Department of Defense role in homeland security needs to be clarified, including issues such as primacy within the department and orchestration of support within the unified and combatant commands.

• *Like the U.S. Army's Louisiana Maneuvers prior to World War II, today we must establish an environment that fosters innovative thinking and embraces a new level of collaboration between the services.*

1. We must increase the flexibility and responsiveness of our forces by assigning joint command, control, communications, computers, intelligence, surveillance, and reconnaissance capabilities (C4ISR) at lower levels.

2. Joint Force commanders and their staffs must understand not only what their own service brings to the joint fight, but also what the other services and coalition partners can contribute.

3. To dissipate the fog of war and enable timely, decisive action by our commanders, we need to exploit our superior information gathering systems and to develop enhanced knowledge management tools.

4. Fielding a Joint Force with interoperable weapon systems and C4ISR (Command, Control, Communications, Computers, Surveillance, Reconnaissance) requirements will facilitate the coordination process and enable timely and informed decisions by operators and commanders.

5. Weapons and weapons systems must be designed for joint and coalition interoperability. The military will have to focus on both upgrading existing systems and ensuring that new systems are "born joint."

• "If a system is not interoperable, if it does not contribute to the joint fight, it's probably not right."

• The military has been forced to cobble together creative work-arounds, because some of our existing forces did not "plug and play" in this joint war fight.

6. The Department is also experimenting with the expansion of joint task force headquarters. The headquarters would be an operational-level head-quarters unit, not an on-call fighting force. It would have robust C4ISR archi-tecture that would be compatible with all future program upgrades, weapons platforms, and communication systems.

Analysis

General Myers identified two theaters in our current war against terror-ism—one in Afghanistan and one in the homeland. In Afghanistan, the mili-tary is clearly in the lead, although that may change as the war is carried to other terrorist organizations and their state sponsors. The military is much more involved in homeland security than before the September terrorist attacks, but still remains primarily in a supporting role to other agencies, notably to law enforcement and first responders. Requirements for both the-aters are significant, but those for homeland security are still in development and responsibility has yet to be assigned for all of them. In both theaters, inter-agency cooperation has improved tremendously since the terrorist attacks, but synchronization of the diverse interagency efforts remains essential. General Myers did not discuss where the war on terrorism will be fought next and what form that fight will take. While it may be possible to expand the conflict to another state and maintain the coalition if another element of national power is in the lead, similar expansion, led by the military, will carry significant risks.

General Myers focused on the importance of information operations over-seas and public information at home. Information operations abroad help with coalition maintenance by providing support to allies and partners in their need to maintain the support of their domestic populations. Maintaining popular support in the United States also depends on other types of actions to keep the public informed and solidly behind the government and the military. The Chairman emphasized that there is a long war still ahead and recommended patience as operations become less visible than those currently being con-ducted in Afghanistan.

General Myers stated his intent to focus on building and improving the interoperability of the joint force. Even in platforms as advanced as the B-2 bomber, there is still interoperability to resolve. He identified the need for the Services to change how programs are developed to ensure that joint interop-erability is inherent not additive. He noted the improvements made as a result of lessons learned in Kosovo, but reiterated that much work remains. Command, control, communications, computers, intelligence, surveillance, and reconnaissance (C4ISR) are the keys to joint warfighting, but General Myers also discussed organizational initiatives—specifically the standing joint task force—that may enable more effective joint operations.

Finally, General Myers discussed the need to transform the military to prepare for future threats. As with the homeland defense mission, many of the parameters of transformation remain undefined, but the Chairman emphasized that transformation must encompass doctrine, training, and organizations, not simply technological enhancements. Although his immediate focus is on joint interoperability, his long-term goal is the transformation of the entire U.S. military. While acknowledging that a joint force with appropriate land, sea, and air capabilities is essential, both in defeating global terrorism and against future threats, General Myers did not discuss how the current war affects the timing or course of the military's transformation.

In closing, General Myers stated that he firmly believes the younger generation will answer the call to serve. All that service will undoubtedly not be military, but service to the nation now seems to have a resonance absent before September 11.

Transcript

ANNOUNCER: Ladies and gentlemen, may I have your attention, please. Our program will begin in one minute. Good morning, ladies and gentlemen, and welcome. At this time, please welcome Dr. Robert Pfaltzgraff, President, Institute for Foreign Policy Analysis.

DR. PFALTZGRAFF: Ladies and gentlemen, welcome to this, the second day of our conference. We have, as we did yesterday, and exciting and informative and very important series of addresses and presentations and discussion for you. I would like at this time to introduce General Shinseki, who will be introducing our opening speaker this morning.

As all of you know, General Shinseki assumed his duties as the 34th Chief of Staff of the United States Army on June 22, 1999. He is a graduate of the United States Military Academy, has a bachelor of science degree. He holds a Master of Arts degree in English literature from Duke University. General Shinseki's military education includes the Armor Officer Advanced Course, the United States Army Command and General Staff College, and War College. Most importantly for us in this room, General Shinseki has been the moving and driving force making this conference and previous meetings in its series in recent years possible. So it is with very great pleasure that I welcome General Shinseki. (Applause)

GENERAL SHINSEKI: Well, good morning, everyone, distinguished guests, ladies and gentlemen. Bob Pfaltzgraff, thank you for that generous introduction and, more importantly, thanks for your services as moderator yesterday. You and Jackie Davis have done it again this year, pulling us all together, getting us off to a great start. Well done.

You know, listening to the several references yesterday to the date 11 September, I could not help as I sat out there in the audience—could not help but recall that very recently, here I stood on the floor of the New York Stock Exchange with other service chiefs, actually this past Monday, the 12th of November. Over that long Veteran's Day weekend, we had rung the bell at 9:30 to begin the Exchange's international trading day. And as you recall, the tragic accident with American flight 589 had just occurred and was beginning to break on the airways. And I had a chance to see the near-immediate effects of the reports of that tragic accident. As it broke on the television airways, and watched the downturn in numbers on the exchange sales boards, and I was struck by the speed with which the trading public reacted. It was instructive—the power of information and the confidence of the American people, and in an unusual way for me, were both visible and almost tactile.

But the confidence of the American people to get up and go to work every day and put their children in school to the care of others, to get on mass transit, to stimulate our large and powerful economy so that they can create the basis of commerce, go about their daily lives, pay taxes every day. How central to the strength of our nation, the confidence of the American people. And I had to wonder, what contributions do we, as the military instrument of national power, bring to the table in nurturing that confidence? To our citizens, but to the citizens of other countries, as well? It is an international trading arena, confidence to go about their daily routines and stoke the boilers of our economic engines. And though we have declared war on international terrorism, it is a war of asymmetry and not the major conflict for which we maintain major standing forces in all services, with the intent of keeping the effects like incidents of the 11th of September from ever again being visited on the American homeland. We must be sure to be able to transition from the unconventional to the major conventional war when and if necessary. That is what makes us world-class in the profession of arms, and that is what will fully nurture the confidence of the American people, no matter what happens, to understand and to believe that we can and will prevail.

That said, it's my honor and privilege to introduce to you this morning the senior member of the U.S. military member of the U.S. defense establishment. He is a visionary, who is committed to keeping our military ready for today's challenges, and also preparing them for those that will arrive in the next century. He is a Kansan, and he brings together those great Midwestern attributes of common sense and hard work, and a great sense of humor. Thirty-six years of service to the nation, eminently qualified to be our Chairman of Joint Chiefs of Staff, great breadth of operational commands, leadership positions, joint assignments. Learned the profession in the skies of Vietnam as a young fight-

General Shinseki

er pilot, today carries over 4,100 flight hours on six different aircraft, 600 of those hours in the F-4 combat hours, commanded U.S. forces in Japan in the 5th Air Force in Yakota, prior service as the Assistant to the Chairman of the Joint Chiefs, Commander of Pacific Air Forces in Hickham, Hawaii, and CINC-NORAD, U.S. Space Command, and nineteen long, valuable months' hard work as the Vice Chairman. And then announcement of a selection to be the Chairman of the Joint Chiefs on 24 August, the President of the United States called him a man of steady resolve, determined leadership, a skilled and steady hand. The SECDEF described him as a man of candor, sound judgment, keen insights, fiber, and good humor. Ladies and gentlemen, I couldn't agree more or describe him any better. Please join me in welcoming my friend, the 15th Chairman of the Joint Chiefs of Staff, General Richard B. Myers. (Applause)

GENERAL MYERS: Thank you. Distinguished guests, and fellow flag and general officers, ladies and gentlemen, good morning. Ric, as you leave the stage, thank you for that introduction. That was very kind. And to Dr. Pfaltzgraff, and to Rick Hogel both for the invitation to join you both today.

I would also like to extend my appreciation to the Army staff, General Shinseki, the Fletcher School, and the Office of the Secretary of Defense for Net Assessment for organizing this important event. I think this event comes at exactly the right time with the right kind of people to discuss exactly what we must be discussing in this time, and the events that we are going through.

You know, last Sunday, like a lot of you—I know Ric was there, because we were seated together—but I had the privilege to participate in Veterans' Day ceremonies over in Arlington Cemetery. Given recent events, for me, anyway, and I think probably Ric, and for others there, it was an especially emotional event as we pay tribute to those who have served in both peace and war to protect our freedom. And I will tell you, no matter how many years I wear this uniform, when they play Taps out there, by the Tomb of the Unknown Soldier, I certainly got some chills up my spine and a tear in my eye. Because it's not only those who have served, but it's those who are serving. And know-

ing at that very moment, we have got
folks in harm's way trying to defend
our freedoms, it was just a very
poignant time for me.

And of course, Veterans' Day,
November 11th, was also significant
for another reason this year. It marks
the two-month anniversary of the terrorist attack on the World Trade
Center and on the Pentagon.

That date is really imprinted on
our minds. We now speak about it in
shorthand. We simply say "Before,"
and everybody knows that we mean
before September 11th. So I think
with that simple word of "before," we
acknowledge that our lives have been
changed forever.

We also acknowledge that we
have entered a new era in international relations and thus, the theme
that you all have chosen for this par-

General Myers

ticular year, this conference, national security for a new era, focusing national
power, certainly underscores that fact. I'm sure you have already discussed
what vision you all had when you picked that theme, because nobody could
have guessed how important those words and how appropriate they are to our
current situation. It's a pretty—some pretty smart folks thought about it and
came up with exactly the right theme.

This morning I would like to discuss three issues that are directly related
and connected to national security in this new era. First one will be winning
the war against global terrorism and second, joint warfighting. And third,
transformation. And we don't spend a lot of time on the last one, but I do want
to make a couple of remarks on that.

After the attacks on September 11th, President Bush declared war against
global terrorism. He did so because of the significant and growing challenge
that presents a direct threat to freedom and to freedom-loving peoples around
the world. He said it was time for action, and we have taken action.

All instruments of national power are now engaged in a just and relentless
campaign that we have named Operation Enduring Freedom. And many
nations around the world have joined the cause. Our objectives in the military
campaign against terrorism are fairly straightforward and simple: first, to deny
the use of Afghanistan as a safe haven by al Qaeda and the terrorist network
they control, and second, to make clear to the Taliban and others that there is

a price to be paid for harboring and supporting terrorists; third, to destroy the military forces of the Taliban and al Qaeda; and lastly, to provide humanitarian assistance to the long-suffering Afghani people.

This truly is a new kind of war. And in this war, we in the military may not play the decisive role. In fact, the war is being contested on many different battlefields, involving diplomats, bankers, law enforcement officials, and customs. Even the IRS is involved. Thankfully, they are on our side. I'm going to get in trouble on that one, I know.

If you recall, the President's remarks in the Rose Garden on the 24th of September, he said, "This morning, a major thrust of our war on terrorism began with the stroke of a pen. Today, we have launched a strike on the financial foundation of the global terror network."

Now, it's also important to note that the U.S. government seeks to coordinate the use of all our instruments of national power with the actions of many countries that make up our working coalition.

In many ways, the new war against global terrorism is like taking down organized crime syndicate. You want to hit them where it will hurt. You go after the finances; you go after the logistics; you interrupt their information flow and their ability to train and recruit new personnel; and you send in undercover agents to gather intelligence. You disrupt their routine and go after known bases of operation. Some of this requires shooters who can kick down the door and engage in firefights where appropriate, and some of it requires green eyeshade types tracking down finances, and some of it requires Generation Y whiz kids surfing the internet.

The key in any case to all of the above is synchronizing these efforts so we can maximize the impact that we have and get the desired effects. Doing so requires a great deal of coordination. Each element is important. Some are more visible than others, but it's the entire package and the combined effects of all of this that generates powerful results. And that's why today, all elements of national power are engaged in this war on terrorism.

I have been involved in interagency debates and operations and the process ever since I was Assistant to the Chairman back under General Shalikashvili, back in the middle of this decade. And I would say so far, the interagency coordination and cooperation has been absolutely remarkable. In fact, I have never seen the different elements of our government work so well together. This is truly national security in a new era.

I recently saw a firsthand example as I was going through the Joint Staff Crisis Action Team space the other day, just to see what was going on. There was a fellow in a suit; he was introduced as our FBI representative to the Crisis Action Team, which is not a normal piece of that team. And I think that was a pretty good optic about what we are talking about here. We are sharing information, we are sharing people, and we are sharing resources like never before. And we need to push this new level of cooperation out to the theaters, as well

There is some debate about this. I'm sure your panel can talk about it later. But we are looking at assigning liaison officers to different agencies to the staff of the combat commands. They want that kind of cooperation. Most of you know that the combatant commands already have good intelligence liaison, whether it be CIA or NSA or DIA or so forth. They have got that part pretty well down. But in terms of Treasury and FBI and others, they do not. A good model here, and maybe the Commandant of the Coast Guard talked about it yesterday—I don't know—but a good model is the way we handled the drug war, for lack of a better term, where we put joint interagency task forces together. Very, very effective, there. And we think they can be effective on this global war on terrorism, as well. And the reason we do that is because this coordination is not only important inside the beltway, but particularly outside the beltway, as well.

So in my view, the interagency process is working well on many fronts. But it obviously has not been perfect. One area in particular I think we've been slow to get going has been our information operations campaign. Despite our best efforts, we took too much time to put together the team, if you will, so occasionally we missed the opportunity to send the right message. Sometimes we sent mixed signals and we missed opportunities, as well. I'm sure you are well aware of all that. Information operations, when I use the term, since it's hard to find a good definition for this particular term—I'm talking about the broadest use of the term, from psychological warfare to public affairs, and the whole gamut of things that we do. It's a complicated and demanding business, and when you move into new territory like a global war on terrorism, the task is made even more difficult.

I think in the future, what we need to look at front-loading our information operations campaign. This can't be done by a pickup team. It takes too long to get everybody up to speed and to figure out who is working for whom. Obviously, we have got to do it a lot smarter, and fortunately, I think we have turned the corner in that regard. In fact, last night, Secretary Rumsfeld walked through some of the information operations activities that are going on in the Pentagon and his 15-minute visit turned into a 45-minute visit. I think he appreciated what they are doing now, and how it's integrated with all of the government agencies and National Security Council.

The IO campaign is also an important element of our coalition effort. I'm very pleased with the remarkable support that we have received form all of our friends around the world in the information operations area, and across the board, for that matter. Our partners in this fight, the countries that want to rid the world of terrorist networks, are willing to do what they can to support the cause. They will support us in many different but important ways. And I can tell you the support they provide, including intelligence, overflight rights, cruise missile launches, logistic support, and access to operational bases, has been tremendous.

Achieving unity of effort and keeping many different countries focused on the primary objectives through the long months ahead will be a demanding task. In fact, it will not be just with our coalition partners, but with the American population. I was asked recently what can we do?—in a mainly civilian audience—what can we do to help? And I said the main thing that you can do to help is to understand that this will be a very long war, and we need patience. And don't expect that if you are not seeing something going on, that means nothing is going on. Some of this will be visible, some of it will be invisible. So patience is what is required.

Given that, in our coalition cracks will inevitably occur. But I think what keeps us all glued together is the thought of the 5,000 innocent victims—men, women, and children from 80 different countries, from essentially all cultural, religious, and ethnic groups. That thought helps prevent those cracks from growing too wide. It's important to remember, however, that maintaining the coalition, while very, very important, is not an end to itself, and we shouldn't allow elaborate consultations to get in the way of operational progress. We need to make progress. We have to find an appropriate balance between those actions necessary to maintain the evolving coalitions and those actions necessary to wage war successfully. I know you have a panel later in the day to discuss coalition issues, and I know who is on your panel, and they are truly experts in this area—far smarter than I am on that. And they will give you great insight. And I look forward to hearing how some of the discussion went, because I think it will give us insight on what is important in terms of our coalition partners. This is about partnership.

Having discussed the larger context, let me turn to the element of global terrorism campaign that I'm most familiar with currently, and that's the shooting war. As you can imagine, winning the war on terrorism is my number-one priority, as is everyone in uniform's number-one priority right now. And while all elements of national power are fully engaged in this war, I want to focus on the military role in just the next few minutes. And then I would like to move to other priorities that I want to advance during my tenure as Chairman of the Joint Chiefs of Staff, priorities that will help us win this war and any conflicts that we face. Those two are joint fighting and transformation, as I mentioned earlier.

But this morning, as we meet here in the Ronald Reagan Building, our armed forces are continuing the offensive on the ground and in the air against al Qaeda and the Taliban that supports them. We are heavily engaged in what will be a long and difficult fight. We have seen some successes over the past few days, but there is much fighting that remains to be done until we achieve the victory that we want. It's important to remember that these military activities in Afghanistan are only the beginning of a global campaign, and perhaps the most visible component, as I mentioned earlier. I think the media reporting of the operation has kept America well informed over the past few weeks

We have all seen in both pictures and words, Navy fighters launching from carriers, Air Force bombers streaking across the skies of Afghanistan, marines coming in from the rolling decks of the amphibious ready group, and Army Rangers and Special Forces units parachuting into enemy territory. These images, I think, tell part of the story, but they are in reality nothing more than individual snapshots that fail to capture the true nature of our operation.

The real story, in my view, is the manner in which General Franks and the entire Central Command staff and team have choreographed and executed the overall effort. In my view, General Franks is an absolutely outstanding commander and leader, and he has effectively called the strengths and unique capabilities that the different services bring to this fight. And he has worked them all together to generate the power and synergy of a truly joint effort. This is really what joint warfighting is all about and why joint warfighting is so important.

I should add that we are currently engaged in a second theater of operations in the war on terrorism, and that's right here at home in America. And I guess you're going to have Governor Ridge speak later after me. That will be a good time to talk about that other front, where we're engaged. Here at home, our joint forces play a key supporting role as well, flying combat air patrols—who would ever have thought it. Providing security at airports and for our critical infrastructure, inspecting ships that are entering our ports, and supporting law enforcement efforts and preparing to assist first responders in case of another tragedy.

Homeland security is another area of cooperation, the likes of which we have not seen in the past. This has been discussed for the last several years, and the Department of Defense's role in homeland security is—and the precise definition and who is going to be in charge inside the Department of Defense, then as we go on down to the unified command and combatant commands, who is going to orchestrate our support, is yet to be determined in its final end state. We know who is doing it today, but the final end state is going to be determined. In fact, that's the subject of a number of discussions we have with the Joint Chiefs of Staff, and General Shinseki has been an active participant in that, because the Army plays such a large role, in particular the Army [Reserve] and National Guard.

Obviously, the amount of coordination involved in bringing all the elements of national power to bear in this current crisis is significant. Coordinating the military aspects alone can be a difficult proposition. In my view, the best way to facilitate the coordination process is to field a joint force with interoperable weapon systems and interoperable command, control, communications, surveillance requirements—C4ISR (Command, Control, Communications, Computers, Intelligence, Surveillance, Reconnaissance). This will enable timely and informed decisions by operators and commanders. If we are going to focus on anything in my tenure, we have got to focus on better C4ISR in a way to give operational commanders the tools they need to make decisions on a timely manner. I'm going to talk about that a little bit more in just a second.

Thankfully, in this current campaign, our systems are, for the most part, working well together, and much better than I would say in Operation Allied Force. We have taken a lot of Kosovo lessons learned, and in the intervening couple of years, turned that around where we have much better interoperability, particularly for fleeing targets. We can attack them much more efficiently than in the past. But in some cases, we've been forced to cobble together creative work-arounds, because some of our existing forces did not plug and play in this joint war fight the way we would like. One example I would use is the B-2 bomber. I visited the B-2 crews out at Whiteman Air Force Base a couple weeks ago on my way to Fort Riley. As you know, the B-2 cruiser participated in the first three nights of the conflict, primarily used there until we beat down the defenses, particularly up in northern Afghanistan.

As you know, these crews flew from Missouri to Afghanistan, and in fact, what they did is they landed in Diego Garcia. The crew would get out, a new crew would get in, the motors would never shut down, they would add new oil to the motors because that was a limiting factor and fly back home. The one-way trip to Diego through Afghanistan would take almost two days, almost two days. The reason I mentioned that is that, if it takes you that long to get to the target, you are going to have some updates along the way. The threats can change; targets can change; and they did. Therefore, you have got to get updated in a timely manner.

You would think that a modern aircraft that cost as much as a B-2 would have this interoperability built in, but, in fact, it doesn't. So how did they do this? They had a special antenna with a special communication setup that came down to a laptop in the cockpit, which one of the pilots would hold on his lap. That's how they did their communications and how they got updates of targets and so forth. Effective, but a lot cruder than we need to do.

So, are we managing? Yes absolutely. They are able to manage. This is one example. I'm sure every service can cite other examples along this very line. But we have got to do, we must do better in the future. So the bottom line to me is the weapons and weapons systems must be designed with joint and coalition interoperability in mind. We have got to do that up front. So we hear this term "born joint," and that's certainly what we would like to do. Of course, we have got to upgrade some of our legacy systems, plug and play, because we are going to have some of these systems around for a long time.

I think the United States Army knows a lot about this as they try to modernize the way they communicate and keep track of forces. This is the point on interoperability that's absolutely essential to ensure the joint force of the future achieves the highest level of effectiveness and ensure our force is agile enough—we've got to be agile to operate inside the decision group of even the most capable adversary.

But we have got to take advantage of our superior information-gathering systems, which we've got some very good information-gathering systems, and develop enhanced knowledge management tools that would give our commanders the ability to see the right data when they need it.

What we are really trying to do here is to dissipate as much as possible the fog of war, to enable timely, decisive action by our commanders. This is a key part of joint warfighting, and all the services need to get it right, and so do we on the Joint Staff as we help facilitate that. So as we move from science and technology to research and development to procurement, we have got to bear in mind that if a system is not interoperable, if it does not contribute to the joint fight, then it's probably not right.

As I said earlier, our immediate and most important goal, and the one I think can have the biggest impact, because it impacts the ability of the commander to command, is interoperable C4ISR. We simply must get our joint task force commanders the necessary tools to fully integrate their combat power.

To help work this issue, we are exploring the idea of expanding Joint Task Force Headquarters. As you know if you have read the QDR Report, that was one of the issues that came up. This is an operational-level headquarters unit. It's not an on-call fighting force like the standing Joint Task Force—that's a different concept, and one that is being studied. This one is a tool to help push greater interoperability. The Joint Force Headquarters would have robust communication, computer, command and control, and intelligence architecture that all future weapons platforms and communication systems and any upgrades to existing systems would have to be designed to plug into it. We're also counting on Joint Requirements Oversight Council, which General Pete Pace, the Vice Chairman of the Joint Chiefs of Staff, chairs for reforms to help in this area. Our intent is that any system brought forward for review must be shown to be interoperable with other systems. And by the way, this is not an easy task. Before you decide how it's interoperable, you have to have the operational concept of how this all fits together. This is the more difficult issue that's before, so it's one that the Oversight Council is working on several different strategic topics.

We want to avoid acquiring new systems that will have trouble plugging and playing in the joint world of the future. A good example here, perhaps, is the F-22. As it was designed, it was designed to know what's going on in a flight of F-22s, but not to tell the rest of the world what that flight of F-22s knows. So it was absorbing lots of data and it received lots of data, but it wasn't sharing other than among its own flight members. Well, today, that's not interoperable, and so the Air Force has been tasked in the next major update to the avionics to make it interoperable so what it sees can be relayed to other folks; that's one of the things I'm talking about, and one of the examples.

As the Chairman, I think it's my responsibility to push jointness and interoperability at every opportunity, and I will do so not only because it's in the statutes that I do so. But I will do so because I believe it really is necessary to fight effectively in this new era. I don't do this alone. I do this with the rest of the Joint Chiefs of Staff, because my statutory authority extends to the Joint Chiefs of Staff when we are meeting inside the tank, when we take off our service caps and try to do what is best for the services and best for this nation.

I also intend to focus on transformation during my tenure. We could pass out a piece of paper and ask everybody to write down the definition of transformation, and I don't know how many folks are here this morning, but my guess is we'd probably get several hundred different definitions. So I'm not going to go into a lot of detail this morning, but speak about it in general terms.

If we are to evolve into a decision-superior force, transformation must spread across doctrine, organizations, training—not just material solutions. This is precisely what the Army did just prior to World War II with the Louisiana Maneuvers that transformed our understanding of armored warfare.

Today we must also establish an environment that fosters innovative thinking and create a military culture that embraces a new level of collaboration between the services. We must also push joint command, control, communications, and computers and intelligence capabilities, C4I capabilities, to lower levels to increase the flexibility and responsiveness of our forces. Joint force commanders and their staffs must understand not only what their own service brings to the joint fight, but also what capabilities from the other services, as well as the coalition partners, are available to plug and play into their system.

All of this is obviously going to take time and a lot of hard work. We are looking at a number of approaches to help, and we will use the experimentation efforts of Joint Forces Command to help synchronize these efforts and to validate them, as well.

There was a time not all that long ago that our military force services, each very capable in their own right, moved along almost separate, unrelated, transformation routes. I think we have come a long way in recent years and the current joint effort in Afghanistan is proof of our progress. But our goal is to accelerate this process so all services move as an entity along an integrated transformation path toward a common vision for the future. This will not be easy, but it's absolutely necessary.

As a pessimist said recently, "Everyone is for transformation, but nobody wants to change." Despite the nonbelievers, I'm confident that jointness and transformation are achievable goals. I believe they are relevant and necessary to this new era with all its danger and all its insecurity. I personally will pursue them vigorously, even as we continue to focus on winning this war against terrorism.

As Exhibit I to some of the things I think we need to work on, when we were going through some of the QDR reviews this last spring, one of the panels on transformation was chaired by an individual who came to my office after receiving each of the services' transformation briefings, and he came in, he said, "Listen, every service sent us two- or three-star generals that were very articulate, with great Power Point slides that could explain their transformation process and their service, and in every case they were brilliant presentations. And as our panel would question them these folks were steeped in transformation, and they would talk about their services." He said, "What disturbed me, and why I'm in your office is—"I was a Vice Chairman at the time; he said, "Not one of the service presentations ever said how what they are doing links to the joint fight. Not one time."

It would be easy to do that. So we've got to overcome that. I think we have in many respects. We have a lot of work to do, as I mentioned.

On September 11th, the terrorists demonstrated to the world that they are willing to kill indiscriminately in pursuit of their goals, and if given the opportunity, I don't think there is any doubt that they would do so again. Of course, our job is not to let them as best we can. So America is again rising to meet a new challenge. As we fight this new war, we will draw our inspiration from the sacrifices made by so many other American heroes in other conflicts, like the veterans we paid tribute to last weekend. One of those honored was a fellow named Rick Raumly. If there's some Marines in the audience, and I know there are, you might know Rick. He went to Vietnam early in his life, enlisted in the Marine Corps and went to Vietnam and—I'm sorry; he went as an officer. He went to Vietnam—stepped on a land mine and blew off his legs. He was selected this year as the Disabled American Veteran of the Year. He is currently in the County Prosecution Office in Phoenix, Arizona. He has got about a thousand folks working for him, and he has got a national reputation, testified in front of Congress and others about fighting crime and so forth.

His story struck me because first of all, he is obviously a genuine American hero, a man of great integrity, honor, courage, and commitment. It was obviously an honor to meet him. He gets around fairly well without his legs, but still, as you watch him walk, it's a reminder of the sacrifice he made for our country. What was especially poignant to me as we were talking last Saturday night at this particular event, he mentioned that his son is a captain in the United States Marine Corps. And guess where he is right now? He's with the 15th MEU (Marine Expeditionary Unit), either on land or sea, over off the coast of Pakistan. I would guess that Captain Romley, now, and others like him, all volunteers, are part of a new generation that has answered the call to service. These are obviously men and women of honor and of courage and of commitment, and they stand ready to defend and protect the freedoms we hold so dear.

When I think about young service members like Captain Romley, I think about his dad before and what he sacrificed, and the challenge that is before us. I'm reminded and inspired by the words of General Omar Bradley who once wrote, "Freedom. No word was ever spoken that has held out greater hope, demanded greater sacrifice, needed more to be nurtured, blessed more the giver, damned more its destroyer, or come closer to being God's will on earth. May America ever be its protector."

Ladies and gentlemen, I just say that we have a new generation of American, once again, fighting to protect our freedom. And let there be no doubt, we will prevail. Thank you very much. God bless you, and God bless America. (applause)

DR. PFALTZGRAFF: Thank you very much, General Myers, for that outstanding, inspiring, and informative address. We now have the opportunity about 20 minutes for questions and discussion. Who would like to open the discussion period? Please raise your hand and wait for the microphone. Yes? Right down here. Please identify yourself.

AUDIENCE MEMBER: Good morning, Erin Winagraham, Washington Publisher. I wonder if you can elaborate on the recent operations piece and how you think it needs to be improved and changed to be more effective?

GENERAL MYERS: What I was alluding to in the presentation was it just needs to get going faster. I think it's put together now in ways that are probably pretty effective in getting our messages out, whether it's in the leaflets we drop over Afghanistan or in the radio broadcast that Commando Solo is broadcasting. The ability to change as those as events on the ground change, coordinating that with people who speak out in both the United States and in our coalitions. I think now it's working pretty well. It was just getting it started— was very difficult, giving birth was very difficult. And it just took time deciding who was in charge, realizing that it is all our departments and agencies that play a role in this. And not only that, but that our coalition partners have a role to play in this, as well. I'd say for some time now, we have been off and running. But most of you probably understand the problems we began with, and when we have missed some opportunities to make some statements. It was going; it just wasn't as coherent and focused as it needed to be. I think we have turned the corner on that now.

DR. PFALTZGRAFF: We have some time for more questions. Who would be the next? What a bashful group. Over here, yes, please.

AUDIENCE MEMBER: Sir, Lieutenant Colonel (inaudible), German Army. I'm a fellow at SAMS. Sir, you talked so much about jointness and how important it is. The question is, could you say few things or share your view on the education, what has to be changed, or if there has something to be changed meaning you want to have jointness. From my perspective, you have to work together, you have to be educated together as soon as possible even to not allow the (inaudible). Could you share?

GENERAL MYERS: Sure, and I'm glad you asked that question, because as I mentioned in the speech a couple of times, this is an issue inside U.S. armed forces. It's also an issue on how we work with our coalition partners. That's a more difficult piece, particularly when you talk about the C4ISR part of it. It's difficult to figure out how we lash together. I tell you it's particularly difficult when our coalition partners don't put a lot of money into the defense budget. You can't move into the 21st century, you can't address security in this new era unless you put the dollars to it. I'm not pointing at any ally or friend. But most budgets, like our budgets, went down. They need to go up, so we can become interoperable.

But you make a very good point. In my upbringing, early in my career, and I suppose the same for Ric, there wasn't much jointness except for some occasional joint training. Professional military education was not near as joint as it is today. We did not have the various courses for our joint staff officers, the capstone course. It took Goldwater-Nichols legislation to kind of force us together in ways we had not been before. I would say that now I have had two Army interns in my office as Vice Chairman and now as Chairman—I've still got one. Their knowledge of joint operations is incredible compared to what my knowledge was at the same point in my career, when I was a major in the U.S. Air Force, which is about where they are in their careers.

I think we are doing a lot of what we have to do. If we put together the standing Joint Task Force Headquarters, a standing headquarters, probably, and I don't know how this is going to come out because it has to be decided through development and experimentation down in Joint Forces Command and so forth, and we all got to take a look at it. But the concept might be that you have 40 or so officers enlisted as the nucleus of those standing—don't quote me that number; it could be a lot more, it could be fewer. Then virtually, you would have a lot of other officers and NCOs connected to it, of all services, that would be ready to go into action if we had a particular action. So we are talking about not a lot of resources in peacetime, but the connectivity that if we had to do something quickly, we could put it together and go to the field and execute.

We might also—I mean, it's perfectly conceivable that you would have coalition partners in that standing Joint Task Force Headquarters. We do essentially that in NATO, but they are not as mobile and flexible as they probably need to be. And so, this is for other parts of the world where we don't have that kind of organization. But I think we are making pretty good progress. Your premise is actually right, absolutely right. Are we where we need to be? Probably not. Are we making progress? I would say absolutely yes.

DR. PFALTZGRAFF: Next question? Please wait for the microphone.

AUDIENCE MEMBER: I'm Ann Scott Tyler with the *Christian Science Monitor*. General, you described Afghanistan as the first campaign in the war on terrorism. What specific roles do you see for the U.S. military in a war beyond Afghanistan?

GENERAL MYERS: As I said in my presentation, this is going to be across a broad area with lots of partnerships with all the elements of our national power. I do not want to specifically, or speculate on where the next military operation ought to be, but if you remember the goal, the goal is to eliminate international terrorist organizations. The goal is to ensure that weapons of mass destruction do not fall in the hands of the terrorists. September 11th is obvious to all of us. Whatever threshold there was for use of weapons of mass destruction certainly passed on that day when innocent civilians were intentionally targeted by a terrorist organization.

So those countries that harbor terrorists, those countries that are in the production and the research for weapons of mass destruction, are all ones that will have to be dealt with, either diplomatically or through other means. I think we know where most of those are. You can read the State Department list of those countries that support terrorism, and we know where weapons of mass destruction are for the most part, and weapons are experimented with or produced. So that's what the war is against. And whether it's military action or whether it's diplomatic action or financial action, I don't know. I think I would opine that the message that is being sent by our actions inside Afghanistan, to rid Afghanistan of a regime that supports international terrorism, is a pretty important message for the rest of the world to listen to. And hopefully some countries will be a lot more cooperative and I will just leave it there.

DR. PFALTZGRAFF: We have time for one or two more questions. So who would like to be the next? We have two—this one back here, is that all the way back? Let's take one on that side for now and then we'll take one or two here. Please identify yourself.

AUDIENCE MEMBER: I'm Pauline of the Associated Press. General, can you bring us up to date on any developments in Afghanistan overnight, any more Pastun defections, any more ground gained by the Taliban?

GENERAL MYERS: Ground gained by the Taliban? They have been going backwards pretty fast. I think things are continuing in the same vein as they were continuing yesterday. How coherent the Taliban is still remains an issue. We know there are pockets of Taliban that are still active in the north around Kanduz. The numbers vary, but it could be several thousand that are still resisting. Part of our effort today will be up there to support the opposition against them. And a lot of focus on the south, to assist the, some of the tribal leaders and consolidating support down there and to see if they will continue to limit their support and deny the Taliban their support. That continues. As we have said, we have got small units in the south doing reconnaissance and interdiction, trying to sort out the good guys from the bad guys and destroying the bad guys' military capability, and that will continue. Humanitarian assistance continues under some of the lead of the United Nations and other nongovernmental agencies. We are going to support that as best we can. It's my understanding now is that the land bridge between Uzbekistan and Mazar E-Sharif in northern Afghanistan is open, and that supplies are starting to come in that way. I need to verify that. But that was an initial report this morning. This is exactly the right time of year to start getting some supplies in there to help those that don't have the food or the clothing or the blankets to make it through the winter.

DR. PFALTZGRAFF: We have time now for only one or two more questions. In fact, we have about three minutes. So what if I do the following: let each of the two of you ask your question, make it very brief, and then let General Myers have the concluding word. You can address both questions. Would that be okay?

GENERAL MYERS: If I can remember two of them.

DR. PFALTZGRAFF: I will try to remember, too. I'm sure I can, but I will try. Go ahead.

AUDIENCE MEMBER: Thank you. David Litt, the State Department, Political Advisor at Special Operations Command. Yesterday, I think it was General Clark who was the speaker, I can't remember, but he said he was somewhat disappointed at the reaction of young people on college campuses and among young people that he's talked to. There's a lot of interest in service, some curiosity, but not a lot of commitment. I have heard some various views about this. But what would be your recommendation of how we translate interest in the part of young people into commitment and service?

DR. PFALTZGRAFF: Okay, now let's go to the next question.

AUDIENCE MEMBER: General, you talked about coordinating instruments in national power. You mentioned the law enforcement agencies. The cooperation with military and diplomatic power is also extremely important. We have made strides—we've got people like Ambassador Litt serving as policy advisers to the CINCs, and in this crisis, we had an Air Force officer on the

State Department and of course in the JROC community and of course CATS. I'm wondering if you could suggest any more specific organizational or management mechanisms we may put in place that coordinates diplomacy and military power.

GENERAL MYERS: I will talk about the second question first and the first question second, if that's okay.

The way we are, as I mentioned in the remarks, what we are trying to do, what the combatant commanders want to do, what Admiral Blair wants to do in Pacific Command, what General Ralston wants to do in European Command, what they want to do with the Southern Command, and what General Frank wants in the Central Command is many more. All elements of national power to be organized in a joint interagency coordinating group, not a task force like the drug war, but a coordinating group to bring these elements of national power out to the commanders as they look at their theaters and they look at terrorist networks that need to be dealt with, that we understand how it ought to be dealt wit by the various agencies and diplomatic leaders at the State Department and so forth; or if they're being dealt with by Treasury, or the FBI's involvement in the criminal investigation, and so forth. So we are going to bring all those elements of power together and coordinate them the way joint combatant commander says, "Mr. Secretary of Defense, here is my plan for combating international terrorism in this theater but you what other people are doing in the theater." It's very important. I have got examples that I simply can't share with you for classified reasons, but where this has worked pretty well, and where it hasn't worked so well, in having the kind of people you talk about in these coordinating groups can be very, very effective. We do pretty well inside the beltway, but we can do it better outside the beltway with the combatant commanders.

On the issue of service, I would—my experience has been different than Wes Clark's. When I spoke at the L.A. Town Hall a couple of weeks ago on a Monday evening, and there were a bunch of high school students there that were sponsored to be a part of the forum. And one of the questions asked was, How can we serve? And my answer is: Serve. It doesn't necessarily have to be military service, but it just needs to be service for your country. There are ways to do that.

I was impressed that that's what they are thinking about. And my impression in visiting campuses in the last couple of weeks is that young people do want to serve in some way. For the most part, they understand the importance of this particular global war on terrorism. They understand that if we don't win it, the impact it can have on our way of life, and on freedom—not just here, in America, but around the world. And this is very, very important. I think it's awakened an interest that hasn't been this active in a long time. At least that's my impression as I travel around. My time outside Washington is somewhat rationed to some degree, so maybe Wes is getting around more to some degree, but that's my impression.

So my answer to the high school seniors was, "Just serve." Just as you start out your life after school, find out how you can serve. Join the military. That's a great way to do it. Find other ways to serve, whether it's with nongovernmental organizations that are trying to make life better in the world somewhere, whether it's public service with whomever, start out that way and have an appreciation for what it means to serve. You will get a lot of fulfillment out of that, and it's so very, very important right now. So I have a little different impression about how young people are looking at this. The enthusiasm I have seen has been tremendous.

DR. PFALTZGRAFF: This is a very suitable note on which to end this opening session. I would like to thank General Myers for taking the time to be with us, to give us the benefit of his insight, his wisdom, his experience, his expertise. And also to tell us what he hopes to accomplish during his tenure as Chairman. We thank you for your service to the nation, General Myers, and we wish you the very best in achieving all of the goals that you have set forth today. Again, many thanks for being with us. Thank you. (applause)

GENERAL MYERS: Thank you, thank you all.

PANEL 4

Employing the Instruments of National Power in a Complex Environment

Chair: Dr. Loren B. Thompson, Chief Operating Officer, The Lexington Institute

The Honorable Frank Carlucci, National Security Advisor and Secretary of Defense, Reagan Administration

General Anthony C. Zinni, U.S. Marine Corps, Retired, former Commander in Chief, U.S. Central Command

Dr. Gordon M. Adams, Professor, George Washington University

Panel Charter

If they are to be employed most effectively, the instruments of national power must be synchronized in support of a shared and unifying security strategy, as previous panel charters have suggested. First and foremost, such synchronization is best achieved when those charged with the task of decision-making are able to work effectively together in an appropriate organizational setting that brings together the various instruments. This encompasses the use of force, together with other instruments such as financial resources and information on behalf of the strategic goals of the nation.

The complexity of the issues facing the United States today requires a reexamination of the interagency process that has evolved since World War II and especially since the National Security Act of 1947, now more than 50 years old. What have been its strengths and weaknesses, its successes and failures? The distinction once drawn between what was considered "international" and what was deemed to be "domestic" has been rendered obsolete by the events of September 11. The creation of an Office of Homeland Security, together with a Homeland Security Council having broad cabinet-level representation, is illustrative of this organizational need. What are the other organizational changes that may be necessary to maximize tomorrow's opportunities and meet future challenges?

This question must be considered with much greater urgency than seemed necessary until the attacks on the World Trade Center and the

Left to right: *General Anthony C. Zinni, Dr. Robert L. Pfaltzgraff, Jr.,
Dr. Gordon M. Adams, Dr. Loren B. Thompson, The Honorable Frank
Carlucci, and General Eric K. Shinseki*

Pentagon. Organizational relationships among the various departments and agencies may require modification to achieve greater clarity in strategy and responsiveness.

In previous eras, the nation has employed its military forces across a broad spectrum of security challenges to fight and win the nation's wars. They have also been used when necessary to respond to natural disasters such as the San Francisco earthquake of 1906 and Hurricane Andrew in southern Florida in 1993. Military forces have been indispensable to crisis management as well as the essential basis for economic development, stability, and crisis management. The events of September 11th point up both the vulnerability of our society and the tasks confronting our military forces across the operational spectrum. How well the use of such forces will be meshed with the other instruments of power from the strategic to the tactical levels will depend in no small measure on how we organize for national security in this new setting.

Of special importance is the integration of the instruments of power represented by financial transactions. The ability to halt the movement of funds to support terrorist operations has become an important national security concern. This trend underscores the need for national security strategy to be based on effective integration of such instruments of power, together with diplomacy and intelligence. All must work in synchronization in the interagency process, based on improved mechanisms that allow each to contribute most effectively to overall national security. The terrorist attacks of September 11th have given heightened importance to such tasks as protecting domestic infrastructure, including airports and air travelers, as well as other transportation systems, ports, power grids, and financial institutions, in the complex new security environment. Last but not least, we need to identify the lessons that can be learned from prior experience, as we develop organizational structures to focus the instruments of national power.

Discussion Points

• What are the essential organizational issues to be addressed to synchronize the economic, military, and other instruments of power? How do the events of September 11th affect the need for organizational adaptation?

• Do the current interagency processes produce solutions that are adequately responsive, flexible, and adaptable?

• How can we ensure that interagency processes produce coherent programs, taking into account issues of responsibility, accountability, resources, and procurement?

• How can policy cohesiveness be enhanced by bringing together diplomatic and military instruments, including the Departments of State and Defense and the various military commands, as well as the numerous other departments and agencies which have an important national security role?

• How can we developing more effective national security organizational capabilities to integrate resources among the various levels of government?

Summary

The Honorable Frank Carlucci, Former National Security Advisor and
         Secretary of Defense

• *Unprecedented teamwork and coordination are required to properly prosecute the war on terror. Victory in this war will be difficult to define.*

     1. The new enemy has no fixed location and seeks to employ asymmetric means against us.

     2. The four main elements of this effort will be covert action, intensive diplomacy, broad-based financial action to cut off the terrorists' source of funds, and coordination of agencies involved in homeland security.

• *The President is the ultimate coordinator of homeland security, but he has a chief of staff, a director of homeland security, and a national security advisor who assist in this effort.*

     1. How well this circle of advisers works together is crucial to the success of interagency coordination.

2. To encourage cooperation among domestic agencies, the Director of the Office of Homeland Security needs the right to review and comment on various agencies' budgets and the authority to increase funding that he believes is inadequate.

3. Like the National Security Advisor, the appointment of the Director of the Office of Homeland Security should not require Congressional confirmation. The Director's sole focus should be to provide unfettered advice and counsel to the President.

• *The NSC serves as an appropriate model for the new Office of Homeland Security, since it is the most capable component of our national security organization.*

1. DOD has been severely underfunded for some time, damaging military readiness and preventing the realization of military transformation concepts.

2. The State Department has been hollowed by reductions in overseas posts and by a 40 percent reduction in authorizations.

3. Overwhelmed with regulations and forced to disclose information threatening sources and methods, the CIA has developed a risk-averse culture and eliminated most of its covert action capability.

4. To be most effective, the Director of the Office of Homeland Security, like the Assistant to the President for National Security (National Security Advisor or NSA), must be capable of handling several delicate interactions.

• Both must have access to the President and be honest brokers in reconciling tensions between different agencies, especially the Departments of State and Defense.

• Both must also have the confidence of the Secretaries of State and Defense and the Director of Central Intelligence, and must ensure that all policy options and agency positions are presented and made clear to the President.

• The NSC has had problems that can serve as a lesson to the emerging homeland security process. In the past, organizational lines of authority and accountability have been blurred, and the NSC has lacked a system of checks and balances.

General Anthony C. Zinni, U.S. Marine Corps, Retired, former Commander in Chief, U.S. Central Command

• *The military is the key foreign policy enabler for development, security, and crisis resolution. The post-Cold War practice of relying primarily on the military instrument of national power has produced mixed results.*

1. The military has had over a decade of experience and can employ different tactics, techniques, and procedures to operate effectively in a variety of environments and locations.

• The military's sheer size, planning and logistics capability, and flexible capacity make it uniquely qualified to deal with a wide variety of problems.

• Our forces have valuable regional expertise, relations with local leadership, and experience with engagement programs.

• The military is capable of quickly stabilizing a crisis situation after domestic political support and commitment coalesce.

• Forces on the ground demonstrate American commitment and help build a "coalition of the willing" because potential partners feel more comfortable contributing their capabilities.

2. However, the military is often distracted by small-scale contingencies (SSCs) that do not have a clear mission or endstate. Rather, these contingencies are often messy, expensive, and asymmetric and often become open-ended commitments.

• *We need better integration of the political, economic, cultural, and humanitarian aspects of national power with the military and security dimensions. This integration is not easily achieved in the interagency process.*

1. The other instruments of power cannot react as quickly as the military, and there is the potential that global commitments may outpace our ability to respond.

2. Political objectives are difficult to translate into clearly defined military tasks.

3. A disconnect exists between strategic decisions made in Washington and the conditions in theater.

• *In the future we will face seven different kinds of missions:*

1. Coping with a possible peer competitor.

2. Dealing with regional hegemons who possess WMD and will try to employ anti-access measures.

3. Countering transnational threats, including terrorist groups and extremists, international criminal and drug organizations, and local warlords.

4. Addressing environmental security issues, such as disease, health control, and illegal migration.

5. Conducting humanitarian and peacekeeping operations in failed or incapable states.

6. Coping with domestic emergencies that exceed the capacities of other federal and local agencies.

7. Countering threats to information systems.

• *The military accepts the need to change but lacks a clear-cut transformation strategy and direction. We have four areas of change to address:*

1. The military's personnel system must foster a more professional and experienced corps of leaders.

2. Modernization must outpace the capabilities of any potential enemies, but we must not overlook proven capabilities such as ground forces. Our CINCs want a balanced set of forces; new technology cannot solve all of our problems.

3. When upgrading systems, the new capability must be online before we retire the legacy system.

4. We need to conduct research and development toward transformation in a way that manages risk and maintains a broad set of capabilities.

Dr. Gordon Adams, Professor, George Washington University

• *Five assumptions shaped the Bush Administration's early national security agenda.*

1. The military needs to be transformed to perform its job of fighting and winning wars more effectively.

2. There will be a deliberate attempt to end overcommitments.

3. There will be increased concern about defending the United States.

4. The U.S. will not "bail out" foreign governments in financial trouble.

5. There should be a reluctance to engage overseas and commit to treaty regimes.

• *September 11th highlighted the homeland's vulnerability to terrorism and asymmetric attacks and focused attention on the integration of foreign and domestic capabilities to fight the terrorist threat. However, the fight against terrorism is not a central organizing concept for American national security policy, but rather one vector in the broader concern about global engagement.*

1. Our vital regional interests lie in Europe, Russia, the Middle East and east and northeast Asia.

2. Issues of regional conflict, primarily ethnic conflict and state collapse, continue to fester despite our distraction by the war on terrorism.

3. Weapons of mass destruction continue to proliferate, along with other asymmetrical capabilities that may be used against us at home and abroad.

4. Globalization in the economy and technology and the movement of people and financial information exacerbate the tension of economic disparity.

• *There are two main policy lessons from September 11:*

1. We need an integrated National Security Strategy to focus attention on a broad set of goals and the instruments needed to achieve them. This strategy must have three critical foci:

• The United States must anticipate, not simply respond.

- We should seek to engage and shape, not just react to, events
- We must be able to engage without leaving the defense forces of the United States deployed indefinitely.

2. We must integrate all the instruments of national power to address the war on terrorism and other vital issues. The military has become the key enabler for integration since we have not developed the other instruments to allow more selective use of the military.

- *Our economic resources remain vital in anticipating and shaping events, but are not integrated within the national security process.*

1. In trade policy, we lack a clear strategy for expanding free-market economies.

2. International development and bilateral assistance programs are not properly integrated with other elements of power.

3. Our capacity to stimulate and develop our domestic economy has a tremendous impact on the global economy, yet domestic economic policy is often overlooked as an international security policy issue.

- *To better manage our economic tools, four areas need improvement*

1. Better integration is needed. Leadership is required to ensure that all agencies are involved in the development of the National Security Strategy and the interagency process.

2. We need better integration of strategic and budget planning.

3. We need better Congressional integration of the relevant subcommittees and authorization committees to streamline the process.

4. The Foreign Service Corps, the Agency for International Development, and other areas of the diplomatic establishment require better funding.

Analysis

The focus of the fourth panel was the organizational and policy changes necessary to synchronize the various instruments of national power. The United States has no peer competitor, but many challengers: we have more global might than any nation in history and more constraints on the use of that power. To most effectively use our great strength to achieve our lasting vision of national security, we must ensure that we are employing our resources optimally in this complex environment.

Winning the war on terror requires more effective utilization of the military, intelligence, law enforcement, and economic tools at the disposal of the U.S. and its allies. In his introductory remarks, Dr. Thompson observed that during the Cold War our government directed its entire effort toward fighting communism in all realms. After the Cold War we thought that the source of future threats would be rogue states; now we are focusing upon terrorism. We used to have ample time to adapt; now we must learn to adapt and change quickly.

The panelists were unanimously discouraged by the current state of interagency cooperation and believe that the continuously shifting nature of the terrorist threat strains that cooperation even more. Dr. Adams, who has served in many government economic agencies including the Office of Management and Budget, described the events of September 11th as a "critical learning moment" that has influenced the current administration to increase its involvement in multilateral and interagency issues. He argued that the current Administration's National Security Strategy should aim to anticipate and shape problems in a region before they become crises, in order to create the ability to engage without the need for interminable military deployments. Economic elements of power are particularly poorly integrated into policy processes, and domestic economic policy needs to be better tied to the National Security Strategy.

Mr. Frank Carlucci, former National Security Adviser and Secretary of Defense for President Ronald Reagan, argued that the new Office of Homeland Security should be based on the model of the National Security Council and that the Director should operate as an honest broker between the responsible departments and agencies. The panel agreed that in order for Governor Ridge to be effective in his new position, he must have budgetary authority over the agencies he is coordinating.

General Zinni explained that the military is "the key enabler" for American activities overseas—despite its reluctance to assume many of those missions—because of its broad capabilities, regional knowledge, and flexibility. The other panelists acknowledged the need for leadership and a coherent strategy to make interagency integration work; however, the lead role for the CINCs and their forces in advancing American interests in their regions was more controversial. Dr. Adams argued that terror is a tactic primarily aimed at U.S. global presence, and, while military presence and capability are important, the proper response requires worldwide engagement on a number of fronts, complemented by more coherent policies involving trade, international development, finances, and technology transfers. Other recommendations included providing CINCs with more interagency representatives and ensuring that other government departments become more adept at the operational level of planning between tactics and strategy. General Zinni noted that military organizations also need to reform and transform, but that they should not concentrate too much on technology and neglect maintaining the balanced joint force, including adequate ground power that is essential for protecting vital national interests.

Transcript

DR. THOMPSON: Good morning. I'm Loren Thompson from the Lexington Institute, and I'm going to be moderating this morning's panel.

which is called "Employing the Instruments of National Power in a Complex Environment." Let me bring on our three panelists. We have first coming out Dr. Gordon Adams of the George Washington University, General Anthony Zinni, former CENTCOM Commander and, finally, former Secretary of Defense, Frank Carlucci. Let me make a few opening remarks and then introduce them more fully and go to their presentations. And, after they've presented, we'll give you an opportunity to ask some questions. You know, it wasn't this difficult in the old days.

Although the threat that America faced in the Cold War was a good deal more serious than the challenges that we face today, at least it left little doubt as to what the danger was. For two generations, the entire apparatus of the federal government was directed to countering the threat posed by communism—not just our defense posture or our foreign policy, but every aspect of federal exertion from the interstate highway program to the space program was justified, at least in part, by the contribution that it made to combating the Communist menace. Other lesser threats were neglected unless they could be linked to that overriding concern. And then, the Cold War ended. Since the Soviet Union collapsed, we've lacked an overriding threat around which to organize our national security preparations. For a decade after Desert Storm, we thought that the threat was rogue states.

Now, in the aftermath of the atrocities of September 11th, we have shifted our focus to global terrorism. But the uncertainty remains. Do we mean the terrorism generated by a scattered fringe of disaffected fanatics, or do we mean a broader cultural phenomenon, perhaps something sweeping the Arab or the Moslem world. Or perhaps what we mean is some sort of technology-driven dynamic that has empowered fanatics of every stripe around the world. We don't know yet. What we do know is that the world is a far more complicated place than it once seemed, a place where every instrument of national power may need to be employed and coordinated, but in frequently changing ways. When the threat was relatively static, we could take years to work out the mechanisms by which various means of external influence were synchronized. But we may not have that time anymore, because the threat shifts frequently and, as we now know, in quite unexpected ways. So, how do we enable five military services, a dozen intelligence agencies, a sprawling diplomatic community and a decentralized economic apparatus to turn on a dime in response to new challenges? And how do we make such shifts mesh with the relevant domestic agencies, with a divided Congress, and with a diverse coalition of overseas friends and allies? That's the focus of this morning's first panel, employing the instruments of national power effectively in a complex environment.

We've gathered a group of three respected scholars here, who make a moderator's job easy. Easy because they are, themselves, admired moderates who need no introduction. Let me tell you a little bit about the three of you

Dr. Thompson

and then we will see a video that introduces the panel further, and then finally, we'll go to their remarks. First there is Frank Carlucci, the Chairman of the Carlyle Group. Mr. Carlucci is one of the most accomplished policy makers of his generation, having served successively as Deputy Director of OMB (Office of Management and Budget); Undersecretary of Health, Education and Welfare; Ambassador to Portugal; Deputy Director of Central Intelligence; Deputy Secretary of Defense; National Security Advisor; and finally, Secretary of Defense. Aside from the fact that Frank remains deeply involved in national security matters, he brings to today's panel an unparalleled range of expertise in diplomacy, in intelligence, in management, and in military affairs.

Second, there is General Anthony Zinni of the U.S. Marine Corps. General Zinni spent the last three years of his career as Commander in Chief of the U.S. Central Command, the regional command responsible for protecting U.S. interests in two dozen countries stretching from the horn of Africa through the Middle East to the former Soviet Union. Beginning as a company commander in Vietnam, General Zinni went on to hold a series of highly sensitive military posts directing operations in Iraq, in Somalia, in Turkey and in the former Soviet Union. Prior to assuming command of CENTCOM, he was Commanding General of the 1st Marine Expeditionary Force.

And, finally, there is Dr. Gordon Adams, Professor of International Affairs and Director of Security Policy Studies at the George Washington University. Dr. Adams was director and founder of the Defense Budget Project, before entering the Clinton Administration, the Associate Director of OMB for National Security and International Affairs. After that, he went on to be the Deputy Director of the International Institute for Strategic Studies in London. Few scholars have exercised a more persistent and a more perceptive influence over the way in which national security affairs are discussed, both in the press and on Capitol Hill. Now, we'll hear from our first panel member, Frank Carlucci.

MR. CARLUCCI: Thank you, Loren. The film really said it, unprecedented teamwork. It's almost self-evident that in the current situation we're going to have to bring about the kind of coordination we've never seen in the past. We're dealing with an enemy that has no fixed address. He's everywhere but he's nowhere. He's in our schools and businesses and in the caves of Afghanistan. He turns our freedoms to his own advantage. And, he devises hideously ingenious ways of inflicting pain and killing on innocent civilians, including the use of suicide. To defeat this enemy will require an extraordinary effort. It's a war like no other that we have been in. Indeed, even victory is hard to define. A large portion of the equation is military, and that seems to be rolling along rather well. But together with our military operations, we have to employ good intelligence, including covert action, effective diplomacy including public diploma-

Mr. Carlucci

cy, and a massive effort to cut off the funding supplies for the terrorists. And after that, homeland security, a new problem for us, which involves reportedly some 40 to 50 different agencies, and you have a coordination task of gargantuan proportions.

The ultimate coordinator, of course, is the President. But he has for this purpose a staff. He has a Chief of Staff, he has a Domestic Policy Council, he has a National Security Council (NSC) and, now, he has a Director of Homeland Security. How these people exercise their authority and how they interact with one another will determine, to a large extent, how effective interagency coordination is. The Director of Homeland Security is a new player, and he'll be speaking to you later this morning, so I won't comment extensively. I'll just repeat what I told the Congress when asked to testify on this. That I think the NSC model is an appropriate model, at least while it's a work in process until we see how it works. But it is true that domestic agencies respond more readily to budget pressures than anything else. So, Governor Ridge has to be a player in the budget game. And, as reported in the papers yesterday, he apparently is. He needs not only the right of review and comment, but he needs the right of escalation should he believe that the funding is not appropriate.

Contrary to the conventional wisdom, I do not think that confirmation would add to his clout with the different agencies. In fact, by having him report to two masters, it may well weaken his influence with the agencies he's directed to coordinate. I anticipate that Governor Ridge will work through the National Security Council, the National Security Advisor's Office in dealing with the defense agencies, partly because that makes sense, partly because that's the realm of the four pillars of our national security that is in good shape and has proved the test of time. The others are in disrepair. Defense has been under-funded, by various estimates from $50 to $100 billion a year, for some time now and we are not reconstituting the first subject, on which Loren has written extensively. Readiness has suffered and transformation is more of a concept than a reality at this point. While there may be some, albeit thin, rationale to demobilize our military, there is absolutely no rationale for demobilizing our State Department, but that's what we've done.

The State Department budget since the end of the Cold War has been cut some 40 percent in real terms. Instead of opening new posts with new countries, we're closing posts. Our people are working in insecure conditions with outdated telecommunications facilities. It's only been a year since the State Department got rid of its last Wang computer—a dysfunctional personnel system and a shortage of Foreign Service officers. Colin Powell is moving to correct this, but it will take time. Worse off, even worse off, is the CIA, which has been used as a political football since the days of the Church committee. We've overladen the process with regulations. We've forced the CIA to disclose information threatening the protection of services and methods. We've created, in effect, a risk-averse atmosphere. We've indicted CIA officers for implementing policy and we've tried to conduct something called open intelligence, which is an oxymoron. We have no covert action capability when the President signs a Covert Action Finding one day and it's headlines in the papers the next. NSC, of course, is a process, not a program. But it works.

And the NSC staff plays a key role. What are the qualifications for a national security advisor? First of all, obviously, some national security background. Secondly, and most important, access to the President. Third, enjoy the confidence of the Secretary of State, Secretary of Defense, DCI (Director for Central Intelligence), and now the National Homeland Defense Coordinator. Fourth, understanding the process and being willing to drive that process forward. Sounds easy, but it really isn't. We saw what happened when the process broke down in Iran-Contra. And, leaving aside personalities, I made a judgment when I came in as National Security Advisor that there were several flaws in the system. One is that the organizational lines of accountability and authority were blurred. Secondly, there was no system of checks and balances. There was no independent general counsel, and we created one. And, third, the NSC was misguidedly involved in operations. And that, for the NSC, is fatal. Less fatal, of course, is upstaging the Secretary of State, but that's not recommended. There are natural tensions between State and DOD. People ask me all the time, "Well, isn't there a fight between the State Department and DOD?

Do Rumsfeld and Powell get along?" My answer is, "I'd be disappointed if they agreed on every issue."

Indeed, the two organizations have different missions, and good policy comes out of an interaction between their points of view. And they generally can reconcile their points of view themselves, but if they can't, that's when the National Security Advisor has to step in. And it's the job of the National Security Advisor to make sure that the decisions are teed up appropriately for the President, that he's given all the options, that he understands what the agency positions are, and that, if necessary, the agency heads have the right to appeal to him. The National Security Advisor is usually asked for his or her opinion, but that should be at the end of the process, not at the beginning of the process. The National Security Advisor has to be an honest broker. Learn to mediate, learn to escalate to the President is always a judgment call. It depends much on the style of the President and the personalities involved. In closing, let me note that the current team is ideally suited to make this process work. They've all been there before. I've had the opportunity of working with all of them. They're superb individuals, and the results are showing, and they certainly merit your confidence. Thank you very much. (Applause)

DR. THOMPSON: Thank you, Frank. Next speaker, General Anthony Zinni.

GENERAL ZINNI: Well, first let me begin by echoing Mr. Carlucci's concern about the under-funding of the State Department—as an unpaid employee of the State Department. My assigned subject line and topic for this presentation was, "The role of the military as a key enabler for development, stability, crisis resolution, and enduring peace." When I looked at that, at first I knew it had been written in Washington, and it took me a while to get through it and figure out what I was going to talk about. But there is one part of that that I'd like to focus on and maybe change a little bit. That business about a key enabler. And I'd like to change it to "the" key enabler, because ever since the end of the Cold War what has happened in issues where we've had concerns about development, stability, crisis resolution, and enduring peace, we have put the military in the position of being the centerpiece, or the key enabler. And that has had mixed results.

There are pluses to the military being the key or the centerpiece, or the key enabler. The first is obvious. The military has tremendous capacity, tremendous resources compared to the other elements of power and the other agencies of government, and tremendous throwaway just in terms of size and ability to deal with problems, to bring the logistics and the planning and all the sinews that help resolve issues. It's good to build around the military. The second is the military knows the neighborhood best. And this may be arguable, but I'm going to say this as a former CINC: No one knew my region of the world better than I did and my unified command headquarters. No one. Not State Department, not anybody back here in Washington. We knew the region best. We lived and breathed there, we knew the leadership, we knew the issues, we worked the streets, we were there in military exercises, and you would probably find a vast majority of our ambassadors out there tell you that we ran the vast majority of engagement programs, not just the military-to-military, by default, and again by virtue of capacity and resources.

The military is capable of changing circumstances very fast and very dramatically. And what happens is we tend not to go into crises when they can be resolved easily, early. We go in when it's almost too late because, by the very nature of the way we are forced to commit, it requires public support and political commitment here to commit to a crisis. And that usually takes some pretty dramatic events on the ground. And the military is the only one that can freeze the situation or reverse it rather rapidly. As someone who has been in the hills with the Kurds, been in Somalia three times, and many, many more operations—humanitarian, peacekeeping, crisis, quasi-war—I can tell you, the military is the one that makes the quickest and best change. If you want to build a coalition of the willing, the military is the best source to have as a core. Because those that want to commit to something want to see American boots on the ground. And they can easily build around it. If I want a show of participation and commitment, I can add a little something to that very formidable presence the military brings. So I can send my truck company or my air-transportable hospital and claim I am part of a major military coalition, obviously led by the U.S.

And the military has had now over a decade of experience. We've been through the Haitis and the Somalias and the Rwandas and the Bosnias and on and on and on. And it is a credit to our military, and let me right here tip my hat to the Army and General Shinseki, in a number of these issues where the Army, particularly, has focused on these. The Peacekeeping Institute up at Carlisle, and many other efforts to come to grips in the form of exercise, doctrine, training, tactics, and techniques to deal with this new different kind of environment that we face. And what are the downsides of the military being the key enabler? The military doesn't like some of these roles. And let's be completely honest. All of us that signed up and joined, we wanted to fight like our fathers. We wanted to fight the Second World War. We wanted the nation mobilized behind us, we wanted to go to war with a clear mission and unconditional surrender, and we wanted a demonized enemy, we wanted to fight the forces in some sort of symmetrical fashion, we wanted to defeat them and come home to our ticker-tape parade. And we have been struggling ever since 1945 to repeat that.

That probably was an aberration in our history. Messy little wars—the Koreas, the Vietnams; unfinished wars like the Gulf War; the vast list of peacekeeping humanitarian and other operations other than war. Since we can't categorize them, we just lump them into "war—good", "other than war—bad". Got to do it. And we have not really embraced those missions. These missions are expensive. They drain our readiness, they pull us off our combat missions and are difficult to deal with. They don't ideally suit the strong suits of our military. They tend to come at us, a popular phrase now, asymmetrically. Third, the military gets stuck. The military is wary of these commitments now because when everybody else goes home, the military is still there. We are still there in the Persian Gulf. Believe me, I know it. Coming out of Turkey and monitoring the security zone in northern Iraq; policing Southern Watch in the no-fly, no-drive zones in the south, Bosnia and the Balkans—these are enduring commit-

General Zinni

ments that, once we get them, we tend to look around and see not too many suits, but a hell of a lot of uniforms around still in place, still marking time.

The integration of the other elements of power are not done well. I really think our interagency process needs a major reform. The political dimension, the economic dimension, the cultural dimension, the humanitarian dimension are still not well blended with the military or security dimension. And we need to find a way to make that happen. It's not easy. We can see in the current situation that the pace of operations where the military piece of this is moving very fast, and maybe the humanitarian and political are on different timelines. Evening them up and getting them synchronized, you know, is going to be extremely difficult, especially when you're thrown into a situation that is breaking fast. The translation of the political objectives and the military tasks in these operations is extremely difficult. These are not clear-cut, easily identifiable military action verbs. We understand "disrupt, destroy" and the kinds of terms that we use on the ground and in the air to get things done. It's difficult when the political objectives are stated in very soft terms. And we're trying to find a way not to be accused of "mission creep," not to be expanding the objectives of the mission. Trying to understand the situation on the ground, not having a very good iterative process back with those that make strategic decisions. And those that make strategic decisions tend to make them here. And I would tell you the battlefield inside the beltway looks very different than the battlefield out there. The way I saw the world as a CINC, and the way you may see it as someone making key strategic and policy decisions back here inside the beltway, are entirely different. I don't get the Early Bird. I don't watch the Sunday talk shows. I'm looking at events on the ground. You are back here being driven by other elements that have to be taken into consideration. And, there's been a lot of discussion about missions for the military, and after the Cold War that we were adrift. Last June, I was given an opportunity to deliver a lecture on the 21st Century U.S. military. In preparation for that, I looked at what can we see as missions for the future. And I came down with seven. The first is the outside possibility that we have a global power with sophisticated military capabilities that we have to face. Will we or won't we? I don't know. Admiral Prueher is going to be speaking, I think, in the next panel and as a former PACOM Commander and Ambassador to China we can talk, I think, to him at much greater length at what the possibilities are. We're second going to face regional hegemons with growing asymmetric capabilities, such as weapons of mass destruction and missiles, all designed primarily to deny us access to vital areas and regional allies. We will face transnational threats that include terrorist groups and extremists. International criminal and drug organizations—we're already engaged in those kinds of operations. We'll fight warlords as opposed to nation-states.

We will deal with new missions that we haven't even thought of yet, like environmental security, issues of health and disease control and illegal migrations. I think we'll see more of that in the future fall our way. We'll deal with the problems of failed or incapable states that require humanitarian peace-keeping assistance, disaster relief, and national reconstruction. We will continue to face a series of overseas crises that threaten U.S. citizens and property that we'll have to respond to, and very quickly, in very short term, and deal with very decisively. We will face domestic emergencies that exceed the capacity of other federal and local government agencies to handle. I wrote this in June, now, I'm not taking credit for it, but I think you're going to hear now, with homeland defense, the new commitment to federal forces. And, finally we're going to deal with threats to our key repositories of information and our systems for moving information. And, we're going to have to learn to deal with that issue and in that realm.

Let me just say in closing that prior to the events of September 11th, the biggest issue we were dealing with was change. The military needed to change. The military needed help. We talked about a transformation. I never quite understood what transformation was because no one defined it the same way. Everybody had their own definition. I felt that the first thing we needed to do was get a clear-cut strategy and a clear-cut direction for the military. We'd been lacking that since the end of the Cold War. And then, when we went about change, I thought there were four areas we had to look at. The first was reform. There are parts of our military that are in desperate need of reform.

One is the personnel system. And I would argue that we throw people out too soon. We can certainly age and give more experience to our people, more time and grade.

We ought to have a radical reconstruction of the personnel system and the way we handle our people and the way we develop a more professionalized and experienced core of leaders. And, that's just one area. There are other areas that I think "reform" is the right term. The second term I would use is "modernization." There are certain capabilities that we have that are damned good where we're going to see them around for a long while. And we need to keep the pace of modernization up, to stay ahead of any potential enemies. And I think we've made some misjudgments about some of these capabilities. There was a lot of talk about reducing ground forces in favor of more sophisticated space and air forces. Well, I hope the lessons of September 11th, one that comes out is "Thank God we didn't do that!" And, I can tell you, as a CINC in the region, that I had a heavy requirement to have a very balanced force, and not an unbalanced force and to rely totally on technology to solve all the problems.

We will have to make the decision about what we eliminate, as a third category. And I would say that we ought to do elimination carefully. In some cases, it ought to be atrophy, it ought to be over time, so that we're careful that whatever's going to replace that capability is online, that we handle our people right as we remove them from service. Not like we did at the end of the Cold War. And the fourth area is truly transformation, as I would define it, a major technological or conceptual leap ahead. Where will we invest the money to do that? Where will we invest the focus and research and development? It needs to be carefully thought out. There are advocates for sensing, advocates for precision, advocates for all sorts of capabilities. This goes back to the point about strategy and direction. That's going to cost a lot, that's going to be high risk, and it must be focused. But change in the military needs to go through all these and look at all these possibilities as to how we change, and not just focus on one element or limit ourselves to just a few capabilities to handle these problems. Thank you. (Applause)

DR. THOMPSON: Thank you, General Zinni. Gordon Adams.

DR. ADAMS: Good morning. I have the unique and difficult challenge in a world that is exceedingly well organized, when it comes to the military side of the issue, to talk about some broader instruments of American national power that need to be part of this game. Let me start by taking a step back, in the direction General Zinni just took us, to the larger question of the agenda. And then talk a bit about how one integrates these instruments, these broader instruments of national power, into that agenda. Let's start with the agenda first. I think we face a very critical learning moment in American national security policy. At the beginning of this particular Administration, the sense that one had about these instruments of power and their objectives, their missions, was that the military was intended to fight and win wars, that it would be transformed to do the job better, that there would be a deliberate attempt to end the kinds of overcommitments that General Zinni focused on, that there would be a concern about defending the United States, that the United States would not bail out other governments when they got into financial trouble and a certain amount of reluctance with respect to treaty regimes and overseas engagement.

In the terms of this agenda, 9/11 has been a wake-up call, a wake-up call that had a very specific focus: the vulnerability of the American homeland to terrorism and attacks with a global reach. That focused attention on the need to fight on all fronts, to integrate foreign and domestic capabilities, to create coalitions that could confront a terrorist threat. I think there is a much larger lesson that we could draw from our current circumstance. Terror, in my judgment, is a tactic used by specific forces, principally seeking the end of U.S. global presence. But the United States is unlikely to tackle terrorists in every case in every country. In my judgment, terrorism represents one vector of a much broader array of interests and concerns that require American leadership and involvement. We are, in essence, on a learning curve for the 21st Century.

The fight against terrorism is not a central organizing concept of American national security policy. It is one vector in that broader concern about our engagement globally. General Zinni's been through a list of the broader agenda issues that the nation faces. I don't disagree with his list. I have a slightly different way of posing what those threats and challenges to the United States and those opportunities may be. They are very broad and they are difficult to pull into one organizing central concept. We have vital regional interests, only some of which concern issues of terrorism—vital regional interests in Europe and Russia, in the Middle East and the Gulf, and East and Northeast Asia—which I would judge to be the three central geographic regions of American vital interest. The focus on terrorism helps with one of those. It has brought the United States and the Russians more closely together in what Samuel Huntington has called a coincidence of interests, but not a major realignment.

Secondly, we have issues of regional conflict, ethnic conflict, and state collapse. Those issues have not disappeared while we focus on this important conflict with al-Qaeda and the Taliban. The Balkans remain unsettled. Central Africa remains in conflict. Zimbabwe is in disintegration. Other states face regional issues of major concern.

Thirdly, we have the proliferation of weapons of mass destruction that, with other potential asymmetrical capabilities, could be used against the United States both at home and abroad, including the cyber conflict General Zinni referred to.

Fourthly, the much broader issue which has been understandably lost in the last few months: the implications of globalization in the economy, in technology, in information, in the movement of people, and finance, and concern about the relationship between the haves and the have-nots, which in turn leads to and fuels some of these other concerns of American national security.

What then is the policy lesson of 9/11? Where do we find ourselves on the learning curve? Let me make three points as to what I think the policy lesson may be. First, 9/11 and the other issues that we face make it very clear that we need an integrated national security strategy. We do not have one yet. We have a Quadrennial Defense Review, which focuses on the Defense Department, but we still need

Dr. Adams

to shape a full national security strategy, using all of the instruments of power. Some dismiss the national security strategy as an anodyne document that ends up in a filing cabinet long before it has even begun to gray. It is, however, a centralizing document, properly managed, focusing government attention on the broadest array of concerns and goals, the broadest array of instruments.

Secondly, we need to integrate, much more than we have, all of the instruments of statecraft, not just for the war on global terrorism but to confront all the issues that I mentioned. It is time to put an end to "calling card meetings," the meetings where you show up and say, "I haven't met you before. Here's my card. I'm with Agency 'X.' I'm with Agency 'Y.' I'm concerned with humanitarian relief. I do disaster relief. I do migration problems. I do the military in a particular situation." The integration of those instruments needs to be stronger. I would suggest, in my judgment, that in integrating the instruments of statecraft, the military is not the key enabler. I agree with General Zinni it has by default too often become the key enabler. But we have not done what we should do to develop and integrate the instruments of statecraft that enable us to use the military wisely and selectively.

Thirdly, our national security strategy needs to have three very critical characteristics. One, it needs to anticipate, not respond. That's the key dimension and one of the reasons you need all the instruments of statecraft to develop that strategy. It needs to anticipate, not respond. Secondly, it needs to shape, not react. So when it anticipates, it needs to engage and shape, not simply react to events. And, thirdly, it needs to be able to retrieve our defense forces, not leave them deployed forever, as the holder of the bag, as General Zinni described it. To put it bluntly, we need to get ahead of the problems and not have the problems come to us. The military goes in too late to fix things when the problems have come to us. Now, what are some of the other instruments involved here? I am not going to speak except briefly at the end about the State Department, but I think that Frank Carlucci and General Zinni have both made very important points. The economic instruments that I want to say something about are key to anticipation and to shaping. And they are not well integrated, not only into national security strategy making, but not even among themselves.

So, I want to make a few very selective comments about those instruments and the shortfall that we may still face with respect to their integration. Trade policy is the first, for the objective there is creating a more open free-market economy around the globe. But it is not clear what the strategy is for trade policy, and too often, in my experience, trade policy is developed by "hiding the hand" from the rest of the national security structure. One of the key problems is that trade and the other economic instruments of policy are not integrated in the Executive Branch. The only place that funding for development and economics and trade and for the military and for intelligence were integrated into a single office, was in the office I occupied for five years at the Office of Management and Budget. There was no other place in the Executive Office of the President where there was a single focus of concern on all of those instruments. Trade policy, in my judgment, was not well integrated as a consequence. It was developed off-line. Secondly, financial relations, and I say financial relations rather than treasury, because there are many instruments for the financial relationship.

Jane Hull talked about controlling money flows. That is piece one. Paying attention to currency value, providing monetary support and crisis response. In all of these areas, too, there is a tendency in the Executive Branch for the agency principally involved, Treasury, to hide the ball and not to seek to integrate those capacities with broader strategy. You can see, however, how the value of currency, how controlling money flows, how supporting monetary shifts, how responding to crises can play a role in anticipation and in shaping, long before we have to leave the military holding the ball. Third, international development programs. We have bilateral assistance, we have multilateral assistance; but in my experience, our bilateral assistance has not done as well in crisis response as it does in protecting long-term "pet rocks" in the development agenda at the Agency for International Development. Now, I know they're in this building, so I'll probably pay for that comment, but the guardianship of pet rocks has systematically, in my judgment, hindered our ability to integrate development assistance into a broader effort to anticipate and to shape.

We have seen a dwindling supply of economic support funds in the Department of State become almost entirely a program for Egypt, Israel, and Jordan, for the peace process in the Middle East. Not an unimportant process, but one which leaves our ambassadorial corps without the instruments they can use to anticipate and to shape, leaving it to the Joint Chiefs of Staff and the CINCs to know the region better and to have more funding for programs that bring people together in the region. That's a money issue and it needs to be fixed.

We have billions of dollars in contributions to multilateral development banks and the World Bank. But, in my judgment again, our bureaucracy does not focus properly on the objectives of those programs and how they can work to anticipate and to shape the international environment. The amount is negotiated, the funding is transferred to the regional and World Bank offices, and yet this is central to our response to the issue of the haves and the have-nots in globalization. The biggest problem we have faced in Bosnia, in Kosovo, is integrating the capacity to develop justice systems, police systems, health systems, education systems, and simply to reconstruct housing and roads because we have not focused on planning for that objective and we do not fund it well.

Fourth, we have domestic economic policy. We don't often think of this as an issue of international security policy, and yet as we look at a global recession currently under way, our capacity to develop and stimulate our own economy becomes part of the capacity of the global economy to recover. We export the most, we import the most. So it becomes absolutely critical.

And finally, technology policy. We don't talk much about this today, but it's an important instrument both of military power and of our economic capability. It involves the diffusion of know-how and how to control what is crucial and how to strengthen allied relationships. Here we have a stultified, backward piece of machinery preventing the American economic machine from global interaction, especially with respect to dual-use and defense related technologies. And we have not seen a focus on technology-transfer reform or export-control reform. It's an important element in national economic and military power that we have a focus on prevention rather than on cooperation.

Finally, how would we handle these tools better? As I've said before, better integration is part of the answer. The only place at the center of the American government where they are integrated is at the budgetary level, where all of those programs are considered in one place. The National Security Council does not integrate them now and has not done so well in the past. The National Economic Council model developed by the prior Administration did not work terribly well and is, in any case, not functioning today. It did not have the heft, organization structure, statutory capability, and credibility with the agencies that the National Security Council machinery has had. There needs to be some regular involvement of all of these agencies and their objectives in the development of the national security strategy and in the interagency process. And the way that happens is leadership. A decision needs to be made at the center that these issues will play their part and be integrated.

Secondly, I've suggested some areas where I think we need better funding. ESF (Economic Support Funds) needs to be rebalanced. Our Diplomatic Corps needs better instruments in Economic Support Funds to play a role of shaping and anticipating; AID needs a more strategic program focus; the Treasury Department needs to focus on the goals and objectives and not just the transfer of cash in the multilateral development process. These are just illustrations of where we need better-shaped as well as more appropriate funding.

Thirdly, we need better budget planning, integrating strategic planning and budget decisions. Fourthly, we need much better congressional recognition of the need for integration. On the basis of experience, the jurisdictional "Rube Goldberg" device that deals with these budgets in the Congress involves four different appropriate subcommittees and a large number of authorizing committees, none of whom work well in harness with each other. Congressional integration ought to be a focus as well. You can integrate the heck out of the Executive Branch, and the Congress can untie your integration and disintegrate the package.

In conclusion, I think this integration only happens with leadership. Leadership is needed in the White House for strategy development; leadership is needed for the coordination process to be done effectively; leadership is especially needed not to allow agencies to wander off in different directions, but to deconflict and make decisions. Those are some of the directions and some of the lessons that I think we can learn from 9/11 that will facilitate our ability to anticipate, to shape, and to recover. Thank you.

DR. THOMPSON: Thank you, Dr. Adams. Before we turn to the audience for questions, I guess I'd like to put one question to all three members of the panel, leveraging off of what Gordon Adams said about leadership. You know the name of this panel is summoning forth the national instruments in a complex environment, using them effectively. Seems as though some of the complexity is out there, but a lot of it is in here inside of the beltway. As long as I can remember, we've been looking for structural solutions to this problem, different ways of organizing the boxes and coordinating the system. Is this an engineering problem or is this principally a form—a problem of personalities that really can't be fixed in the absence of what Gordon calls leadership?

MR. CARLUCCI: Well, I'll take a crack at it. It's both. I mean you have to have the proper organizational structure with lines of authority and accountability lined up. And there, if I can take a leaf from Gordon's book, the Congress, too, has been unhelpful because they tend to divorce accountability from responsibility as they pass laws affecting the Executive Branch. But a lot of it does impend on personalities and just the leadership function. A good leader can make a bad organizational structure work. But if you have—if you line up your organizational structure a little better, a good leader can do even more. I think—at one time in my career I was appointed a czar to a disaster relief effort. I had argued against it. I was in O&D at the time, Gordon, and I thought it was a bad idea. But, Nixon thought it was a good idea, so I gave in. And I went out for the coordination of the Adenas disaster and I had control over the agencies' budgets at the same time. Well, they fell into line very quickly. So, once again to emphasize Gordon's point—you get a hold of their budgets, the domestic agencies will begin to respond.

GENERAL ZINNI: I agree with Mr. Carlucci that it's both, but I would focus on the structure because I think, especially in terms of dealing with crises, that the structure is ad hoc. Go back to the point Gordon made about calling-card meetings where you meet people for the first time. When people come into the middle of a crisis they are looking for the map, so you may have, for example, people on the military side that have been watching the crisis for years and have a much deeper understanding, and someone that's going to make some critical decisions in another element of national power that is just discovering the crisis. So, the structure needs to provide a more enduring organization for dealing with issues, and one that is cross-fed and cross-populated so that we have a better understanding of each other.

DR. ADAMS: Loren, there's just one dimension I think you left out, which I also mentioned, which is strategy. You can set up the best coordinating mechanisms in the world, but if you don't know where they're going to go it's very hard to direct them and decide which the priorities are. So, in choosing who you want to do what, when, in engineering terms, it's important to have a sense of what it is you want them to do, what the mission is, which is why I also would emphasize strategy. There are some engineering issues here. I truly continue to believe, because I was the guy who had to integrate 16 to 20 agencies on the foreign policy side at the Office of Management and Budget, that our foreign policy machinery is riddled with complexities, defects, lack of coordination, lack of a common sense of strategy. We struggled with that through the strategic planning process as required by congressional legislation, but we are not home with that, and it really requires leadership.

That's where people come in. I share Frank's point here. To give you one example, one agency that was fundamentally broken the early '90s, was the Federal Emergency Management Agency. And the will and capability of one man at the head of that agency, Jamie Lee Witt, created an instrument that can respond as effectively as it can today. So, leadership is very important. Accountability is too. We have [a] peculiarly weak process of government in the United States where we let the elected legislators really work in between elections. If you go to almost any other country in the world with a parliamentary system, the legislatures rubber stamp more than they work in between elections because they've elected the majority and the majority becomes a kind of a dictator in the implementation of policy. Our legislature's separate. It's the glory of American government. What we don't always do well is integrate the two so that they can work together. I do think there's room for structural change in the Congress.

And just to put it on the table as an alternative option, I think it's worth discussing whether something like homeland security needs a statutory basis of existence so that Governor Ridge can effectively, over time, continue the process of making decisions and implementing those decisions and can work with the Congress rather than be at war with the Congress about who is in charge here, which is an awful battle to continually have with the United States Congress. You know, if they are your enemy, bring them close to you and hug them. Do not try to keep them at arm's length. Last point, I really share Frank Carlucci's point about budget control. Governor Ridge may be acquiring some of this over time. Right at the beginning of the process when Governor Ridge was appointed I would have married Mitch Daniels to his hip and said, "All of the decisions that Governor Ridge is going to have to make are going to be implemented by this guy over here," because there's no greater authority for focusing the minds of agencies than saying, "Your budget is at stake."

DR. THOMPSON: All right. Well, we have the opportunity now, for those of you who are interested, in the audience to ask a question. Could you wait until the microphone comes to you and when you ask your question could you identify who you are? I didn't say the microphone had to work. (Laughter)

AUDIENCE MEMBER: Stephen Biddle, Army War College, Strategic Studies Institute. I have a question on organizing for homeland security. If you think in terms of the larger objective of homeland security and keeping Americans safe from terrorist attack, that presumably includes both defense at home but also counter-offensive action overseas. Ordinarily, we try and integrate defensive and counter-offensive action as closely as possible within the military dimension of power, much less integrating across the military and the non-military dimension of power. I was wondering if the panel could comment on the implications of organizing for homeland security by establishing an institution that focuses on the defensive home element and does it outside of the Department of Defense and the National Security Council.

MR. CARLUCCI: I'm not sure I understood the question. You're talking about a separate agency?

AUDIENCE MEMBER: Yeah. I mean, to the extent that the home—that Governor Ridge's institution eventually becomes a substantial outside agency with this responsibility that's neither subordinate to nor superior to the Department of Defense and the National Security Council, does this promote tight integration of all of the elements that we need in order to provide homeland security or not?

MR. CARLUCCI: Well, I personally have a knee-jerk reaction against the creation of more agencies. I think we've got too many already. I think we have to give Governor Ridge a chance to make the coordinating role work. And if he has sufficient budget clout and if he's got access to the President, which he clearly has, the agency should fall in line. If you create another agency, then somebody has to coordinate that agency. So I think what Governor Ridge is going to have to do, and he has obviously the capability to do this because General Downing apparently reports to two masters, is integrate his activities with the activities of the National Security Council, which after all does include the Secretary of State, Secretary of Defense, and the national security components.

GENERAL ZINNI: Before September 11th, I participated as a senior mentor in a series of exercises regarding what amounts to now has become known as homeland defense, but reacting to crises much similar to what we're preparing for now. What struck me in that was some of the other agencies, like Justice and FEMA, go from the strategic here down to the tactical on the street where the event's occurring and have nothing in between. The military attempts to match up, or the DOD has tactical operational strategic levels, and there were mismatches. There was confusion on intelligence sharing, there was confusion on regional direction, tactical direction and then strategic direction from here. So, I do think something like this organization that Governor Ridge is putting together is necessary to fill that void. If you have isolated events that local agencies handle and then states reinforce and then federal come in, sort of the traditional come as soon as it gets beyond the capability of the level before you, that could be handled by the way things were before. If there are going to be a series of events, or they're going to have strategic implications, or they have to be married and seamless with counteractions overseas, I do think we need something to pull it all together, because there are missing levels and missing elements of coordination that are obviously necessary if you deal with something on that scale.

DR. ADAMS: My response is first an observation about one of the interesting features in the current response to the terrorist attacks, and that is that the capacity to plan and act. There's not a lot of degrees between policy making and street action in some of these other agencies. There certainly is in our military capability. It's organized to provide this kind of capability. After the terrorist attacks when we had to develop fiscal requirements for what we needed to do to respond and recover from the attacks, what struck me was the enormous capability of the Department of Defense and the Services to identify what they needed, to prioritize what they needed, to establish those goals, and to communicate them to the Congress, something that we do enormously effectively in the Pentagon.

What was also striking was the parallel inability of the domestic agencies concerned with the same kinds of responses to develop that kind of integrated set of requirements. These agencies have lived so long in an atmosphere of fiscal poverty and just getting along that they have not figured out how to aggressively and ambitiously define what is needed, what the priorities are, what the requirements are, what funding is needed to provide them. It's quite striking that the development of that kind of package has fallen to the ranking minority member of the House Appropriations Committee, Dave Obey, who himself put together a set of requirements for domestic agencies, as well as intelligence agencies, that might be needed to deal with the terrorism crisis. There are a couple of things that I think we'll need to think about. I certainly agree that starting with Governor Ridge's operation is a good place to start.

I am concerned that he does not have appropriate budgetary authority and, as I said before, I'm concerned that I don't think he has the right kind of congressional wiring. That, in my view, should lead us to consider whether or not there should be a statutory responsibility located in the Executive Office of the President. That's worth discussion, perhaps not haste, but at least discussion to coordinate these things more appropriately. And, finally, I think it's worth thinking as well about what kinds of capabilities we need to have at the federal level to protect the domestic American homeland. I'm not entirely persuaded that the option defined by the Hart-Rudman Commission to combine a Border Patrol, Customs, and the Coast Guard in a federated agency focused on homeland security is quite right, but again, it's the kind of option that may need to be considered so that we know people aren't overlapping, duplicating. They're coordinated and they fit a strategy.

DR. THOMPSON: I think we have time for one more question, if we could have brief responses from the panel. Here in front.

AUDIENCE MEMBER: My name is David Strizen. I'm with JSA Partners. It's a consulting company. My question is primarily directed to Dr. Adams regarding your comments on export controls and technology policy. Although if the other panelists have a good opinion, I'd be interested in that too. And, particularly, when you said the focus right now is on prevention, not cooperation. I just want to know if you can explain a little bit better what you mean about that, particularly in light of weapons of mass destruction, etcetera.

DR. ADAMS: It probably requires a longer answer than we have time for at this point, but we have two problems simultaneously—really three. One, technology and the capability to develop not only weapons of mass destruction, but all kinds of instruments of war, is amply diffused and highly dual-use at this point. Two, we have an issue involving the capacity of the U.S. and its NATO allied forces to interoperate. And so, three, we have a question of what do we protect and what do we cooperate on. Right now, we have a piece of machinery operated largely in the Department of State. They process 45,000 to 50,000 license requests a year, mostly for things that in no way engage major military capability that could be directed against the United States. What we have not done is prioritize very specifically what technologies we can, need to, and should protect, what kinds of regimes we need to establish with our allies so interoperability and tensions over defense trade don't become a source of friction that weakens the alliance, while being sure that we're not providing the capacity to other countries to develop capabilities to be used against us. It's a very difficult problem, but right now we're going at it in a way that doesn't control technology, doesn't allow interoperability, and therefore, doesn't strengthen our national security.

DR. THOMPSON: Well, we are out of time. Let me just say by way of conclusion that even mushroom clouds can have silver linings. We may find that this war against global terrorism that we're all so preoccupied with right now is a relatively transient thing. But in the aftermath of what happened on September 11th, the distinction we've traditionally drawn between domestic and foreign affairs, between homeland and foreign defense, I think that's gone forever. So I want to thank our panel members for offering their insights into how we deal with a radically transformed world and a different kind of defense in a new millennium. Thank you. (Applause)

SPEAKER: I want to thank the panel as well, and to its moderator and to announce that we now have a 15-minute break. Please be back in precisely 15 minutes so that we can resume.

PANEL 5

LEADERSHIP: ACHIEVING UNITY OF EFFORT—ALLIES, COALITIONS, AND INTERNATIONAL EFFORTS

Chair: Dr. Robert L. Pfaltzgraff, Jr., President, Institute for Foreign Policy
Analysis

Admiral Joseph W. Prueher, U.S. Navy, Retired, former Ambassador to the
People's Republic of China

Dr. Keith B. Payne, Chairman and President, National Institute for Public
Policy

General Montgomery C. Meigs, U.S. Army, Commanding General, United
States Army, Europe, and Seventh Army

Air Vice-Marshal John Thompson, Defence Attache and Head of the
British Defence Staff, Washington

Panel Charter

Our greatest successes in foreign policy have been based on the ability to
mobilize the support of allies and others sharing common interests. This has
been demonstrated from the American Revolutionary War to the alliances and
coalitions in which the United States participated or led over the last century.
We are now in the process of utilizing existing alliances such as NATO and at
the same time developing new coalitions in response to the events of
September 11. Such cooperative arrangements provide political as well as military support, together with access to overseas facilities, intelligence, and information. The need for the United States to work closely with allies is growing
as a result of the proliferation of the means for asymmetrical warfare.
Increasing levels of lethality available to a variety of states and other actors are
producing important implications for deterrence and thus for alliance/coali-
tion operations.

Alliance/coalition cooperation in military operations requires a high level
of synchronization among the forces of contributing partners. However, unity
of effort extends to the national level as well. The need for joint operations that
bring together the capabilities of each of the military services places a high

premium on synchronization within military organizations. At the national level we need to assure unity of effort within and among joint forces.

Achievement of international unity when the partners have shared, but also distinctive, national interests and objectives is challenging. Whether or not it is the dominant alliance/coalition member, the United States still faces formidable problems in forging, sustaining, and maximizing the potential for collective international action. The United States has participated successfully in military campaigns with a variety of allies, coalitions, and partners and, in most cases, is the leading member, as in the current campaign against terrorism. In other situations the United States may have a supporting role as in East Timor, where Australia has played the leading part.

The coalition against global terrorism exemplifies the challenge and complexity of achieving a unity of effort with diverse nations. Coalitions are shaped by the issues that draw members together. In the present terrorist crisis, the United States seeks to include states with which there have been fundamental differences in the past. How to maximize areas of agreement, while recognizing the inherent limitations on such cooperation, is a problem of continuing importance. The inherent relationship between diplomacy and military operations must be considered at the alliance/coalition level. In the present crisis, the issue of NATO participation has come to the fore. For the first time in its history, NATO invoked Article 5 of the North Atlantic Treaty in support of the United States after the events of September 11. According to this provision, the attack upon the United States is regarded as an attack on all Alliance members. NATO cooperation has many important dimensions. In addition to transatlantic military cooperation, such as having NATO surveillance aircraft (AWACS) patrolling U.S. skies, the alliance furnishes an important basis for diplomatic synchronization. Such international efforts provide a unique set of challenges. The United States faces the need to determine how and when coalition efforts may support U.S. goals and how and when they may be less than beneficial.

As demonstrated in the U.S.-led NATO *Operation Allied Force* in 1999, the transformation of America's military poses a challenge for future combined operations. There is a growing gap between U.S. forces and those of allies as a result of disparities separating the United States and its Alliance partners in military technology investment. This gap is symbolized by the Revolution in Military Affairs—the vastly greater U.S. investment than that of its allies in information-age technologies for its armed forces, together with the potential for a major change in the nature of warfare brought about by the innovative application of new technologies leading to new military doctrines. If allies lack the advanced military technologies required to make them useful coalition partners in military operations, their ability to act together will be diminished, and the overall collective effort will be weakened. How the United States and its allies address this issue will shape the future of Alliance relationships. In those efforts in which the

United States chooses not to act as the leader or principal contributor, other challenges must be faced. These include the type and level of support, together with arrangements for continuing consultations and necessary levels of coordination of military integration among Alliance/coalition members.

Discussion Points

• NATO as an organizational framework for combined action. What are the lessons of recent operations, from southeastern Europe to the war against terrorism?

• What is the likely extent of support and the potential for discord between the United States and its allies?

• Will the RMA and the emerging technology gap between the United States and its alliance and coalition partners hinder cooperation in the future?

• What are the implications for designing deterrence concepts for the United States alone and in concert with Alliance/coalition partners?

• What are the priorities and tasks facing the United States in achieving agreement among allies/coalition partners? What is the role of diplomacy, and how does diplomacy relate to other instruments of power?

• What lessons can be drawn from the events of September 11th for future alliance/coalition cooperation?

Summary

General Montgomery C. Meigs, U.S. Army, Commanding General, United States Army, Europe, and Seventh Army

• *Multinational operations are notoriously difficult due to the domestic politics, military cultures, and unique strategic interests of the countries involved. Personalities of subordinate commanders can also complicate these operations. Multinational political consensus on clearly defined strategic objectives, a shared sense of danger, and a common purpose in confronting the threat are required for unity of effort in coalition operations.*

• *The coalition commander is simultaneously responsible to a domestic political constituency and to the political leadership of the coalition for the results achieved by its elements individually and collectively.*

1. Contingent commanders are bound by orders from home; their ability to act depends on the degree of commitment from their political leadership.

2. An aversion to risk in the United States, for example, severely constrains American commanders' actions. Asking contingent members to accept a higher level of risk than is carried by their own nation's troops will undermine the cohesion and morale of the operation.

- *Military commanders in multinational operations must constantly balance influences and pressures from their own nations, from other nations, and from international organizations.*

    1. They must be able to balance competing military and political pressures and understand the unique operational priorities of the coalition members.

    2. To foster mutual respect and confidence among senior allied officers, multinational commanders should routinely address the concerns and seek the advice of officers from other nations.

    3. Commanders must exhibit and demand impartiality, patience, and a strong sense of moral responsibility.

    4. Subordinates must trust the coalition commander to accept personal responsibility for all coalition actions.

Admiral Joseph W. Prueher, U.S. Navy, Retired, former Ambassador to the People's Republic of China

- *Coalition operations require alignment between the coalition commander and the political leadership of his own country.*

    1. The leadership and commanders must fully exploit the political, information, military, and economic instruments of national power.

    2. Sun Tzu wrote that a great general maintains forces that are prepared to prevail in combat, yet avoids combat while other means remain available.

- *An important lesson of September 11th is that fundamental security issues, such as homeland defense, form the basis for our broader national security strategy and organization.*

    1. The cabinet's interagency problem-solving approach should be applied to other levels of military and civilian interaction.

    2. The military's role in focusing the instruments of national power is to create conditions—stability, time and space—that will give the other elements of U.S. national power the opportunity to function.

- *Although common threats and fears bring coalitions together, common objectives and goals are needed to maintain them. Common values, shared culture, and open communications make it easier for a coalition to function as a cohesive organization.*

    1. We must develop interagency engagement plans, similar to CINC theater engagement plans, to foster the necessary trust among coalition members before a crisis begins.

    2. The United States is seen as a competent, confident honest broker and leader. The United States must respect its coalition partners as sovereign equals to facilitate coalition building and teamwork.

3. In the early stages of an operation or campaign, it may be counter-productive to define an exit strategy, but it is necessary to identify our criteria for success.

Air Vice-Marshal John H. Thompson, Defence Attache, British Embassy

• *The attacks of September 11th were perpetrated against the entire world and affected the priority, organization, and goals of international relationships. The United States was able quickly and masterfully to unite a broad range of countries that were ready to join in our coalition.*

1. While NATO responded first by invoking Article 5 of the North Atlantic Treaty, individual countries followed with concrete offers of assistance. The rapid response improved NATO's credibility, but the coalition against terrorism must also include non-NATO countries to be fully effective.

2. Groupings such as the EU and the G-8 have also contributed by attacking the terrorists' funding sources and denying them safe havens.

3. The United States has also wisely recognized the essential role of the United Nations, which can bestow legitimacy on coalition operations and provide a forum for developing antiterrorist measures.

4. The current campaign demonstrates the readiness and capacity of the majority of countries to work together and the unprecedented opportunities for cooperation to address other global threats.

• *The leadership of the United States has been admirable; the challenge will be to sustain the coalition-building efforts. The United States can continue to expect strong support as long as it finds ways to involve those extending help. The United Kingdom welcomes the extent to which the United States has made use of these multinational bodies to promote its counterterrorist strategies.*

1. Even the United States cannot act alone in confronting the wide range of transnational threats.

2. The vigorous approach taken by the United States to expand international cooperation in the fight against terrorism has been welcome, particularly in the cases of Russia and Pakistan.

Dr. Keith Payne, Chairman and President, National Institute for Public Policy

• *The trend toward increasing lethality in the hands of small groups has grave implications for deterrence and coalition warfare.*

1. The dramatic decline in the cost of weapons has increased their availability to small groups. The increasing lethality of weapons and the increasing density of urban areas have reduced the number of participants necessary to inflict immense casualties.

2. Biological and chemical weapons are threats today and nuclear weapons may be a realistic threat soon.

• *A wide array of agile and adaptive military capabilities is needed to deter threats across a wide variety of contingencies.*

1. Attacks by small groups armed with WMD can inflict mass casualties anywhere in the world.

2. Predictable policies of deterrence have become much more difficult to establish.

3. Familiarity with opponents is critical to fashioning effective deterrence by knowing what to threaten, how to threaten it, and how best to communicate that threat to an appropriate decision maker.

Analysis

The task of integrating the instruments of power on the international level is complicated by the need to synchronize the efforts of multiple coalition members, as in the current war on terrorism. Military, diplomatic, and political goals must be balanced at the coalition and national levels, taking into account partners' distinctive national interests and objectives.

Dr. Payne noted that a broad spectrum of coalition capabilities is needed to deter and defend against multiple threats across a wide variety of contingencies, a situation that is exacerbated by the increasing lethality of small groups using weapons of great power in asymmetric ways. He remarked on the importance of thoroughly understanding the threats in the new security environment in order to construct effective deterrence policies.

Air Vice-Marshal Thompson discussed the importance of expanding the coalition against terrorism outside the NATO alliance, for example the European Union and the G-8, and continued involvement of the United Nations, and emphasized that no nation should act alone in the emerging security environment. He highlighted the need for the participation of economic and political agencies as well as military alliances. Air Vice-Marshal Thompson suggested that the unprecedented level of support following the terrorist attacks could create opportunities to address other global threats cooperatively. However, Admiral Joseph Prueher cautioned that common threats and fears, while effective at bringing coalitions together, were insufficient to maintain them. For this, common objectives and goals are necessary, and shared culture, values, and communications are desired. Indeed, there was broad agreement that unity of effort in coalition operations requires multinational political consensus on clearly defined strategic objectives.

General Meigs discussed the challenge coalition commanders face in balancing competing influences, pressures, and demands from partner nations, from their political leadership at home, and from the organization sponsoring the coalition. Contingent commanders' actions are in turn constrained by the degree of commitment from their political leadership, and the extent to which they have the trust of their superiors.

Admiral Prueher emphasized the importance of domestic politics to effective coalition operations and suggested that the cabinet-level problem-solving approach be applied to other levels of military and civilian cooperation. He also noted the need for jointness at all levels, the increasing importance of non-military dimensions of national power, and the importance of seeking non-military solutions to avoid the unnecessary waste of national resources in combat. In planning operations, he argued that while we should not insist on exit strategies before using force, we should nevertheless think through desired end states in advance. We must also retain our confidence but remain humbled by the terrorist attacks in our participation in and command of coalition operations.

Whereas the speakers uniformly emphasized the importance of broad coalitions to establish the legitimacy of U.S. actions and to gain access to intelligence and other resources where partners' strengths complement our own, others have identified important disadvantages of coalition operations, primarily the restriction on states' freedom of action that comes with the need to maintain a coalition. Balancing the two in a complex, global conflict will remain a major challenge.

Transcript

DR. PFALTZGRAFF. Again, welcome to Panel Session V. Our concluding panel discussion today will focus on alliance coalition issues. How do we achieve unity of effort?

We have structured this panel to address a series of very important issues that face us and our coalition and alliance partners in the early 21st Century. They include a discussion of NATO as an organizational framework for a combined action. What are the lessons of recent operations in southeastern Europe, indeed, the last decade of NATO experience in the post-Cold War era? What are the implications of lessons in southeastern Europe for the war against terrorism, for example? Are there any lessons that can be drawn? We hope also in this panel to address the significance of the RMA, the Revolution in Military Affairs, for alliance cooperation between the United States and its alliance coalition partners. Is there an emerging technology gap that will hinder our allied cooperation in the years ahead?

Another issue for this panel includes the implications of proliferation for our ability to design deterrence concepts for the United States, acting alone or in concert with its allies and coalition partners in this new world of the 21st century. We also have in this panel an opportunity to begin to think about some of the lessons that are beginning to emerge and the issues that we will need to address that can be drawn from the tragic events of September 11th for future alliance coalition operations.

So, with those brief introductory comments and urging that you read the Charter for this panel, which is set forth in the program, I would ask each of the panel members now to come out and be seated so that we can proceed. I am going to introduce each of the members as they speak. First on the list will be General Montgomery Meigs, United States Army. General Meigs is Commanding General, U.S. Army Europe and Seventh Army, Heidelberg, Germany. This is a position that he assumed in 1998. He also served as Commander of the Multinational Stabilization Force in Bosnia, Herzegovina, beginning in October 1998, and therefore, he is especially able to talk to us about some of these alliance issues that are on our agenda with respect to southeastern Europe. He has held a variety of appointments in his distinguished military career. I'll only mention one or two of them: Commander 1st Squadron, 1st Cavalry Regiment; Strategic Planner on the Joint Staff in Washington, D.C., and on and on the list would go. I would also mention to you that he is a Ph.D. in history. He received a Ph.D. in history from the University of Wisconsin in 1982, so this is no mean achievement. It is with great pleasure that I welcome General Montgomery Meigs to this meeting and look forward to his presentation. Monty, the floor is yours.

GENERAL MEIGS: Bob, thank you. Thanks for the opportunity to be part of this very impressive series of presentations, and thank you and all of the people in the back rooms and out in the reception areas that do all the work to make this such a great event.

Coalition warfare, or multinational operations, the term we now seem to be using in our recent contingency operations, remains, as always, fiendishly difficult. Domestic politics of individual members, their unique diplomatic and strategic interests, personalities of subordinate commanders, the military cultures of the contingents all create frictions that complicate and frustrate the lives of the commanders who lead multinational formations.

In the last 60 years, some rules of the road have been hammered out in hard experience; they're worth revisiting here as the structure for our discussions. Multinational, political consensus on a clearly defined strategic objective provides the ambient necessary condition for unity of military effort in a coalition. The complexity of the task of the commander of a multinational formation depends on the strength and shared sense of danger and a common purpose confronting a threat.

Clearly stated and well-understood strategic objectives help to reduce the ambiguities the commander must confront. This shared consensus at the political level provides the basic foundation of action, of coalition, by doing several things. It buffers the self-interest generated by the domestic politics of coalition members. It supplies the support from national capitals, sensed by the senior military representative of a national contingent in the multinational force. And as Secretary of State Powell noted about Desert Storm, "every country is sovereign and wants to know how its forces will be used."

National commanders in the formation feel this pressure directly, from the specified language of their national instructions and from the informal direction from the leaders, as well as from their own personal loyalties and experiences. The coalition commander's subordinates must also report home and report home often. Only to the extent their orders and guidance allow can they accept decisions on their own authority. Only to the extent they are trusted by their own senior military leadership can they expect to justify to their own masters decisions taken in the coalition that carry operational risks requiring explanation to their national political leaders.

General Meigs

This same relation between clarity of collective intent and operational initiative applies to the coalition commander himself. If his own nation is not completely committed to the goals of the coalition, if it is a reluctant leader, if it is squeamish about the tactical risks that must be accepted in the campaign to attain operational success, he has problems on several levels. As the senior officer of his nation, he remains responsible in the court of public and political opinion back home for the perceived successes and failures of his own national force. As the commander of the coalition's combined military force, he is responsible to the political leadership of the coalition for the results achieved by all elements, individually and collectively. He cannot often ask the units from one coalition member to take risks toward common goals that are higher than the risks that he is allowed by his own nation to assign to units that wear his cap badge. The perception that a commander's own contingent may not be pulling in the traces as hard as some of the others can quickly undermine morale and cohesion.

Multinational commanders must constantly balance three factors against military necessity. They are the pressures from individual nations, the pressure from his own nation, and instructions of the organization sponsoring the coalition. Occasionally, one's own nation will forward guidance not in concert with what the commander sees as the best way forward, or ideas he knows he cannot sell to the coalition. In these times, his relationship with his own national leaders determines how far he can lean into the wind to argue for the case of the coalition. At times, individual nations will ask for special considerations. His support at higher multinational headquarters is critical to deflect these requests. And at other times, coalition headquarters will generate pressures that he knows are contrary to what his own or another nation can accept.

On those issues, subtle pressure on the political leadership of the coalition by his national leaders and those of other sympathetic nations, alerted by their commanders in his formation, are indispensable. Let me be clear at this point that I'm not talking about duly constituted orders. Within specified and implied intent, commanders must follow the orders they receive. They also must adhere to the limits imposed by binding national instruction. But before orders are published, during the process within the coalition in which courses of action are being developed, the commander must be able to make his views known. Further, he must have the political skill, the military competence, and clout to make these views tell.

The combination of shared purpose, political will, and credibility of the commander defines the degree to which he can be effective in that role. Let me give an historical example to highlight the issue. In the summer of 1944, after the invasion of Normandy, General Eisenhower planned for a second invasion into southern France—Anvil, later renamed Dragoon. The prime minister and his commander in the Mediterranean, General Wilson, opposed this course of action. Eisenhower knew that to bring the necessary logistic weight and additional divisions from the U.S. into the offensive across France into Europe, the Allies needed another large port. He also believed an attack up the Rhone Valley would draw forces away from the thrust toward Germany and the German defense of Italy.

The British argued for either of two options: reinforce the main effort out of the Normandy beachhead with a second parallel thrust from the French Atlantic coast, or unhinge the Germans in Italy with an attack around their flank threatening the Balkans Trieste, and eventually Austria. The debate lasted from June to mid-August, with the Prime Minister finally complaining to Franklin Roosevelt that the Americans were being arbitrary and that the invasion in southern France risked ruin of our great affairs in the Mediterranean. And we take it hard that this should be demanded of us.

On 9 August, Ike met Churchill in what he called one of the most difficult sessions he had during the entire war. Churchill was adamant, as only Churchill could be. Ike stood his ground, advising the prime minister that if there were political reasons for a campaign in the Balkans, Churchill should take the issue up with the President. Obviously, Ike knew he had solid backing in Washington. The support of Marshall, King, and Hopkins was crucial to him. Not only was he careful about husbanding his case with Marshall, he had a unique ability to argue his points with his allies without alienating them, a quality in which Ike remains an exemplar for all—for all of us students of this business. Had there not been a clear intent and shared resolve to defeat the

Axis Powers, and had not Eisenhower retained the support and confidence of his national leaders, and in the final analysis of Churchill himself, he would have lost his case, or having won, might have seen his allies reluctant to come onboard at the last minute.

In short, if we want to set conditions that enable a military success of a multinational coalition, we must ensure the mission is clear and understood and well supported by all the participants. In addition, we should ensure that the military commander has the support and confidence of his national leaders and that the other members of the coalition have properly accepted him. But at this point, we have only stated one of the necessary conditions of success, one of the additional sufficient conditions that derive from the role of the commander himself and how he conducts his management of military affairs.

Given the best of multinational support and clarity of strategic intent, a commander can still make a mess of things. What then must he do to enhance the chances of success? What personal qualities must he exhibit? He must have political skill to balance the competing military and political pressures. He must gain quickly an understanding of the operational idiosyncrasies of his allies. He must always show complete impartiality. And finally, to the point of mind-numbing frustration and then beyond, he must have patience, and more, and then more patience, and then in those dark hours of embarrassment and frustration, a profound will to do what is right.

I've already described Eisenhower's ability to marshal support from his own capital to ensure he preserved the strategic initiative and the courses of action upon which he believed success depended. We can find a number of military figures that successfully led coalitions. They include Marlborough, Wellington, Mountbatten, and many others. All had the ability to gain and keep the respect of allied military leaders and, equally importantly, the loyalty of their troops. Other leaders like MacArthur and Stilwell had tremendous military ability, but either because they alienated their political and military leaders back home or caused irreparable fissures within their multinational formation, they were removed.

Simply put, coalition leaders must have the political skills to garner support back home in their own national capital. They must have the human touch that allows them to gain the support of the leaders of the national contingents in their formation. And they must be good enough at the business of soldiering to exact loyalty from subordinates of whatever uniform and to execute a campaign that promises to win. The circumstances of MacArthur's relief by President Truman are well known. Stilwell would probably have been a terrific army or army group commander in the European Theatre of Operations. He was temperamentally unsuited to the vagaries of dealing with the National Chinese in coalition warfare, despite his great skill and character.

One must also understand the idiosyncrasies of the units assigned to the coalition. As I began my duties as COMSFOR (Commander, Stabilization

Force) in Bosnia, I noticed that one contingent generally expressed discomfort with orders that had some risks, or that interpreted Dayton in a newly expressed aggressive manner. The question was in the verbs. As I got to know my unit commander and the member of his army on my personal staff, I began to understand the issue. In the case of his national law, if any plaintiff from Bosnia went to his home country and gained acceptance of a judge to apply jurisdiction, and then examine a legal complaint, that leader could be liable to a civil or criminal suit for decisions made and executed in good faith in Bosnia in ensuring compliance in Dayton.

My lawyer and I quickly adapted a procedure in which we accompanied orders with a written legal finding from my Staff Judge Advocate, outlining how the order fell within the language of Dayton. In addition, we learned to keep the language of orders within semantic forms of the Dayton Agreement already accepted by parliaments. Normal military terms would often get us in trouble unless we had screened them very carefully. In these ways, we removed concerns about personal legal liability and about political risk back home, but creating the proper environment meant moving quickly past one's frustration and an impulse to be critical, in seeing the problem from our subordinates' point of view. Once we addressed the hidden risks, there was never again a reluctance to act.

If I were to give any one piece of advice to a newly appointed multinational commander about how he must conduct himself, it would be never to say anything untoward about one of his contingents. Truly the walls have ears. General Eisenhower said it best when Lord Lewis Mountbatten, newly appointed to command the China/Burma/India theater, asked for his advice. I quote, "Never permit any problem to be approached in your staff on a basis of national interest." To that I would add, never criticize or belittle a contingent, even in what seems to be the most private setting.

In addition, one must spend the time to address the concerns and advice of one's deputies and senior staff officers from other nations. Again, Ike's words say it best: "The thing you must strive for is the utmost in mutual respect and confidence among the group of seniors making up the Allied Command." Remember, once one gets agreement on a course of action with some risks that yet promises gains, these seniors must sell it to their own masters in their national capitals. They must also advise the coalition commanders of problems in selling the option and the attainable middle ground. To do that enthusiastically, they must be confident in the commander and his operational skill, and they must want the decision to work. This kind of confidence means that one must be convincing and competent. One's allied subordinates must believe that if things go wrong, that he will—that the multinational commander—will shoulder the blame as his own. That he will do, in the public—will do so in the public domain, even if one of the national contingents caused the plan to go awry. In fact, it does not hurt if early in one's command there is a failure caused by a coalition member for which the commander can take personal blame. His capital knows the game, as do the senior officers of the nation involved.

Finally, the other quality coalition commanders must have is extreme patience. Marlborough provides one of the best examples. It is 1705. Marlborough had already campaigned successfully for several years and in the previous year had won the decisive battle of Blendheim. He had just maneuvered the French Army into a disastrous position in Belgium between the Oich and Overish Rivers—his combined Dutch and English army was one-third larger than the French and had them pinned into a disadvantageous defensive posture.

But the conditions of Marlborough's command required that representatives of the Estates General, the Dutch government, accompany the army. And they had final authority in the field over Marlborough's decisions. The senior Dutch general, Overkirk, agreed with Marlborough that the Army should attack the French immediately. But some of Overkirk's reluctant subordinates appealed to the so-called field deputies, who then had to give their approval before Marlborough could attack.

I'll let his words tell the story. This is his report back to London, his own government. "After a four days march, I found the enemy encamped as I expected so that I thought we should have a very glorious day. But as the deputies would not consent without first consulting the Generals who were all against it, except Mr. Overkirk, we have been obliged to retire from the enemy. Notwithstanding, where we were at least one-third stronger than they, which I take to be very prejudicial to the common cause and scandalous for the Army and against all discipline." In a postscript in his parallel report to the Estates General he added, "My heart is so full I cannot refrain from representing on this occasion to your High Mightiness that I find myself here with far less authority than when I had the honor to command their troops last year in Germany." Marlborough was furious, frustrated, embarrassed. Yet he persevered. He stayed in command and in 1708 won the battle of Ramillies and conquered Belgium for the coalition. He went on to win the battle of Oudenarde and, by 1710, had fought the French armies and their allies to a standstill.

In Bosnia, in December of 1998, SFOR (Stabilization Force) began an operation against an organization with criminal links within Herzegovina, and it backed into Amsterdam, called the Renter Company. And General Shinseki will get a wide grin about this. With the help—because he's the one that started it—with the help of corrupt Bosnian and Croat secret police and hard-liner politicians Renter misappropriated Bosnian land and set up a market, a construction company, and a used car business—read that, stolen—in a reasonably important town called Stolitch.

In October of the next year, a very difficult trail with many fits and starts led us to Mostar. This trail included assaults on SFOR soldiers, evidence of war crimes, violent disruption of returns to Stolitch by Bosnian landowners, the murder of the Federation's Deputy Minister Interior, a Bosnian Croat, by leaders of his own faction, and an attempt to buy the Bosnian Croat leaders to manipulate the public shock and anger about the murder to damage the Federation government. Its final phase involved SFOR's occupation of the headquarters of the Bosnian Croat Intelligence Service and the headquarters of its money-laundering front in Mostar, and confiscation of records, computers, and evidence pursuant to further and successful investigation of the murder and indictment of the individuals that are accused.

I'm not suggesting in any way that this small operation resembled the significance of Marlborough's doings, but it did—did it ever—require mind-numbing patience and again-and-again efforts to keep all the allied contingents on plan and to refocus the effort after setbacks. In short, if we want a multinational formation to have the best chance of success, we need to give it clear, strategic guidance and ensure that the member countries to the coalition understand the goal and support it in a way that will stand the parliamentary stresses in their governments, vice those in our own government with its fixed terms of office.

Coalitions must select a commander who possesses convincing military competence and an ability to work sensitive political issues with his host nation with the coalition's sponsor and civilian entity, and, with civilian—and with national capitals. He must be a quick learner with sensitivity to the political and cultural issues affecting his units. He must always enforce impartiality in his staff and must, in his own conduct, reflect total confidence in his subordinates and their units to the point of accepting their mistakes as his own and quietly taking the flak in public, I might add, sometimes stoically. Finally, in addition, he must have the patience of Job and the will to press on no matter what gets in the way. Thank you.

DR. PFALTZGRAFF: Thank you very much, General Meigs, for giving us the benefit of your operational experience, as well as your very impressive historical perspective, as much that we could discuss. This has been a very important contribution to our deliberations today.

I now turn to our second speaker, who is Admiral Joseph Prueher, United States Navy, Retired. Ambassador Prueher served as United States Ambassador to China from December 1999 until earlier this year. Before that assignment, he completed a 35-year career in the United States Navy. His final assignment was as Commander-in-Chief, United States Pacific Command, clearly a command that requires a great deal of understanding of alliance and coalition issues and cooperation. I cannot fail to mention, however, that during his career in the United States Navy, Admiral Prueher flew over 5,500 hours in 52 types of aircraft with over 1,000 carrier landings. Think about that! So, it is with very great pleasure that I welcome Joe Prueher to our meeting today, and welcome him to the podium.

ADMIRAL PRUEHER: Thank you very much, Bob. For those of us who are somewhat technically oriented, airplanes are nice; when you push, it goes in the direction you want, unlike coalitions. So, it's a good background to have on things that actually act the way you think they are. It's a great treat for me to be here today.

I need to tell one quick story about Ric Shinseki, the main sponsor of this conference. We met when we were senior O-6s a few years back, and we were talking about the advantages that accrue to increased rank in the military services. And I was talking about on ships, you get a chance to, instead of living in the stacked bunks, you might get a stateroom, small, but have a single bunk. I said, "How does the Army go?" This was part of our cultural exchange. He said, "Well, when you're in the Army and you get to be an O-6, you get to sleep on the hood of the Jeep." So I think that was—imagine, Ric, I think, has stepped out to do other stuff now, but he probably wouldn't mind sleeping on the hood of the Jeep instead of some of the other things he does these days too.

I'm not going to give a series of stories here, but I would like to give a couple of examples. And one has to do with a person who Monty mentioned, Lord Louis Mountbatten, who, after World War II, was the head of the British Mediterranean Fleet. And at that time, he had a guest on what was a new flagship for him and he had a new communications suite on the flagship. He brought the guest into his cabin and was explaining the advantages of this modern communication that he had, and he drew a comparison to one of his predecessors, Lord Nelson, on his flagship, *Victory*, which happened to be anchored down south of Crete in the Mediterranean. He talked about when Nelson wanted to communicate with London, he would write a message, he would hand it to his orderly, they'd get it to a courier, they'd row a boat ashore, ride horses across Crete, do some more boat work, horses or carriages through Europe, sail across the Channel, horses to London. And he said, "And Nelson, under the best circumstances, would get a response back in about eight weeks." "And so," he said, "Now, I have this great new modern capability. I've got a radio room just one deck up on the ship. When I want to communicate with London, write out a message, I hand it to my orderly, he takes it up, it's instantly transmitted to London and in about eight weeks, I get a message back." So, aside from being an instructive story on a number of fronts—when you think about it, if you're a technology buff or anything else, one we all appreciate a bit because of the cultural aspects of it.

The other part that it brings to mind is: we understand bureaucracies. Both Dick Myers and Gordon Adams made the point today that before you can have coalitions, before you can have joint warfighting, before you can do these things at the lower levels where the rubber meets the road, you must have alignment at the top. Bosses must agree that the plan is a good thing to do. Otherwise, coalition partners or joint warfighting partners cannot work together if they have a boss that's pulling in one direction and you, as a joint commander, are pulling in another. So I think this is a good lesson that we can take away from this.

I would like to take a moment to get a little bit of a backdrop so we can be sure of what our terms of reference are. Because this whole pitch, this whole meeting—which has been so well put together—is about focusing national power. Now, for those of you that took Political Science 101 many years ago, you had a book that listed elements of national power. It's critical stuff. And yes, they talked about geography, they talked about natural resources, they talked about military, they talked about the quality of government. And there's a list of five or six, seven, eight elements of national power. I don't think we're necessarily talking about all of those things here when we we're talking about focusing national power. What the handouts have talked about, have talked about diplomatic, military, economic, and cultural.

I would quibble just a little bit with that definition. I think it's useful to talk about that some. The Joint Forces Command—Tony talked about doing some mentoring work—uses a term called DIME. They call it Diplomatic, Information, Military, and Economic. Tom Friedman, who was here last year, wrote that great book (because it's easy to read) *The Lexus and the Olive Tree*, where he discussed the political, military, economic issues and then he would add, cultural, environmental, and technical. This is an arguable point. But I think the ones we should be talking about for the purpose of this discussion are—I would change "diplomatic" to "political" because diplomatic connotes diplomacy; it connotes overseas work. Political, I think, embraces that, but also embraces what commanders must deal with in their own nations and the local politics, and that is very important. Domestic politics have a tremendous effect on how we can bring to bear the elements of national power. The military part I think we understand. That's traditional security. The economic part we understand, though we don't necessarily do it very well. And the fourth thing I think is useful to add in is information, and add that one in. So, if we talk about political, military, economic, and information, I think those are the elements of national power that we are largely talking about as we go forward here in this conference.

Now, I'm—one of the things that you're going to have to suffer with a little bit here with me today is, if you look in your program, I was supposed to be the moderator, not a speaker today. I found out I was going to get to speak about 10:00 pm last night, and I was already past my useful conscious time by then. So, in the spectrum of prior preparation prevents particularly poor performance and the improvisation mode, I'm a little closer to the improvisation side today, but I think maybe I can contribute a bit. I have, since about 1962, off and on, studied Sun Tzu fairly hard. My Army advisors have told me that gives me about the qualifications of an average Army major in knowledge of Sun Tzu. But we quote Sun Tzu a lot. He was not a simple soldier. He embodied a lot of the same principles that Clausewitz has, a lot of the bringing to bear

the elements of national power. In
China, in Sun Tzu's time, the great
admiral--in Chinese, admiral and
general are the same words, so it con-
verts really nicely to admiral--he
talked about the foremost quality of
the--of the great general. I'll concede
in this audience. The great general
wins the objectives of his nation without engaging in combat. Now, this is
a sophisticated view because it does
not mean that we are not--that the
armies are not--immensely capable
of engaging in combat or warfighting.
But he said that is a squandering, usually, of the nation's resources in terms
of time, in terms of money, in terms
of lives, and other assets. So, if the
great general can win the conflict
without engaging in combat, that's
the ultimate goal.

Admiral Prueher

So, you can snooker your way
into a victory, but you do, in this sense, if you are a general, you have to have
either control or a strong influence over all these elements of national power.
And so, this is going to get--or it gets now into the discussions of how much
horsepower should Dick Myers have as Chairman? How much horsepower
should CINCs have to bring these elements to bear? And it's a good point. And
as we look through--as we look at Sun Tzu and we look at what we're trying
to do in this nation, you look at the various elements of national power, and
we've talked about--Dick Myers talked about joint warfighting a bit--the ultimate interagency group is the Cabinet. And when you really want to talk about
interagency things, you end up with a Cabinet meeting. And in the current
Administration, that occurs. They talk and work through things. If you take
this mode of jointness, or interagency stuff together, the military is one part of
that through Secretary Rumsfeld, in our case the Secretary of Defense, and
Dick Myers. But the other elements all come together.

How do you bring these elements to bear? One of the things is to bring
this interagency approach to solving problems. You bring it all the way down,
and if you bring it down to the military, or you bring it down to a country team
in the case of the State Department at a well-functioning Embassy. Then you
bring this interagency group approach all the way down to solving problems,
and it keeps you from stubbing your toe as often. It keeps you from having as
many unintended consequences as you might otherwise have had.

So, it's imperative to bring this interagency notion to even low-level planning and actors. And the Joint Forces Command is now talking about a JTA, a
Joint Tactical Action, down at a very low level in the military, which will consider and have in mind these many things that we've been talking about today.
I think that's important. Let me give you an example. In Asia, it happened
when I was there; in 1997, the biggest crisis in Asia was an economic one. And
it had important security implications.

It started off with the baht crisis in Thailand in 1997, when the baht
crashed. The smaller nations in Asia came tumbling down, and that was the
start of the Asian economic crisis. Thailand is not only a coalition partner of
the United States; they're an ally. We have a formal treaty with Thailand.
Thailand has given us access to their air bases and their real estate, in times
when no one else would. And yet their biggest problem in 1997 was an economic one and we ignored them. We paid no attention to it; we dropped the
ball. In talking to Sandy Berger at the National Security Council, the Treasury
Department was looking at U.S. problems; they were not looking at the international economic problems. This is an example of what happens when you
do not focus international power in a sophisticated way.

Another point that I think has been brought home by September 11th is
that when you look at bringing to bear the elements of international power,
the idea of traditional security undergirds the other ones. General Shinseki
brought this up in his comments this morning when he talked about the confidence of the American people. Dick Myers brought this point up when he
talked about the security issues in the United States. Lee Kwon Yu in
Singapore talks about security being the oxygen for the economic engine of
Asia. When you have security, people feel confident about themselves, that
they can invest, that they can send their children to schools, that they will get
a return on their investment, that their house is going to be there when they
come home, those types of things. The fundamental security issues undergird
the basic, stable conditions that allow people to do long-range planning for a
business plan for example, that allow people to peacefully pursue prosperity.

So, as we look at the political, military, economic, and information elements of security, we must not lose sight of the fact that traditional security,
brought home to us in the most tragic way on 11 September, is the fundamental issue.

What breeds the need for coalition? A common threat? A common fear?
What makes coalitions stick together? Common goals and objectives. These
are buzzword terms, but when you have common values, shared values, and
shared cultures, it's much easier to make a coalition cohesive than it is trying
to bring together coalition partners who have very different cultures and very
different fundamental values.

An instance occurred in Hawaii when Jiang Zemin was making his visit to
the United States, and after the Straits crisis in 1996, where we brought some

aircraft carriers out there, one of the things we realized at PACOM is that we had communications with every nation in the theater. We could pick up the phone and talk to somebody, every nation, absent one, and that was China. So, crises were going to occur because we didn't have communications. We set about a plan, which got critiqued in a lot of ways, to build up communications with China so that we would not miscalculate. Anyway, Jiang came to the U.S.; Hawaii was his first stop. We were out on the barge, going out to the *Arizona* Memorial, and he put his finger in my chest and said, "What are you trying to do with the PLA? How come you're hanging around with my guys?" I said we were trying to build up a modicum of trust so that we don't miscalculate and so that we can solve issues between us. When you think about it, you can't solve any problems without a modicum of trust. You can't buy a car unless you really think the person is going to come through on their deal.

You've got to have some element of trust with the people you're dealing with. Monty brought this out in his presentation about coalition leaders. Jiang talked about the Chinese in the U.S. and he said, "Our countries are very different. We don't have trust because our cultures are different, and we don't understand each other. And not only that, we can't have understanding without communications." So his point was, there needs to be a hierarchy of communications, of understanding the other culture, and then you can build the trust that is essential to starting to solve some of the problems that you might have.

Now, I would argue that, as you take this point and talk about coalitions, that the real work for coalitions is done during precrisis time. If you've got a spectrum of time of relative peace to crisis, it's in the precrisis time when you build the foundations for these coalitions that are so important. If you're a Steven Covey fan, it's Quadrant 2 work. It's important, but it's not urgent. You do this important work when you've got time to have communications and you've got time to build.

That's what a CINC theater engagement plan is about. It is about building these ties so that in times of stress, when the system gets stressed, you can build a coalition, you can come together, or maybe you can avoid the crisis. I think we have a CINC theater engagement plan. What we really need is this interagency group type of engagement plan.

With regards to September 11, the United States, from a vantage point of having lived overseas both in Europe and in Asia, is seen as confident. One possible positive side effect from 9/11 is it's been a very humbling and tragic experience for the United States. And as we continue to keep a firm eye on our national interests, if we go forward to other nations with confidence, with competence, with the issues of leadership, but not the "we've got the power; we've got the money; we've got the technology; let's do it our way," I think these coalitions are going to work much better in the future.

Like Wes Clark mentioned yesterday, what I see overseas is a lot of people saying, "We really like you all on an individual basis, but, you know, as a nation, it doesn't appear that you care much about us." And I think this will make the coalitions work better. The other part as we look at coalitions, and this gets a little bit to Tony Zinni's points that he made. The role of the military in this focusing of national power, the military doesn't solve the fundamental problems. The military creates room and time and space for issues to get resolved. And so, when we look at things that have long-range, underlying issues, we need to realize that the military piece of this, which is very important, goes in and creates some time, temporary stability, and space. But into that time and space have to come those who are represented by these other elements of national power to help solve these problems.

I could not possibly agree more with the comments that have been made earlier, and Gordon Adams made it and Frank Carlucci made that at the earlier pitch, about we need a strong State Department. We need a magnificent State Department, and I think they're on the right track, but they have been underfunded a long time. And the attrition of what they've been able to do over time has been something tragic for our country. And we need those things to work very well.

The other part that is in addition to the room, space, time argument is the idea of going into a mission, a coalition, or a task, with the idea of an exit strategy. Now, I forget who talked about exit strategy, but I tended to agree with what they said. When you start defining your exit strategy too well, or you won't go in unless you've got one, I don't believe that's where we want to be. However, we do need to define the task sufficiently so we can at least tell when it's over. Under what conditions can we say we're through? And it may be that that answer is "never." Like this war on terrorism. I don't foresee, in our lifetimes in this audience, of being able to say it's complete. It will always be there. Maybe it will diminish. We will get a big bite out of it, but it will always be there. And when you think about history, about World War II and the Marshall Plan, we went into World War I, we fought everybody, at the end of the war we dusted off our hands, we went home, turned our swords into plowshares, and 15 years later, bang, we're at it again in a major way. At the end of World War II, we started with the Marshall Plan, which is still going and has bred both coalition friends, allies, shared values. It's been a wonderful thing. At the end of Korea, the war didn't stop, but we stayed and we preserved the peace. In Japan, the military stayed and preserved the peace. I do not think in history this is the natural condition of things for that to happen, for the military to take on this chore, but I think it has, almost by default, but the issue of we're still there may be true.

But I think what we need to argue, instead of the military still being there, is the United States interests being there with our elements of national power in a supportive way with the coalitions. And maybe that supportive way is providing enough sustenance to another coalition or the other government can be self-sustaining. So I think it's very beguiling, in a way, to think about time to leave, but we need to think more in terms of what are the conditions under which we can remove some of this. When are these things going to be over?

I think these are some useful thoughts. And some of them are arguable as well, and I look forward to questions later. Thanks a lot.

DR. PFALTZGRAFF: Thank you very much, Joe, for showing and giving us insights into the need to integrate the various instruments of power, and of course, recalling for us the work of Sun Tzu.

Our next speaker ought to feel very much at home by this time in the panel because over the last few minutes, if you've listened carefully, you know that we have heard the name Nelson, Mountbatten, Slim, Churchill, and, of course, his great ancestor, Marlborough mentioned. And we began the panel with a Commanding General in Europe, whose first name is Montgomery and goes by the name Monty. So I hope, John, you feel suitably at home. We arranged this all for you here as our closest ally.

It is with a great pleasure, therefore, that I welcome Air Vice Marshal John Thompson. He is presently the Defense Attache of the United Kingdom, based here in Washington, D.C. He is a Harrier pilot. He has had extensive coalition experience. He spent 10 years of his military career in Germany. He has had NATO experience also in Bosnia. And I might add, just to complete the circle here, that he served as British Advisor to General Zinni at CENTCOM. So, welcome, John, we're delighted to have you with us.

AIR MARSHAL THOMPSON: Thank you very much indeed, gentlemen, and thank you, General Shinseki, for accepting me, an Air Force officer, to stand in for the Ambassador.

Certainly, I feel in this Army setting, I'm barely qualified, but I have done a course where, for those of you who don't know, the British Army—and we heard some of the history—is very keen on its regimental system. And the regiments and the history of the regiments is very much a part of how the British Army works. When the Chief of General Staff opened the first—gave the first address—to the course I was on, he asked a rhetorical question, which was, "Why do we have an Army?" I'm afraid I answered it by saying, "Is it to preserve the regimental system?" So my Army credentials are not that good. I'm also, as you can see from that, not particularly good as a diplomat.

But my subject today is "Focusing International Power to Achieve a Common Cause." And really, I want to talk about operational diplomacy amongst allies. I take Admiral Prueher's point about politics and diplomacy, but as you know, as a serving officer, I can't possibly talk about politics, so I'll stick to diplomacy and use it in broadest sense as I go through.

I do have some minor qualifications for doing this, and I've served twice in unusual jobs. Once was in Zagreb when I was for four months working as a liaison officer between Admiral Leighton Smith, who was CINC South, and

General Bertram De la Presle, who was a French General running UNPROFOR (United Nations Protection Force). And at that time, there was always a British officer, and it was usually Air Force, who was put between the sailor, the American sailor, and the French Army officer, and I don't think anybody else could have done it but a Brit. I still carry some of the scars. I then worked, and I know somebody in this room has seen me in a suit, working in Sarajevo where I worked for Carl Bildt as one of his military advisors on the civil side of the Dayton process. And again, there, persuading people the difference between mission creep and mission accomplishment from a slightly different perspective, again, left some scars, which I remember.

The 11th of September shook the kaleidoscope, not just in the United States and Central Asia but in the configuration of foreign policy, around the world. As the Prime Minister has said, "The outrages committed that day were perpetrated against the whole world." The international response bears testament to that. The initial outpouring of shock and sympathy was coupled with an understanding that the threat of international terrorism affects us all.

As a result, the U.S. in the days after 11 September found that a wide range of countries was ready and willing to join the bold coalition. And in a masterful display of operational diplomacy, the Administration moved quickly to pull it together. In some countries, the response was not so surprising, but no less welcome for that. NATO was first off the blocks with the invocation of Article V, followed by specific offers of military support by individual allies. Much attention has been paid to the British and their contribution. But other allies—France, Germany, Italy, Spain, Belgium, the Netherlands, Turkey—and those farther afield—Australia, New Zealand—followed up with offers of concrete military support.

If before 11 September there were still any skeptics around on either side of the Atlantic who doubted the value of the NATO alliance, this display—this instant display of solidarity must have silenced them for good. But as President Bush made clear from the outset, the coalition—or rather, the coalitions, to fight international terrorism will need to be multifaceted, and we've heard some of the facets mentioned today, we begin to draw on the full range of international instruments, not just military. Groupings, such as the EU, the G8, have also been mobilized to take on key aspects of the fight, closing off, for example, the sources of terrorists' financing and denying terrorists safe haven.

The U.S. has also wisely recognized the essential role of the United Nations in countering terrorism. As the global body, the United Nations not only bestows international legitimacy, but can also provide a forum for drawing up and enforcing measures to tackle terrorist networks. The UK welcomes the extent to which the U.S. has made full use of these multinational bodies to promote its counterterrorist strategy. It has long been clear to us that in this globalized, interlocking world, no country, not even the United States, can

PANEL 5 235

hope to act alone in combating the
range of transnational threats confronting open democratic societies—
terrorism, of course, but also the proliferation of weapons of mass destruction, international crime, international narcotics networks, and disease,
where, as we've seen in the case of
disease here in Washington, has been
a close connection with disease and
bioterrorism.

But what has been particularly
remarkable and very welcome has
been the proactive fashion in which
the Administration has responded to
what the Prime Minister has
described as the vigorous shake of the
kaleidoscope of international relations, which September 11th brought
on. There's clearly a number of examples which fall into this category, but
indeed I can't possibly name them

Air Marshal Thompson

all. But two, Pakistan and Russia, are worth mentioning, both for the impact
they have had so far and for the potential that exists to extend cooperation
against terrorism into other areas. I won't say much about Pakistan, other than
to observe that the future of their counterterrorist campaign, the presence and
support to Pakistan in this international coalition, is absolutely vital. As for
Russia, the Crawford Summit is living proof of the distance that the United
States and the Russian relationship has traveled. As well as the prospect of a
new strategic framework, there is now a tremendous potential to forge a new
and more substantial partnership with NATO and Russia.

So, 11th of September and its aftermath have demonstrated vividly both
the readiness and capacity of the overwhelming majority of countries around
the world to work together to combat terrorism, and the opportunities this
unprecedented support offers to tackle other global threats cooperatively. The
leadership of the United States' reassurance so far has been admirable. Looking
ahead, the challenge will be to sustain the coalition-building efforts. The
United States can continue to expect strong support so long as it finds ways to
involve those extending help. By the same token, it cannot afford to spurn
those offers. Going it alone is simply not an option. Thank you.

DR. PFALTZGRAFF: Thank you very much, John, for pointing us in the
direction of understanding more fully the need for coalitions to be multifac-

eted, where to draw upon all of the elements of national power, and for bringing to bear your experience and expertise.

As our final speaker, we now have Dr. Keith Payne. Keith Payne, who has been a friend of mine for many, many years, is President and Director of Research at the National Institute for Public Policy and an Adjunct Professor in the International Security Studies Program at Georgetown University. He pursues not only a very active career in the policy community, but also he is active in the academic setting. He is the Editor-in-Chief of *Comparative Strategy*. He has authored many, many articles on deterrence and on strategy, and in particular, books recently on deterrence in the second nuclear age and peacekeeping in the nuclear age. These are all wonderful publications, many of which I use in my classes at the Fletcher School.

So, it is with great pleasure that I welcome Dr. Payne, Keith Payne, as our concluding speaker in this session this morning. Keith.

DR. PAYNE: Thank you. It's a pleasure to be here, and thank you for the introduction. Let me first offer my congratulations to you Bob, for a first-class conference. I will keep my remarks fairly brief so that we can maintain a schedule here.

Let me take just a few minutes to address an issue of increasing importance, including to coalition warfare: that's the trend toward the increasing lethality of relatively small groups. I would then like to examine what this trend may mean for deterrence and coalition warfare.

The increasing lethality of small groups has taken on a greater visibility since September 11th, as we all know. But it actually was an important emerging trend before then. The increasing lethality of small groups is a function of the increasing lethality of weapons that are available to smaller and smaller groups and the increasing population density of urban areas. There are several seminal works discussing this trend. I recommend Dr. Kathleen Bailey's path-breaking 1991 book called *Doomsday Weapons in the Hands of Many*, and Yale Professor, Martin Shubik's, 1997 *Comparative Strategy* article entitled "Terrorism, Technology, and the Socioeconomics of Death." These are shocking titles, but they're meant to be wake-up calls for this community to the emergence of a very new and dangerous trend. This trend is the dramatic reduction in the cost, the organization, and the number of participants required to inflict immense casualties, particularly on advanced, civil societies.

Professor Shubik offers, in his article that I mentioned, a quasi-numeric graph, which I show here with permission.

This is a political science graph, which usually means that the numbers involved are for show only. But Professor Shubik has provided an unusual political science graph that takes numbers seriously and has something actually behind them. His graph suggests—let me just summarize it—that for thousands of years, small groups in a single operation typically could inflict maximum casualty levels measured in the high hundreds. But as the chart suggests, in the near future, relatively small groups, with limited organization and resources, may be capable of inflicting casualties in the hundreds of thousands and possibly the millions.

This point doesn't ignore the fact that in the past large, organized, and well-disciplined groups could inflict mass casualties. In the 55 B.C., for example, Caesar's legions efficiently and totally annihilated the Usipetes and the Tencteri Germanic tribes. And the Mongol invasions under Ghengis Khan probably led to the death of between 8 percent and 12 percent of the earth's total population. But even with these types of past examples of mass casualties, a real revolution in military affairs appears

Dr. Payne

to be in the making, as illustrated by Professor Shubik. This revolution stems from this trend toward the capability of small groups, at relatively low cost, over a relatively short period of time, to inflict casualties at levels many times higher than has been possible in the past.

The main instrument for this, at least as we see it now, will be biological weapons. As the war against al Qaeda and the Taliban has demonstrated, however, nuclear weapons may become part of this concern sooner than many of us thought possible. I'd prefer not to take a lot of time either critiquing or defending this proposition that the capability to inflict mass casualties is coming to smaller and smaller groups.

Rather, let me just ask that you suspend possible disbelief, and let's explore some of the deterrence implications of this trend. There are three that I will summarize very briefly.

First, because in Dr. Bailey's words, "Doomsday weapons will be in the hands of many," the reliable, predictable functioning of deterrence will become much more important for the United States and our allies. Why? Because in the past, if we in the U.S. failed to deter, we were powerful enough and far enough away from most opponents to be relatively safe from catastrophic consequences. Historically, we have indeed failed to practice deterrence and coercion effectively many times, and survived to tell about it. In the future, we may be less fortunate.

As increasing numbers of states and even terror networks acquire nuclear and biological weapons, we will need to deter an entire spectrum of opponents across a wide range of contingencies. Deterrence will need to work with the same reliability, the same predictability we hoped for in the Cold War, because a single failure could lead to hundreds of thousands, even millions, of casualties. In short, in the future, a single failure of deterrence may be intolerable. That's a standard of deterrence effectiveness that has never been achieved in the past over an extended period. Unfortunately, at the same time that the functioning of deterrence must be more reliable, the establishment of predictable policies of deterrence are going to become much more difficult.

It's wrong to think that deterrence will be easier in the post-Cold War period because the Soviet Union is gone. In fact, predictable policies of deterrence will be much more difficult to establish. Why? Because to deter reliably across a broad spectrum of possible opponents and contingencies will require detailed information about, and familiarity with, a broad spectrum of opponents and potential opponents. Absolutely critical questions for deterrence in each case will include, for example, what has to be held at risk for deterrence to work? How can deterrence threats and conditions be communicated reliably? To whom? And how determined will the opponent be under what conditions? Answering these types of questions in each specific case will be crucial to any predictable functioning of deterrence. Deterrence isn't like men's socks. One size is not going to fit all.

I'm reminded, for example, of what we now know about the 1962 Cuban missile crisis. At that time, Fidel Castro and Che Guevera both urged the Soviet leadership to use the nuclear weapons in Cuba against the United States. They were willing, according to their own words, to become martyrs and for Cuba to be martyred. The Vice Premier of the Soviet Union at the time Mikoyan, responded to Fidel Castro and said, "We see your willingness to die beautifully, but we do not believe it is worth dying beautifully." In the Cold War, we had the relatively easy task of trying to establish a reliable policy of deterrence against only one relatively cautious and familiar opponent, the Soviet Union. In the future, there may be many opponents, including some with extreme goals and hatreds. Establishing reliable policies of deterrence will not be easy, and may be impossible. The predictable, reliable functioning of deterrence certainly will be problematic.

Finally, identifying the military capabilities necessary to support deterrence across a wide range of opponents and contingencies will involve considerable uncertainty, and we will need the broadest possible spectrum of force options. We no longer have the luxury of structuring our forces according to the deterrence requirements of a single opponent who we know fairly well. We will need a wide spectrum of capabilities and the agility to adapt our deterrence threats and policies to address a wide spectrum of contingencies, including the unknown. The old triad and SIOP, as measures of deterrence, are a luxury of the past. Flexibility and adaptability will become the keys to deterrence in the future.

I'm going to move right to the conclusions. One, there appears to be a trend toward much greater lethality in the hands of fewer and fewer. Why? Because of the spread of nuclear and biological weapons and the attendant capability to inflict mass casualties. As Professor Shubik calls it, the "socioe-conomic of death", is becoming much less costly, requiring much less organi-zation, and far fewer people. This trend, if not readily countered, will make the working of deterrence much more important across a variety of opponents. Unfortunately, at the same time, deterrence is likely to become much more uncertain and difficult because of the variety of opponents. To support deter-rence, we will need to maintain a very broad range of capabilities, including nuclear, and be capable of highly flexible and adaptive planning.

Thinking about this trend toward the enormous lethality of small groups, is unpleasant and sobering. But if this trend is real, and I suspect that it is because all the evidence seems to be pointing in that direction, we need to become very sober about these possibilities. Thank you.

DR. PFALTZGRAFF. Thank you very much, Keith, for demonstrating to us in your work, your writings, and of course, discussing with us the dramat-ic reduction in the cost and the greater availability of weapons of mass destruc-tion, and what this will mean for deterrence as we move forward. Now, we have only a very few minutes because we must prepare for our next presenta-tion by Governor Ridge who will be here shortly. But we will take—I believe we can take one question, if that would be appropriate. Who would like to have that one opportunity? Right back here, you've got it. One question. Please announce yourself.

AUDIENCE MEMBER. Thank you. Miranda Hoffsetter, former Marine. I now work for Tulane University's Center for Disaster Management and Humanitarian Assistance. We've heard a lot on the panel, and the last one, about integrating the team, the military, the diplomatic corps, the economic apparatuses into a single team. We've even heard about the new C2, coopera-tion and coordination. But we haven't heard much about the other critical team players and the other key enablers who may already be in the conflict zone, that is, those nongovernmental organizations (NGOs) who are invari-ably involved in development, advocacy, other missions in overseas conflictive areas where the U.S. military and its coalition partners find themselves. NGOs in my opinion are, realistically, the answer to the military's own stakes. I've been to many conferences where the topic of discussion is how to integrate these NGOs into military planning, not to mention sharing of information and things of this nature. From your perspective, what is really being done to incorporate and integrate these very important partners into your own plans because their operations affect your operations, as much as vice versa, even though they're not structured, they don't look like, they don't smell like, they don't act like the military?

DR. PFALTZGRAFF: OK, now, we're going to have to stop because this is a—this is not a statement, but a question. So, we're going to—and we have 30 seconds for the answer unfortunately. So, I think that's—excuse me for interrupting, but we do have to get a quick response here. So, let's go to—let's start with the Air Vice-Marshall.

AIR MARSHAL THOMPSON: Yeah, I would say that we certainly exercise in the British forces—all exercises we do involve just how we address this problem with humanitarian aid. I know at the moment we have a coalition liaison team in Pakistan doing this, and there's talk of them being deployed elsewhere. So, I think the military is really alert to the fact that this is an area where the NGOs should lead, but there does need to be coordination. It's always something we have to work at. And as far as I'm concerned, it is high on the priority of all the commanders' lists all over.

DR. PFALTZGRAFF: General Meigs, can you give us a 30-second answer as well, based on your experience in southeastern Europe? Thank you.

GENERAL MEIGS: We know the importance of NGOs. We've learned that it's very critical to work with them in the field. If you come to our mission rehearsals, you'll find the NGOs represented by actual NGO personnel that create all the frustrations and frictions that you have. One has to remember that NGOs are vital. They're patriotic, idealistic, and do things that the rest of us cannot do. However, they often have goals and missions and processes that are opposed to what we're trying to do in a larger coalition. And sometimes they've been infiltrated by factional elements, and even supporting elements of terrorists that make them subject to be—to be watched very carefully. On the other hand, I do agree with your premise that they're fundamentally critical, and we do work that very hard.

DR. PFALTZGRAFF: Well, thank you very much to the panel, and my apologies to the rest of us—all of us would have had many, many questions, but the excitement of the panel is that we were not able to do all that we'd like to do with it. So, keep that in mind. We have many issues. We very much have enjoyed the opportunity to discuss alliance coalition issues with this outstanding panel. Please thank them very much for their presence.

SPECIAL ADDRESS

HOMELAND SECURITY

The Honorable Tom Ridge, Director, Office of Homeland Security

Summary

• The principal challenge for homeland security is focusing our resources—federal, state, local, and private—to maximize U.S. security. The events of September 11th created a shared sense of urgency and a common sense of purpose that has fueled an immediate and comprehensive national response.

• We cannot focus exclusively on response and recovery efforts. We must also continue developing a comprehensive, forward-looking strategy for homeland defense, by maximizing our innovation, discipline, patience, and resolve and by maintaining a willingness to reconsider traditional missions and relationships.

1. We must force our adversaries to respond to our strategy, instead of our responding to their actions.

2. We must detect and deter terrorist threats before they happen and employ a seamless system of rapid response and recovery.

3. To develop a comprehensive strategy, we must base our goals on performance, not process, and resolve discrepancies between our current and future capabilities.

4. This strategy will be national—not federal—involving all levels of government and will include the public and private tools of national power.

• Based on the National Security Advisor model, every future President needs an assistant to coordinate the multiple departments and agencies involved in homeland defense.

1. The Office of Homeland Security, working through the Office of Management and Budget, is sufficiently involved in the budget process to synchronize these efforts.

2. The Homeland Security budget will use the DOD model to create a multiyear plan that cuts across all agencies. The President has instructed the Office of Homeland Security to focus on the immediate needs of the agencies, while incorporating longer-term needs into the annual budget process.

• *The Defense Department has been essential in responding to the terrorist attacks, and its future role in homeland security is evolving.*

1. The National Guard should have a primary role in domestic security. The Office of Homeland Security will work with DOD and individual states to determine the National Guard's appropriate role and force structure for this mission.

2. The President and the Secretary of Defense view the use of regular forces for homeland security as a last resort.

3. The DOD's valuable experience in combating biological, chemical, radiological, and nuclear threats will be critical as we develop our domestic capabilities.

• *We must enhance cooperation across the federal government, and we may merge some agencies with overlapping responsibilities.*

1. We need a stronger biodefense strategy that strengthens the public health system, increases the ability of local hospitals to handle major public emergencies, and better protects the nation's food supply.

2. We must find better ways to share intelligence quickly, not only across the federal government but also with state and local officials, especially law enforcement.

3. Our domestic first responders need standardized training, procedures, and equipment to communicate with each other and operate together in crisis.

Analysis

Governor Tom Ridge, Director of the new Office for Homeland Security, identified the need to focus on both the current situation and the longer-term aspects of the war on terrorism. The tragic events of September 11th provide an urgency and purpose to the difficult task of responding and recovering. That effort is both extensive and impressive, but the long-term view brings added challenges into focus.

Terrorists must be made to respond to American initiatives, rather than the United States reacting to their attacks. To meet these challenges, it is essential that we develop a comprehensive national strategy that provides direction beyond the federal level to all government agencies and that coordinates and integrates the efforts of the private and public sectors, including state and local governments.

To develop this strategy, the Office of Homeland Security must coordinate an effort to identify goals, needs, and ways to meet those requirements. The strategy must be forward-looking and include a biological defense strategy. Current processes and institutions must also be analyzed to find ways to make them more effective in the war on terrorism.

An essential part of the strategy must be the provision of tools, such as equipment and standardized training, to first responders. Sharing of intelligence must also be facilitated and that intelligence must get to state and local governments in a timely fashion. Governor Ridge stated that he saw the National Guard—perhaps reorganized and reequipped—as the most obvious candidate to lead the military effort in homeland defense.

Recovery remains the priority for homeland security while this strategy is developed and refined. Governor Ridge stated his belief that broad public support will carry America to victory in the war on terrorism. Many details of the national strategy and the implementation of that strategy remain to be defined and executed before the path to that victory becomes clear.

Governor Ridge

Transcript

DR. PFALTZGRAFF: This pleasure is very special, because I am also a Pennsylvanian, and lived in Pennsylvania nearly all my life. Governor Ridge—Tom Ridge, as we all know in this room—was appointed Director of the Homeland—of the Office of Homeland Security in October of this year. Previously, he had served as Governor of Pennsylvania. He was elected Governor for the first term in 1994. He was reelected in 1998, and served there for nearly seven years as Governor. As Governor of the Commonwealth of Pennsylvania, he focused his efforts on education, land conservation, and reconfiguration of the state's fiscal management. And I can tell you that taxes are still very low in Pennsylvania. It's a good state to be in.

Prior to becoming Governor, Director Ridge served six terms as the first Vietnam veteran elected to the United States House of Representatives. He has also served as an Assistant District Attorney in Erie, Pennsylvania, and as an infantry staff sergeant in Vietnam, where he won the Bronze Star for Valor. So, it is with great pleasure that I welcome the new Director of the Office of Homeland Security, Governor Tom Ridge, to this meeting. (Applause)

GOVERNOR RIDGE: Thank you. Just had to thank Bob for that kind commercial on Pennsylvania. Still where the roots are. Well, thank you for that kind introduction, and I also want to thank you for your thoughtful invitation to spend some time with you today. I want to thank General Shinseki and his staff for organizing this very timely and relevant event and, taking a look at the list of speakers and extraordinary public servants that you have invited to participate in this event, I feel very honored to address such a distinguished meeting.

All of you share the President's goal of making America a safer place for all of us to live and to raise our families. It seems fitting to be at a conference, then, with the theme of focusing the instruments of national power. The principal challenge for homeland security is, in fact, to focus all of the resources at our disposal, federal, state, local, and private, to safeguard our country from those who try to do us harm.

Unfortunately, nothing compels us to focus like a tragedy. The events of September 11th created a shared sense of urgency and a common sense of purpose. That sense of purpose has fueled a national response that has been immediate and comprehensive. Recovery efforts in New York City and at the Pentagon, handling the anthrax challenge, identification, treatment, decontamination, investigation. Addressing urgent economic needs, airlines, insurance. Restoring effective commercial services, air travel, mail. Restoring public confidence while instilling vigilance.

For two months, we have been focused on our response and recovery from the terrorist attacks on our country. Federal agencies have mobilized to protect our critical infrastructure. The FAA took immediate steps to secure our airports. We've improved—aviation security has become a national priority. Hopefully we—Congress—will listen, and we need Congress to take action now to pass the Aviation Security Bill. The FBI has stepped up its counterterrorist efforts with watch lists, threat credibility assessments. The Federal Emergency Management Agency is running a 24-hour Operation Center and staffing health service support teams. The FBI has taken on a new mission with the intelligence community that is prevention of terrorist attacks. The Department of Energy has accelerated its oversight and joint coordination on nuclear material control and security enhancements. The Environmental Protection Agency has significantly increased its efforts to protect our water supply. The Coast Guard is patrolling our nation's harbors, nuclear power plants, and other critical infrastructures. And, in addition to pursuing our nation's military objectives overseas, our Department of Defense is making a critical contribution to protect our nation's citizens and infrastructure, as well. Army National Guard soldiers and airmen are protecting our airports and patrolling our skies. The Department of Justice has created our new Foreign Terrorist Tracking Task Force, which will help us in our effort to protect American citizens from the shadow enemy that we're up against: people who would use America's open and welcoming tradition of hospitality and generosity to hide their real motives, their real intent, committing atrocities against innocent people.

So, as I've said, we are working to respond and recover from the events since September 11th. It is crucial, as response and recovery efforts are, the country can't focus exclusively on the present and, therefore, neither can the Office of Homeland Security. We must seize and maintain an initiative. We must begin to improve and strengthen our domestic security for the long term. Our adversaries must respond to our game plan, instead of us responding to theirs. So, as we make this transition, we must focus on the larger mission of the Office of Homeland Security, and that is to create a comprehensive, national strategy for homeland defense. Notice I said national, not federal. The national strategy the President envisions will involve all levels of government, federal, state, and local. It will tap the creative genius and resources of both the public and the private sector. We have begun working on the national homeland security strategy. The ultimate plan will include a comprehensive statement of all activities to secure the United States from terrorist threat or attacks. That's the language the President used in his Executive Order establishing the Office. We need to be able to detect and deter terrorist threats before they happen and, if America is attacked again, to be able to trigger a seamless system of rapid response and recovery.

As all of you know, the first step in developing a strategy is to identify your goals. This is as true in homeland security as it is in the military. Our national strategy for homeland security will identify our objectives in both precise and, as importantly, measurable terms. What does that mean? It means performance, not process. We're going to know exactly what needs to get done, and we're going to know when we got it right. The second step in developing a strategy is identifying your needs. This means find the gap between where we are today and where we seek to be tomorrow. The third step is to fill those gaps. Our national strategy will focus all the instruments of national power at our disposal. Where we find cracks in the system, we will repair them. Where we find strengths in the system, we will work to enhance them. When you're dealing with people as audacious and as calculating and as determined as—and as evil as—terrorists, no system will ever be 100% failsafe and perfect. But we're going to try to get as close to perfect as possible. Our strategy will be forward-looking. This will require doing things a little bit differently than we have in the past. This will require innovation, discipline, patience, and resolve, and a willingness to rethink traditional mission and traditional relationships. The Defense Department takes a long-range approach to its budget needs. Homeland Security will do likewise, with a multiyear budget plan, a plan that cuts across all agencies, a plan that addresses—not only addresses present urgent needs, but also works to get ahead of the threat. In other words, we will prepare not to fight the wars of the past. We must create a blueprint to win the wars of the future. I know a lot of speakers during this conference have identified many of the challenges that the country faces, and I look forward to—on a personal and professional level—to continue the conversation and the dialogue that they had and began with you, with those who are working with us in the Office of Homeland Security. The effective solutions to these challenges must combine the best contributions from professionals across government and the private sector. Let me give you just a few examples of what must be done as we develop a national, comprehensive, long-term strategy.

We need to give our nation's first responders, the firefighters, the police, the medical professionals, and other emergency officials the tools to do their jobs better. Before September 11th, many in our country never thought of these men and women as first responders, as the first line of defense in our homeland security core. Today, every American understands their critical mission. We would never send soldiers into harm's way without proper training and without proper equipment. We owe the same commitment to our domestic first responders, our domestic first line. Our first responders nationwide need standardized training, procedures, and equipment that allow them to communicate with each other in crisis. We intend to enhance cooperation across the federal government. We're even considering merging some of our agencies. We also need a stronger national bio-defense strategy that strengthens the public health system, increases the ability of local hospitals to handle major public emergencies, and better protects the nation's food supply. We've got to find better ways to quickly share threat information, not only across the intelligence community, not only across the federal government but—with my experience over the past seven years—but to spread it across and then down to Governors, states' Attorneys General, Mayors, and local and state law enforcement.

Obviously, there is much more to be done, and our plan will address that. Creating a national homeland defense strategy has never been done before. The challenge is great, but I'm absolutely confident we will succeed. Much has changed since September 11th. But one thing that hasn't changed is our resolve as a nation. Those who attacked us thought it—to crush our spirit—might bring us to our knees, make us cower with fear. But they misjudged us, and not just a little. They so thoroughly miscalculated our response that it gives a whole new meaning to that classic comeback, "you'd have to be living in a cave not to know." They know now, and with all of us working together, we will prevail. So, I think we need to get to work. Thank you very much.

DR. PFALTZGRAFF: Thank you very much, Governor Ridge. We now have an opportunity for some questions. Who would like to be the first? Please raise the lights in the room so we can see. Announce yourself here. Let's take this one here, and then second one will be from here. Wait for the microphone, and please give us your name and proceed with your question.

AUDIENCE MEMBER: Thank you. Adam Nixon with NBC News. There's word that the House and Senate conferees may have just moments ago reached an agreement on airport security. So I'm wondering, in light of that, how quickly do you think that we'll be able to establish a sort of acceptable risk in airports and in air travel, and how quickly will passengers begin to see an improvement in that regard?

GOVERNOR RIDGE: Well, I think—first of all, I'm very encouraged by this late-breaking news. I just asked for them to speed up resolution of this matter 10 minutes ago, and they've responded. (Applause). I think it's pretty clear that the anxiety and concern that consumers have that's shared by the President and everybody else to enhancing as quickly as possible our airport security will give this a momentum that will expedite not only this measure, but some of the other things that we're doing in relationship to aviation security. So, I'm very encouraged by that, the fact that they've reached an agreement. I know that it's something that the President—we've had several conversations about it, and the President is very much engaged in what's going on in Afghanistan. But he is very much engaged in what's going on in this battlefront, as well, and that'll be good news received by all of us. I might add, they won't put it in place by the time I fly to New York this afternoon, but I'm still pretty comfortable flying to New York, though.

DR. PFALTZGRAFF: Next question is over here?

AUDIENCE MEMBER: Erin Winegrad, Inside Washington Publishers. Yesterday, General McCaffrey suggested that the National Guard ought to be redesigned to focus on homeland security. And that may mean, for instance, dissolving heavy armor units and increasing military police, WMD response teams, and medical teams. Could you please give us your assessment of that proposal, both as a Governor and as Director of Homeland Security?

GOVERNOR RIDGE: Well, as Governor, I'm very proud of my 28th Division, my crew back in Pennsylvania. They've worked very hard; they've got some of the highest marks in the National Guard Bureau for readiness. They've been deployed to 30 or 40 countries over the past six or seven years. So, I appreciate very much their commitment and their resolve and their desire to be part of the national effort, whether it takes them overseas or keeps them protecting their—the homeland of Pennsylvania or the United States. One of the individuals that I noted was on your speaker's list was General McCaffrey, and I'm anxious to talk to him about that and a variety of other matters.

I think as we look at the role the Department of Defense plays in homeland security, at least at first blush, the most obvious component of the DOD force structure to have a role with domestic security will be the National

Guard, and we will have to work within DOD, with the Governors and others to identify what that role would be. And if it requires changing the configuration of some units or redeploying some of the assets in a different way, certainly that's got to be something that we want to consider, and we will consider. Not going to resolve it right now, but clearly integrating in a more complete and, perhaps, even some aspects a different way, the National Guard and the Homeland Security is something we need to consider and will consider.

DR. PFALTZGRAFF: Who would like to have the next question? Right over here, yes, please? Wait for the microphone, please.

AUDIENCE MEMBER: Good evening. Avon Williams, with the Department of the Army Office of General Counsel. I've been reading a lot lately about how certain members of Congress are ready to load up the money truck and back it up to this concept called homeland security and dump a load in your lap.

GOVERNOR RIDGE: Well, as long as they dump it out in front of my office, it's okay with me.

AUDIENCE MEMBER: But it seems to me that—and I also heard a lot yesterday about how much is needed to strengthen our national security and especially to improve the status of our forces and commit assets to the Army hopefully. But the President seems to be a little bit more reluctant to just turn on the spigot and start spending money willy-nilly, and I was just wondering if you could shed some light on what some of his budget priorities might be in this regard?

GOVERNOR RIDGE: Well, first of all, the Congress of the United States, both caucuses, both chambers, are trying their very best to assess their priorities and be a part of our country's effort to beef up homeland security. So they've identified some priorities, and there's some fairly large price tags associated with the kinds of things that they want to do, both in the short and the long term. The President has made it very, very clear from the first day that I was introduced to the Cabinet, the first day we had the homeland security meeting that—over which he presided, that the priority for the country for the time being is the war against terrorism, and that has, you know, one war, two battlefronts. We're engaged right now in Afghanistan, we're engaged in the United States. And I think the President asked, and it's reflected in the supplemental—the agencies to say what do you need to accomplish? What are the additional funds you need to get between now and the next of the year, the first part of the next calendar year? They responded. I think there's somewhere between $8 and $9 billion that are going to be available for law enforcement

They're beefing up the public health capacity, infusing some technology into different departments and agencies. They'll expend those dollars in the next 60 or 90 days.

You probably heard—you probably even use—the expression, "if you have 100 priorities, you don't have any." I mean, you really have to decide what's the foundation when you're developing a national strategy. Build the foundation, and then the floor is on top of that. What the President has asked and instructed me to do is, is having identified the immediate needs of the agencies, taking a look at the budget that the White House is preparing now for fiscal year '03, and take a look at that. And then, he has kept open the possibility, if I get back to him, of a—since that budget would take a year to be implemented, if there's some other immediate needs that I thought were worthy of consideration in an early year supplemental, to come back to him with that kind of proposal, as well. So, I think the President is saying we need to address the response and recovery effort completely. We did that. We need to address the immediate needs for the next 60 or 90 days. We've done that. Take a look at next year's budget, and if you think there's some needs that need to be met but can't be met—shouldn't be met waiting a year, then come back to me with that proposal, and that's exactly what we're doing.

DR. PFALTZGRAFF. Is there a question from over here? Let's go to that side of the room, then, please.

AUDIENCE MEMBER. Governor Ridge, as a former Fire Chief, I applaud you every time I hear you talk about the value of the first responders in this war on terrorism. I applaud your resolve there. The critical need of the first responders is the—is to have the ability to communicate with all the federal, state, and regional agencies that are brought to bear in bringing events back to normalcy. The Federal Communications Commission has allocated a radio spectrum that is not yet usable because it's blocked by the broadcasters. There's 10 percent of that spectrum that is set aside to be used one day for interoperability. But our best estimates are it's going to be, at best, 2006 before that spectrum is available to be used. Is there any resolve now to move that deadline forward so those local agencies and federal agencies can use that spectrum? Thank you.

GOVERNOR RIDGE. It's a very appropriate question, because that total seamless communication system is really integral, not only on the front side with sharing the intelligence so you can detect and prevent an incident, but it's also critical, frankly, on the down side, if a terrorist act occurs, so you—enhances your ability to respond to it. The only resolve that I can give you is mine, because I believe that interoperability is critical to the completion of either task. And I'm going to do everything I can to make sure that that process in some kind of seamless communication system is developed ASAP. I mean, I just—it's a very high priority within our office. We've talked to mayors, we've talked to police chiefs, we've talked to Fire Departments, we've talked to emergency management agencies. I'm very proud of Pennsylvania's. We had a good one. We had a good communication system down to our 67 counties and down to our local communities. Not everybody has that capacity. And even if they had them, they weren't necessarily interoperable. So, FEMA is out there taking an assessment of the 50 states. Part of the assessment is the communication capacity, because we do want to make it seamless as quickly as possible.

DR. PFALTZGRAFF: Yes, sir? Yes, over here? Please?

AUDIENCE MEMBER: Hi, Governor Ridge. Bob McClure, Army Fellow at the Council on Foreign Relations. During your talk, you mentioned the possibility of perhaps merging several federal agencies under your plan for homeland defense. Would you care to indicate which those might be, and would that include possibly also the Coast Guard or the INS Border Patrol, which now report to separate Cabinet secretaries?

GOVERNOR RIDGE: I think it's very important for the Office of Homeland Security in conjunction with both the Executive and Legislative Branch, as I said in my remarks, to take a look at how we did business in the 20th Century and how we want to do it in the 21st Century. I'd like to put it in this context: on September 10th, we had agencies and departments who had missions—to deal with national security and economic security and personal security. And that mission has been complicated by the new threat that we see evident since September 11th. So, as far as I'm concerned, wherever you have multiple organizations that seem to be tasked to the same general area, for functional improvement, for economic improvement, for security enhancement, we ought to at least take a look whether or not we need to merge functions, merge agencies. And I may say that's not necessarily on the borders. I mean, you've got—you know, you've got agricultural inspectors across a couple different agencies. One agency does chickens and pigs, and another agency does vegetables. We need to have inspectors. We need to have food inspectors. But the question is, and we need to consider this in light of homeland security, whether or not we want to have multiple organizations basically tasked with the same responsibility, or if we couldn't be—enhance our security, improve our efficiency, and maybe save a few bucks and put them someplace else for enhanced security if we merged functions. And the nice thing about realigning some of these agencies, there'd be more direct accountability, too. So, I like—so, it's an intriguing idea we're going to this year or next year be looking at a couple variations.

DR. PEALTZGRAFF: Okay. Next question? Right down here, please.

AUDIENCE MEMBER: Thank you, Governor Ridge. David Litt, State Department Political Advisor, U.S. Special Operations Command, and a native-born Pittsburgher. Have you had any...?

GOVERNOR RIDGE: You didn't move down here to become a Redskin fan, did you?

AUDIENCE MEMBER: That's enough. Have you had any thoughts or discussions about how the State Department might help you do your job better, for example, enhancing the way consuls adjudicate visas, and—or other ideas?

GOVERNOR RIDGE: Well, just some preliminary thoughts. You can well imagine when you're a group of men and women in the military, the idea is to push the perimeter for your enemy out as far as you possibly can, just keep pushing him and pushing him. And if we could push terrorists into the North and South Pole, that's—I mean, or maybe even off the planet. But the idea is that we've got—if we can expand that perimeter and identify potential risks and potential terrorists outside our borders, outside the Northern Hemisphere, I think we will have enhanced homeland security. It's interesting, a couple of things that are already going on now. Again—a lot of times, I think the government is accused of being slow to respond to a challenge. But I know that your consular offices and the INS have already begun to share different kinds of information so that once you've identified somebody that's getting a visa, you can make sure that when that person shows up allegedly with that visa is actually the same person. There is where we have enormous opportunity, I think, over the years ahead to infuse technology as we expand our perimeter and reduce the risk of terrorism. I mean, biometrics used as far out as possible to make sure that people who get the visas get them, and that they are the same people who show up at our doorstep with the visas. Biometrics can help us with aviation security, biometrics can help us as we try to move and facilitate goods and commerce across borders. So, the infusion of technology, again, with talented, dedicated people will help us a great deal. But certainly, the State Department is a significant part of the equation. We are open. We invite. We're welcoming. We trust. Millions and millions of people come across our borders, so—and we want to change that—because we are—but for Native Americans, we're a country of immigrants. And that's very unique. That makes us very special. But it also, I think, has made us very vulnerable. So, the State Department will be an integral part as we try to push that perimeter forward.

DR. PEALTZGRAFF: Next question? As you think of additional questions, one question that I would have for Governor Ridge is to ask him to reflect upon the public information issues that arise that arose when the anthrax problem came upon us a few weeks ago. What is the balance that one draws in giving information to the public in order to inform the public, but at the same time, not to alarm the public unduly? How do you reconcile that dilemma, Governor, if I might ask?

GOVERNOR RIDGE: I basically, if I could just frame that question, believe the greatest fear is fear of the unknown. And so if you can give appropriate and timely and relevant information to the public, generally, dealing with that kind of crisis, while it may not be complete, and it remains even incomplete as we speak today. But, as we have discovered more information, we revealed more information. And I think that's in—I framed the large answer to a question, obviously. It may be on an ad hoc basis. We're not going to necessarily share all intelligence.

DR. PFALTZGRAFF: That's good.

GOVERNOR RIDGE: And all the things we're doing to enhance homeland security. But, on something like that, a public health crisis, I think our ability— we are best served if we fill in the gap. Where there is no knowledge in public information, I think more often than not we're better served if we fill the gap.

DR. PFALTZGRAFF: Thank you very much. Is there one more question, or two? Yes, please, back here.

AUDIENCE MEMBER: Bob Branna, National Security Fellow from Harvard's Kennedy School. Welcome aboard today, Governor Ridge. We're glad to have you. Several previous speakers have indicated what—at least in some of their views may be a very serious requirement for your office to be able to influence the budget priorities, or perhaps even the budgets themselves.

GOVERNOR RIDGE: Correct.

AUDIENCE MEMBER: Of other agencies that you seek to coordinate. Well aware of the political minefield that this question must pose. I wonder if you care to comment?

GOVERNOR RIDGE: Sure. Actually, I've addressed this question with everybody on the Hill, because members of both parties, some friends of mine whom—with whom I served several years ago—say you need statutory priority, you need budget authority. And my request to them at this point was, for the time being, based on my belief that I've got all the statutory authority and all the budgetary authority I need. I've got the President of the United States saying very specifically to the Cabinet, we're fighting one war, there are two battlefields, one overseas, one in the United States. And we work, and have worked very, very closely with Mitch Daniels. I mean, we have—and I think you're going to see a budget, the first budget. We did—obviously we're not involved six months in advance in planning the budget, but we're intensely involved right now. And you will see this budget reflect the work of the Homeland Security Office, and the priorities of the Homeland Security Office. And to that extent, the President has given instructions, and OMB Director Mitch Daniels has been very cooperative. I would say this, and I've said to my—again, I said this to my former colleagues on the Hill. At some point in time, even if they decided to merge some of these agencies and create an office that, in part, dealt with homeland security, every President in the future should be assisted by someone serving in this capacity. The model's after the National Security Council. There are multiple departments and agencies that are integral part of our national defense. You have Cabinet heads responsible for them, but you need someone as an Assistant to the President to coordinate much of that activity. And, given the fact that so much of homeland security cuts across multiple departments and multiple agencies, you're never going to be able to create a single unit or, from my mind, even two or three units where you just can silo homeland security functions. So I think you're always going to need an Assistant to the President for Homeland Security. And if they choose to create another agency, if they choose to create a Cabinet position, that's fine. But I'm not applying. I already have a job, and I like it. I've already got a job.

DR. PFALTZGRAFF: Is there a final question?

AUDIENCE MEMBER: Governor Ridge, I have a question up here, sir.

GOVERNOR RIDGE: Yes?

AUDIENCE MEMBER: I'm Lisa Burgess, the *Stars and Stripes* senior Pentagon reporter. I'm up here.

GOVERNOR RIDGE: Yeah, I got you. I used to read *Stars and Stripes* back in the late '60s.

AUDIENCE MEMBER: I realize it's early in the process, but could you give us a little bit better idea of what you're looking to the military for in this? What types of questions are you asking, and what parts of the military are you looking to for some answers?

GOVERNOR RIDGE: Well, first of all, we've already looked for support from the Department of Defense. Many of the assets that they have as part of their force structure have been—will be deployed, at least on a temporary basis, for homeland security. We will look to the Department of Defense because of the nature of the BCNR threat, the biological, the chemical, the radiological, and the nuclear threat. The Department of Defense has been looking at those issues, and doing research in developing equipment because of potential use of those kinds of things on the battlefield. Obviously, there is enormous knowledge and experience to be gained and applied to helping, for instance, our first responders. And I think you can go down to potential integration in a different way of the National Guard into homeland security. So the Department of Defense has been a great ally as we've responded to September 11th. And since that time, we've used their laboratories, in many instances, on the anthrax investigation. So, we've deployed a lot of assets and a lot of people and, frankly, we've been working in some areas for application overseas that we have to pull back and see what you've learned, and what you've done, and how they might be applied here as well. So, we've got a great partner in the—in Secretary Rumsfeld, a great leader, and we've got a lot of work to do together, and I'm confident it'll get done just that way.

DR. PFALTZGRAFF: Believe we have time for one more question. Is there one more question? Over here, yes, please? Air Vice-Marshal Thompson.

AUDIENCE MEMBER: John Thompson, UK Defence Attaché. Governor Ridge, that was extremely interesting. Earlier in the year, we had a crisis in the United Kingdom with Foot and Mouth Disease. We don't have any problem with calling in our regular servicemen rather than just National Guard, to help out the other agencies in a situation like that. Do you ever see the Title 10 being changed to enable regular forces to be deployed?

GOVERNOR RIDGE: I think the use of regular forces probably be at the very—would be the last resort. I mean, there are so many other ways that we can respond, including the Guard and the Defense and, candidly, in—with—one of the unique challenges I have is that when you create a national system, not a—you create a national system over a federal government, which means that you've got other governments and other levels of government that we have to work with and coordinate that activity. There are some places that some of my governor friends would prefer to use law enforcement officials or National Guardsmen—excuse me—are presently being deployed, just because they think there is a division of labor that's more appropriate for law enforcement in one area and National Guard in the other. But I do think that the long-term, the use of Regular Army, the—a force is absolutely in my mind, the Secretary of Defense's mind, the President's mind. That is the last deployment. We've plenty of other resources we can deploy first or in intermediate stages.

DR. PFALTZGRAFF: Let me now, on behalf of all of us, express our heart-felt gratitude to Governor Ridge for being with us today. I know that he has a very busy schedule, and is going to New York, I believe, after this. We appre-ciate your being here, Governor, and we thank you very much for this inform-ative talk, and we wish you the very best. We're going to miss you in Pennsylvania, but we know you're doing good work here in Washington, D.C.

GOVERNOR RIDGE: Thanks a lot. Thanks so much. Thanks, all. (Applause)

DR. PFALTZGRAFF: We will now resume the luncheon, or go to lunch, at 12:45. We have a few minutes in between, so please be there at 12:45 for lunch. Thank you.

CLOSING ADDRESS

THE MILITARY'S ROLE IN HOMELAND SECURITY

General William F. Kernan, U.S. Army, Commander in Chief, United
States Joint Forces Command

Summary

• *The United States needs a national strategy for homeland security. Each
agency and department needs a clear role, mission, and an understanding of who
has primacy in each area.*

  1. We must avoid arbitrary change in favor of a systematic plan of
requirements and actions.

  2. Homeland security is hemispheric. The United States has a trans-
parent relationship with Canada but needs to improve its cooperation with
Mexico.

  3. Sustaining national will is essential to combating terrorism.

  4. Americans view terrorist attacks as immoral. The terrorists have a
different value system and culture and do not abide by the rule of law. They
consider their actions to be military operations.

  5. Synchronization and integration of the interagency process are
essential. We must fuse our intelligence resources to better assess threats and
determine how to defeat them.

• *The primary mission for military forces is to fight and win wars.
Historically, our forces have trained to defeat a conventional attack outside the
United States. The military must now address the asymmetric threat of terrorism.*

  1. The military must be postured to prevent an attack on our homeland.

  2. Primacy for homeland defense belongs to the civil authorities and
first responders. The National Guard is legally permitted to undertake law
enforcement responsibilities to augment the civilian effort. The reserve and
active military components are legally restricted to a supporting role in this
mission.

  3. We must have complementary plans and communications. We
have to identify local, state, and regional capability and be prepared to augment these capabilities where required.

4. We need a regional command-and-control architecture to accomplish the necessary fusion within the ten FEMA regions and national headquarters.

5. We have to align the Unified Command Plan to achieve the synchronization needed for homeland security. There are five CINCs involved in homeland security. We do not want to create new organizations but use the existing structure to streamline command and control.

- *Joint Forces Command has combatant command of 83 percent of the general-purpose forces in the United States and has great synergy among the services*

1. Because of its location and role as the primary force provider, Joint Forces Command is well prepared to assume the mission of land and maritime homeland security on an interim basis.

2. JFCOM's primary focus is to undertake experimentation, transformation, and concept development to support the evolution of the Joint Force.

Analysis

General Kernan noted that the events of September 11th inspired a move from simply talking about homeland security to significant action on the issue. He asserted that it is important to define homeland security to ensure that each agency and department properly understands its roles, missions, and responsibilities. He noted the two elements of homeland security are homeland defense and civil support (with significant focus today placed on consequence management). The former recently received much more attention—and resources—than earlier, but the requirements for each element demand definitive identification. The civil support element is well defined and understood through the lessons of many civil-military operations in our nation's history and again on and after September 11, but General Kernan argued that there is both a need and an ability to improve our capability and capacity to execute this mission.

While homeland defense is an enduring military mission, its primary focus has long been to counter a conventional attack from overseas. General Kernan recognized the military's continuing leadership of the external portion of the mission to defend the nation, and noted that the military has been—and will continue to be—the supporting agency in the execution of homeland defense in the continental United States.

Like many speakers and panelists, General Kernan commented on the need to synchronize and integrate actions between active and reserve components, between the CINCs and Services, and in the interagency process. He proposed that Joint Forces Command assume responsibility for land and maritime homeland security to facilitate the streamlining of the homeland security process during the transition period.

General Kernan's views on homeland security tracked well with those of other speakers, particularly Governor Ridge. Like the Director of the Office of Homeland Security, General Kernan advocated the development of a national campaign plan to integrate the agencies and other organizations working at various levels of government. He noted the particular importance of synchronizing foreign and domestic intelligence to assess threats in order to combat them. He also reiterated that the National Guard is legally permitted to undertake law enforcement responsibilities if needed. Therefore should provide the bulk of military support for homeland defense.

General Kernan

General Kernan, again as many others, said that the maintenance of national will is an essential task for all. National trust and confidence must be built and maintained, resources applied to homeland defense will assist materially in that effort.

Transcript

SPEAKER: Ladies and gentlemen, please welcome Dr. Pfaltzgraff.

DR. PFALTZGRAFF: Ladies and gentlemen, I hope that you have enjoyed, as I have, a very good meal here, a good lunch and, of course, some wonderful conversations around the tables here as we have at our table, but now the opportunity arises to hear our concluding speaker. Our concluding speaker for this conference is General William F. Kernan or Buck Kernan, United States Army. General Kernan is Commander in Chief, United States Joint Forces Command. And he is, as they say, dual hatted, because he is also Supreme Allied Commander, Atlantic. He is responsible to the President and Secretary of Defense, National Command Authority, through the Chairman of the Joint Chiefs of Staff for JFCOM's mission of maximizing the nation's present and future military capabilities to ensure that U.S. forces continue to move forward in a multiservice, multinational mission capacity in these two hats that he wears. He also provides ready U.S.-based Army, Navy, Air Force, and Marine Corps forces to support the command's geographical area of responsibility, its domestic requirements, and, of course, other unified combat and commands around the world. I might also mention here that General Kernan entered Officer Candidate School as a staff sergeant. He has worked his way up in the Army, gaining a commission as infantry officer in 1968, and he has had many other command assignments and other appointments during his illustrious career in the United States Army including leading the Rangers' parachute assault into Panama in 1989, Commander of the 101st Airborne Division (Air Assault), and Commander of the XVIII Airborne Corps. So it is with very great pleasure that I welcome General Kernan to give our concluding address and to speak about the role that JFCOM plays in the integration of our military forces in the homeland security mission. So welcome, General Kernan. (Applause)

GENERAL KERNAN: Thanks very much. It is great to be here. I appreciate the opportunity, and I hope it really is an opportunity. I am a little concerned about doing this after Secretary Ridge, Governor Ridge and, you know, after lunch. (Laughter) I know you all have probably been worn out by now. I just warn you ahead of time that—caution you that my voice has been known to lull many folks asleep so—(Laughter) I have about eight slides and I don't have a prepared text, so I am going to speak to this thing from some notes. In doing so, I want to talk about the topic of Homeland Security from a DOD perspective and from the perspective of Joint Forces Command.

It was a great lead-in from Governor Ridge because he is talking about it at the national level. I was elated to hear him say that we need a national strategy. An awful lot of what I am going to talk about today hopefully is embedded in with the vision he has for the future. So, I want talk a little bit about the homeland security mission and specifically our responsibilities for homeland defense and military assistance to civil authorities. I want to help all of us come to grips with it and begin to address what we are doing right now and provide some thoughts on the way ahead.

I think all of you recognize the fact that the primary mission or the primary reason for having a military force is to fight and win our nation's wars. We know that. Likewise, it has been reiterated time and time again that our number one mission is protection of the homeland. And we have always recognized that as well. But I will tell you that we have traditionally focused on that mission starting with the assumption that the attack would emanate from outside the United States and was primarily a conventional threat.

The challenges and focus on homeland security reminds me of the story of the Cajun and the game warden. This Cajun had been extraordinarily lucky fishing, and the game warden was a little suspicious as to his fishing prowess. So he accompanied him one day out in the boat and rowed right out in the middle of the lake, and the old Cajun reached in his bag and pulled out two sticks of dynamite, lit them both. The Cajun threw one overboard and handed one to the game warden. So there the game warden was holding this lit stick of dynamite, lecturing the Cajun on how totally illegal and unsportsmanlike using dynamite was . . . all the while the fuse burned lower and lower. Finally, the Cajun looked at the game warden and said, "Are you going to fish or are you going to talk?" (Laughter)

You know, many of you in this room and others, if you think about it, you relate to the Cajun. He knows there is a lit stick of dynamite and knows what to do with it. And you know we need to focus on homeland security and on the actions necessary to defend this great nation. There are also an awful lot of people who are like the game warden. They see that lit stick of dynamite in their hand, but they are more interested in just talking about it, instead of doing something about it.

Well, 11 September has got us all fishing, I have to tell you. I think that we recognize that post-11 September we were going to have to refocus our efforts. We are all focused and we are moving forward. This is a dynamic and rapidly evolving mission area. We were going to have to re-focus away from what we saw as a conventional threat against the United States to an asymmetrical threat called terrorism, and on how we were going to address it and be prepared to respond.

It only made sense that on an interim basis we take on the land and maritime pieces of the homeland security mission. Joint Forces Command has combatant command of 83 percent of the general-purpose forces in the United States. So, we own the forces and have had the military assistance and consequence management responsibilities for quite a while. And we get great synergy at Norfolk. Three of the four components are colocated right there at Norfolk. Air Combat Command, CINCLANTFLT and MARFORLANT are right in Norfolk. And Forces Command is only an hour away in Atlanta. I might add that the Coast Guard Regional Commander responsible for maritime security on the Atlantic and, as directed by the Commandant, Admiral Jim Loy, as the coordinating commander for maritime security for the continental United States, is also in Norfolk. So our location in Norfolk really provides great synergy.

I don't know if anybody has gotten into the business of defining homeland security, but I think it is important. Definitions are very important. They are essential because they clarify roles, missions, and responsibilities. This slide depicts the current working definitions. They have yet to be fully embraced by the Office of Homeland Security and codified within the Department of Defense, but they are the ones we are working with right now. The overarching umbrella term that we use is homeland security. The military's piece of it is homeland defense and military support of civil authorities. Those are our two primary roles. Homeland security focuses on preparing for, preventing, deterring, defending, and responding to aggression. We focused on that. And it specifically mentions consequence management. This is an area where the military has a big role to play. In the area of homeland defense, we are focused on protecting our population and critical infrastructure against external threats and aggression. As well, you will notice that under civil support, consequence management is not specifically identified. That is not by accident because it is really subsumed up underneath that phrase support to civil authority for natural and man-made domestic emergencies.

Dealing with the internal threat is primarily a law enforcement responsibility. Now, we are prepared to augment and support where necessary, but doing anything preemptively, doing anything primarily inside the United States, we see as a law enforcement mission. Now, in the current environment we find that our adversary crossed a threshold on 11 September, and it wasn't what we normally expected. It wasn't a hijacking. It wasn't a kidnapping. It wasn't a small-scale bomb. He basically used a weapon of mass destruction, albeit one of our own systems, against us and created a high-yield explosive that caused a catastrophic and horrific event. And we shouldn't forget that. And I know we won't, but we should not forget why he did it. We oftentimes look at these acts as criminal. We are horrified by it and consider it amoral. But we are looking at it from our value base. This enemy doesn't hold the same values that we have, he doesn't have the same culture. So we see it as criminal and amoral while he sees it as a military operation. He is also not bound by the rule of law. And he is definitely not bound by the law of warfare. But we clearly are. That creates some opportunities for him and some challenges for us. He will continually be assessing our vulnerabilities and the seams created by those challenges.

As the President said, this war on terrorism is going to be a protracted campaign. We are talking globally focused. There is no reason why we have to live this way, and there is no reason why our citizens have to be subjected to this kind of fear. It is going to take a long time. As vigilant as we might be, our enemy will be equally vigilant, and he is going to look for the seams and gaps. He is going to look for our vulnerabilities. So we have got to "red team" ourselves and identify our seams and gaps before he does. In parallel, we have to look at what we can do to improve, and at same time we have to practice sound operational security. Let me assure you, we know how to do this mission. Military support to civilian authorities, we have been doing it for a long time. We are good at it, and we recognize that we must get better. We learn how to do it better every time we have been employed in support of civil authorities. But now the mission area has changed and expanded dramatically. But again, we are ready now. We can do the mission, we are postured to do the mission, and we will continue to improve.

You heard Governor Ridge talking about the interagency, and I think at last count we deal with about 46 different agencies, and there are probably many more out there. Those are government and federal agencies. There are all kinds of nongovernmental agencies that are involved in this. Our National

Guard, our Reserve, our active component are also principal players. Different authorities, different responsibilities, and in many respects those authorities give some of our forces great flexibility. The Unified Command Plan right now has about five CINCs involved in homeland defense aspects of homeland security. Of course, given Pacific and Southern Commands' geographic responsibilities over Hawaii, Alaska, the Virgin Islands, Puerto Rico, it makes sense that security be handled there. So are there seams? Sure, there are seams. But this is something we are used to—it is part of any military operation.

We have done a great deal to minimize those seams, and we have seams operationally all the time. And we are used to dealing with these. Can they be streamlined? Can we do a better job? Yeah. And we are looking at that, and I will talk a little bit about that later on.

Our own mission at Joint Forces Command is evolving. And I say it is evolving because I said we have interim responsibility for land and maritime security. The bulk of our mission statement preceded 11 September. We have added the last part of it to account for our land and maritime homeland defense responsibilities. Whether or not we stay with that mission area is yet to be determined. Prior to September 11th, our primary focus in Joint Forces Command was to look out to the future, do the experimentation, the transformation, and do the concept development that looks to the evolution of the joint force. So, the sequence we address, the "nation's future and present military capabilities," is intentional and that focus is key to assisting the Secretary of Defense, the Chairman and the Services with the transformation of the Joint force. We drive this transformation, first of all, by determining the operational concepts required for the future. We test them. We validate them. We identify the requirements necessary to satisfy them. We get those requirements in front of the Joint Requirements Oversight Council (JROC), and ideally we get them fielded very rapidly. I will submit to you that this war on terrorism and homeland security has put us in a transformational posture. In fact at Joint Forces Command, what we did to address this has been very transformational as we stood up the Homeland Security Directorate.

Homeland security requires a thorough mission-area analysis. You heard Governor Ridge allude to that earlier today. You want to make sure that what you are doing is right. The intellectual change must lead physical change. Don't just arbitrarily change. Determine what you want to do, and then what is required to do it, and then have a game plan to very systematically make it happen.

These are a number of what I call the homeland security keys to victory. I think they complement what Governor Ridge said. First, synchronization and integration of the interagency arena is essential. We have many masters out there. Ideally what we would like to do is have some kind of funnel where all these things poured through and we had one taskmaster. We've got a sieve out there right now. We are bombarded from everywhere. The fusion of that effort, the synchronization of that effort is very, very important, particularly with intelligence, both foreign and domestic intelligence. And I know we have some domestic oversight issues that we have to wrestle with, and we are looking at those right now. The general counsels are doing that. We have done a remarkably good job netting ourselves with law enforcement to be better postured, to be proactive rather than reactive, but there is an awful lot more that needs to be done.

Second, we must integrate the active, Guard, and Reserve, to ensure unity of effort. There are roles out there for all of us. Netting all that together is going to be very, very important. I personally believe that the Guard has a primary mission here. The Guard is a Title 32 force. It has different responsibilities, different authorities, and different flexibility than Title 10 federal active and reserve forces. But making sure that we all understand what it is that we are doing and who has responsibility and who has primacy is going to be extremely important. We are moving in the right direction. I just had a meeting the other day once again with the Chief of the Guard Bureau and a number of the state Adjutants General. I talk with Lieutenant Generals Russ Davis and Roger Schultz routinely on the integration of active and Guard efforts. We are in this together. I guarantee there is no light between us. We have locked arms. We are going down the same road together. We are going to make the right decision. You know that principle of war—unity—has served us very, very well. Focusing on the common objective gives you mission focus. Making sure that there is unity of effort, unity of command, and making sure that it is as simple as it can be is some of the keys to success.

Third, we need fused, all-source predictive analysis. We must have that. Otherwise we are going to be reactive. If we want to get in front of this, if we ideally want to be able to deter and prevent rather than react, we have to fuse all this information, the domestic intelligence and the foreign intelligence, together. And we need the analytical tools and we need the specialists out there to be able to assess where this threat may come from, what it might be and how we can best posture ourselves to avoid it. We are moving forward on this. We would all like to do it a lot faster than we are able to do it right now.

Fourth, we have to preserve our force and the capabilities of the nation. This includes disciplined execution of the force protection conditions and protecting our priority capabilities. Protecting our power-projection platforms for the military, protecting our critical infrastructure in large measure is what we are doing right now.

We are prepared to respond to security of civilian critical infrastructure, but we are protecting our power-projection platforms right now. We need to have the flexibility, the freedom of movement to be able to rapidly deploy forces to prosecute this war overseas. It takes a tremendous effort on our part to do this right and it is manpower intensive. In the future, I think one of the things we need to do is look to see where technology can enable us to do things that right now require people so that we can be better—we can be more secure on the home base.

Fifth, this mission requires we begin streamlining the command and control system so that we can be more responsive. We are working through that right now. There is a major Unified Command Plan study going on. We understand what needs to be done. We also know that, as much as possible, you don't want to create new organizations. If you have organizations, if you have structure, and it just needs to be modified, morphed into something that is more relevant to the mission area that you are addressing today. That is probably the ideal solution and that is one of the things that the Joint Staff, the Service staffs and the other CINCs are looking to achieve here in the next couple of months.

Sixth, we must ensure we have trained and ready forces including trained and ready civil forces. There are 11 million first responders out there. You heard Governor Ridge talk about the criticality of trying to fuse all that together to the standardized procedures, to make sure the right equipment is out there. In the future, one of the things we must be able to do is make sure that we work together. In order to work together, we need complementary plans. We need the communications architecture that supports operations. We must be able to identify local, state, and regional capability and where there are deficiencies and be prepared to augment that where required. We have to look at this thing very holistically, and we can't look at it just from the military. The military augments those 11 million first responders out there, but in order to be prepared to do that, we need to know what their current capabilities are and what their deficiencies are.

Seventh, we have to have ready-reaction forces that can immediately respond to the needs of our civil authorities. Right now those rapid-reaction forces are coming out of the active component forces. In the future, one of the things we need to look at is whether or not they should come from the National Guard and, if so, how do we resource those to be able to do that?

This is all very, very key, of course, to sustaining national will, and our national will is essential to combating terrorism because that challenges one of our enemy's centers of gravity. His charismatic leadership, which feeds the will of his supporters, is vulnerable to our own resolute, unified national will and action. Our steadfastness and unity of purpose are major combat multipliers for us in combating terrorism at home and abroad. To sustain the support of our nation, the military must be ready to respond instantaneously wherever the threat might be.

Let me address the roles and authorities of Title 10, Title 14, and Title 32 forces. Title 10 includes federal active and reserve components. The Coast Guard comes under Title 14, and Title 32 forces are the National Guard, in their state militia role.

There has been an awful lot of talk about whether or not the federal forces should take this over. No, I don't believe so. The governor should retain primacy within each state. They know what needs to be done. They have a state militia—the National Guard—that is postured there to support them. That state militia can do law enforcement things if required to augment the police and other functions that federal forces like the active military and reserves cannot. There are limitations imposed on the active components under Title 10 that, unless the Insurrection Acts are invoked, restrict us from doing those kinds of things, and rightfully so.

I see the active component as sort of the third team in this. Those 11 million first responders are the first ones out there, and are able to react or deter then the National Guard, and then lastly the reserves and Active components where required. Now, there are an awful lot of things that I think we can do and should do. We need to look at those authorities that either give us flexibility or constrain us. Take Title 14 as an example. The Coast Guard works with and for the Navy. They can take a naval vessel, put Coast Guardsmen on it, and go and do law enforcement-type operations.

In a similar fashion, we need to look at what makes the most sense to be able to be more proactive out there in the states and the regions. We require a regional command and control architecture, I believe, so that we can get the fusion that is necessary within the ten FEMA (Federal Emergency Management Agency) regions all the way up to the national headquarters. Likewise, the military needs to be both complementary to that process and to each other. As with these reaction and response forces I talked about earlier, right now, there is a limitation as to what the Guard can do, and the active duty personnel are doing it. Once we identify and do this mission analysis and determine precisely what is required out there, and then we look at what kind of capability we need at the state level to satisfy that the requirement and further determine what can come from the National Guard, from the reserves, from the active component, and so on.

At Joint Forces Command, one of the first things we did was restructure the headquarters to immediately address our number one mission—homeland security. We created a 90-person Homeland Security Directorate by the Joint Forces Command—the nucleus, if you would like, of the standing Joint Task Force headquarters specifically focused on homeland security.

We recognized that is a no-failure mission. If we are going to protect our citizenry and maintain their trust, confidence, and national will, it is essential that we be postured militarily to deny the adversary the opportunity to do something here to hurt our civilians. So we have done an awful lot of training. Training continues in combat. It is happening right now throughout all the CINC AORs (Areas of Operation), in particular, over there in southwest Asia. You continually hone those skills. And here at home, we had to do the same thing. We took those 90 people and put them through a very deliberate training regimen that continues today.

In fact, we have a week-long staff exercise going on right now that is going to culminate in a major CPX (Command Post Exercise) next month, for two reasons. One, to solidify our efforts on homeland security, and also to be properly postured because we have to support the Olympics that are upcoming in Salt Lake City on 2 February, so we are less than 50 days away from a major international event that could also be a major terrorist target.

In forming this new headquarters and in planning and training, we have used the things we learned in transformation and experimentation to restructure ourselves. We didn't do this along the normal staff relationships. We looked at the fact that we had to interface with the inter-agency arena. We created an entity for that. The plans and operations continued, but then we looked at information and intelligence, and they are two different things, and how we were going to fuse that, and lastly knowledge management and what was necessary to support that. We have got a wide variety of communications apparatuses out there. We have a limitation on collaborative tool suites to support all of that. We are identifying what we believe needs to be done for the U.S. military, and ideally with Governor Ridge, if we can make sure that we have a compatible system, that is going to be the key to success in the future. We are reviewing these issues right now and making recommendations as to what needs to be done, in particular in the command and control arena.

The military is in a supporting role and should remain so. Primacy resides with our civil authorities, those first responders and then secondarily to the National Guard. But ensuring we have identified plans down at the state and local level and making sure we have complementary plans built at the national level are extremely important. We must align the Unified Command Plan to address how we are going to get the synergy that we need to focus on homeland security.

I was elated to hear Governor Ridge say that we needed a national strategy. Not only do we need a national strategy, we need a national campaign plan. We are right now in the process of developing a campaign plan. We are doing that in parallel with the Joint Staff, the Service Chiefs, as well as the components out there. We think we have it right at our level. If we are going to get a redirect, I would like to know it early on from Governor Ridge.

But it is very important, as you can appreciate, that we have complementary plans. And we need to get those plans all the way down to those first responders, and we need visibility on them, and then we try to nest these things together so we can weave this thing into a tapestry that makes sense.

Moreover, this is a hemispheric mission and must be approached from that perspective. We have a good relationship with Canada, we have good visibility on Canada's defense posture, and we have great cooperation. We have a lesser visibility on Mexico. We need to look at that. We need to look at how we interact with Mexico; how we ensure that our plans are complementary to their plans just as with Canada. We probably need something along the lines that we have with NORAD (North American Aerospace Defense Command) right now. We enjoy this aerospace protection with Canada, but we do not have a similar relationship with Mexico.

I don't know what the way ahead is. That is something that State needs to look at and Office of Secretary of Defense. I think I will close there and see if you have any questions. I will tell you that we understand what needs to be done. We have a war on terrorism, and as Governor Ridge says, it has two fronts, one overseas and one right here in the continental United States.

We have to make sure that we have visibility on the forces, and as a primary force provider, I am very sensitive to this, that I can, in fact, provide the combatant commanders of those forces what they need to do the theater engagement and prosecute military operations wherever they may be and at the same time have trained and ready forces available and immediately responsive to whatever threat may exist here in the United States. That is not an easy task.

One of the advantages we have in Joint Forces Command is, because we do have all those forces, we are able to look at that. We know precisely what their readiness posture is, we know right now who is being deployed, who is anticipated to be deployed, and who is ready and available to go. Being able to anticipate gives us the ability to look at what needs to be done in the way of mobilization and bringing people up in case we anticipate a greater need than we have currently. So, ladies and gentlemen, I will open for your questions right now.

DR. PFALTZGRAFF: Thank you very much. Thank you very much, General Kernan, for this outstanding presentation. We now have an opportunity for discussion and questions. So who would like to be the first? Right over here. Right here. I can give you my mike.

AUDIENCE MEMBER: Yes. General, this is a question about money. NORAD has through a window a pretty substantial budget for aerospace security. I think it is going to be seven and a half billion dollars is what is in the new Title 9 suggestion. If I look at ports, harbor, waterway protection—and we have to do a lot of work with the Coast Guard. I have to be honest. I don't think they have anywhere near the kind of money needed to protect the harbor or just the port of, say, Houston, Boston. We are from Boston, so look at the problem they have in terms of LNG tankers going into Boston, and the question is what are you going to do about it? And the answer is we don't know because we don't know where the money is coming from. Can you comment, because you got the poorer part. Your cousin in NORAD got the most of the money.

GENERAL KERNAN: Right up front, we don't know what it is going to cost. We are going through the analysis right now, and we are doing it as we conduct operations. Coast Guard probably has a better feel for that than I do right now as to what it is going to cost for maritime security. There are a lot of unknowns here also because how are you going to deploy? One of the things we need to look at, though, is if there are new skill sets, if there is new equipment, and obviously the training that is going to be required to support this all has to be factored in. We do not know what this is going to cost yet. Right now we are reactive in that. We are doing it because it is essential that we do it. And we are ready to do it right now. But as we are doing it, we are basically getting information that will help us, hopefully, put together a budget to address this. And I have no idea what the cost is going to be.

AUDIENCE MEMBER: I am Hardev Lidder from the Indian Embassy. Sir, I have not been able to understand what is the inhibition for using the armed forces at a time when it is critical for you to respond. I will give you an example. You have first responders to a crisis. They have research. They don't have adequate response capability as desired. You then go on your next line in which you have to mobilize the National Guard to be able to place units. In between this period you have organization that is best equipped. It has excellent transportation, it has premier manpower, beautiful communication, and it is waiting because somebody hasn't put it into the plan to call them up to fill that gap before the National Guard can take on. I just want your comments on this. I haven't been able to figure out the inhibition that lies behind this.

GENERAL KERNAN: I want to make sure I understand precisely what your question is. Are you talking about the active component that is not being employed right now?

AUDIENCE MEMBER: Correct.

GENERAL KERNAN: Okay. As you may be aware, there is an awful lot of different war plans out there. There are units that are being used—that are being trained. There are units that are identified for commitment in other theaters of operation. Right now, we have not been tasked by the National Command Authority to do anything inside the continental United States. There has been a few cases where we have had some specialty skills go forward, some explosive ordinance demolition teams, some dog handlers, and some other things, but we have not been tasked to do that. So their primary focus is still training, being prepared to go in support of other combatant commanders. The National Guard is heavily tasked right now in the states to supporting security at the airfields and guarding other critical installations. So right now, we haven't employed the active component because the National Guard has a good handle on that current mission. Now, one of the things—we talked about nesting plans and identification of assets at state and local level. As we look to the future and as we look at what is available in the National Guard within each state and we look to the Reserve that might also be in that state, being able to access that Reserve without mobilization and employing them in response to an incident is also something that needs to be factored in, but we don't have a requirement right now to employ the active components inside the continental United States. Did that answer your question?

AUDIENCE MEMBER: I think I better clarify myself. I am not talking about this particular incident, but what we were discussing, a methodology of how to respond in the future. I reckon that the whole thing is up for discussion and examination. It is in this context that I framed my query. It is the time period between the occurrence of the incident and when the National Guard can be mobilized, if you have active components which is available for you as for planning that you may do in various different parts of the country and they do respond, handle the crisis, then mobilization takes place and those components come and relieve the active components from duty. I think [each of the components] should be able to fill in the critical gap that would exist between the first responder and the mobilization of the National Guard.

GENERAL KERNAN: We have done that many, many times and we don't really have to mobilize the National Guard. The Governor just simply calls the National Guard out and the employment of state militia. They do not go through mobilization. So we have done that in the past, and we are pretty well practiced in doing that. Now, what does need to be mobilized right now are the Reserve Title 10 forces, and that is one of the authorities we need to look at. And maybe there is some changes that we can do that gives us a little bit more agility out there that can augment the National Guard before you use the active components that are being used by the combatant commanders elsewhere.

DR. PFALTZGRAFF: Let's go on that our next question right now, and we will take this question right now. Wait for the mike, please.

AUDIENCE MEMBER: Lee Ewing with homeland defense. Sir, for many years the active forces heavily depended on the reserve forces in the National Guard routinely. Now we are talking about significant new roles for them at home.

GENERAL KERNAN: Possibly, yeah.

AUDIENCE MEMBER: How do you take care of this potential mismatch if a unit is protecting airports here and flying CAPs (Combat Air Patrols) over our cities and they are tasked to go to North Korea or to Korea or something?

GENERAL KERNAN: That is a great question. That is a question because that is one of the things we are doing right now. We built a matrix and I know what the various combatant commanders are requiring right now. I know what they have identified they may need in the future. I also know what my force pool looks like, and I know what the readiness posture of that force pool is. We are trying to anticipate what is going to be needed and where they come from. And you need to be able to do that ideally long range enough that if you require mobilization, that you do it in sufficient time that you have been able to bring those forces up, put them through the mobilization center, train them, and do all the last minute things that you need to do before you employ them. So one of the value added, I guess you could say, of being a Joint Forces Command is right now with the—we have got 83 percent of the general-purpose forces, so we are primary mission of doing the force provider role. So we are looking at that all the time. And is it a challenge? Yeah. It sure is. And as you look at what we are doing right now in the CAPS, as you pointed out, and the airport security, those are some of those same forces out there that are maybe force listed to do something else, so we then have to look another layer deep. And we are going to have to look at the mission analysis and the force structure to support that in light of this new, emerging mission area that we are experiencing right today.

DR. PFALTZGRAFF: Our next two questions will come from over here. Right back here, please, and then another one.

AUDIENCE MEMBER: Sir, Tim Buck, former soldier. The Unified Command Plan, as I understand it, is being reviewed right now and there appear to be several scenes in our current structure when we look at it from a homeland security perspective. In particular, you are dual hatted as the Supreme Allied Commander, Atlantic—I think a first for an Army officer. It may be time to pass that function back to another NATO ally to free you to function or to emphasize two other areas, experimentation and homeland security. You have said a couple of times that you control 83 percent of the general-purpose forces in the United States as opposed to 100 percent because you split those forces with Pacific, who does not have, my understanding is, homeland security responsibilities. NORAD has air defense responsibilities. You have, as you said in your slides, maritime and land. Is it not time to pull together some of these U.S. responsibilities into a beefed-up Joint Forces Command, possibly with another name, to shed some of the old NATO structure, put it back where maybe it belongs now?

GENERAL KERNAN: Let me ask you a question. Where does it belong?

AUDIENCE MEMBER: Sir, I was hoping that a Four Star would have a whole lot better insight than a former—(Laughter)

GENERAL KERNAN: Yeah. All those things that you talked about are being looked at. Unquestionably, they need to be looked at. Yeah, Pacific

Command has forces in the United States and you say, you know, doesn't have the homeland security mission, but he does. He has it for his geographic area of responsibility, as well as the fact that I have tactical command where required of those forces in the continental United States. So we have removed some of that scene. This is not unlike what we experience in combat operations, you know. You have a joint force commander out there. He has a JPAC that supports him. He has an air, land, and maritime component out there. There are sort of seams, if you want to look at it that way, but it is more than one individual. It is a team approach to this. And the unity of effort and unities of command is there, I believe. No, I don't have combatant command of those West Coast-based forces. Should I have? That is one of the things that is going to be looked at. Yes, I am dual hatted as Supreme Allied Commander of Atlantic right now. Is that one of the things being looked at? Sure. NATO and the transatlantic bridge are extremely important. We are leveraging NATO right now, you know. This invoking Article Five was a big shot in the arm, it was extremely important. We got five AWACS (Airborne Warning and Control Systems) flying right now to support and protect our airways. That is solidarity. That is trust and confidence. That is important. When you talked about—when you sort of alluded to—interoperability, how we are going to do that as we transform, as we modernize, and do that in conjunction with our allies and so on that we can do these coalition-type operations and make sure that we can all work together, a large part of that is done through this SACLANT hat I wear because SACLANT does have the responsibility to look at, in conjunction with General Ralston, the futures piece. We have responsibility for looking at combat development and experimentation and DCI (Director of Central Intelligence). So what is the way ahead on that? I don't know. I think that we have all made some recommendations, and we are looking very hard at what needs to be done.

DR. PFALTZGRAFF: We have another question from over here. Was there another question here? I thought I saw another hand up. If not, then who would like to ask the next question? Over here again, please. All the way back

AUDIENCE MEMBER: Sir, I am Dan Day from the Army Space and Missile Defense Command. Other regional CINCs have intelligence center central support from the national agencies to help them do the job. Will your command have such a center and, if so, will Governor Ridge's office have a piece of that?

GENERAL KERNAN: I couldn't tell you what the future looks like on Governor Ridge's office. I believe we need something like a national interagency coordination center—I think that is essential—that feeds the joint interagency coordination centers that right now the combatant commands are standing up. I believe that whoever has homeland security needs a similar type joint interagency coordination group to focus on protection of the home-land, and, like I said, ideally it need to be linked to a national interagency coordination center. But I don't have one now, but we are going to look at building one and, of course, this is another one of these things that requires resources, people, money, equipment, and the communication architecture to support it all.

DR. PFALTZGRAFF: We have time for perhaps one or at most two more questions. Would anyone like to take advantage of this opportunity? Apparently not. I take your silence as being that we have exhausted the sub-ject matter. If not, certainly not—we have exhausted at least the participants. How is that? (Laughter)

GENERAL KERNAN: That might be true.

DR. PFALTZGRAFF: Well, let me on our collective behalf, then, express thanks to you, Buck, for being with us. General Kernan has given us a won-derful overview of the important challenges and responsibilities of the recent-ly stood-up JFCOM and has provided us with a suitable culminating experi-ence as we try to think our way through the many issues that we have dis-cussed over the last two days. So many thanks for being with us, General Kernan, and for giving us these concluding remarks and presentation.

GENERAL KERNAN: Thanks, Bob. (Applause)

DR. PFALTZGRAFF: Now, ladies and gentlemen, I would like to offer just a few concluding remarks. Obviously there is a great deal that one could say about a meeting of this kind coming at the time that it has, the first being that the fact that we were even able to hold it is itself, I think a remarkable cir-cumstance and experience, but we have indeed succeeded. We have done a great deal in the past two days. We have talked about a wide range of issues. We have been video streaming this meeting as we have proceeded. Transcripts, as I said last evening, are already available. And, of course, we will be produc-ing a report, a printed report, to give broader dissemination to the broader community of the many issues with which we have dealt here.

It only remains for me in closing this conference to express my profound thanks, my profound gratitude to the Army leadership and, of course, to General Shinseki again for his leadership, his vision, in making this possible and allowing this meeting under these circumstances to go forward. I would thank the Army staff, his staff. I would thank the various speakers, all of the speakers, every one of whom has added a new dimension, reinforcing each other and supplementing and filling in gaps as we proceeded over the last two days. I would also thank you, the participants, for all that you have done to help in the synergism of this meeting, the excellent questions, the discussions that we have had, both in the formal sessions and, of course, in the corridors outside.

There are, of course, many, many people who have made this conference possible, logistically speaking. We know that amateurs deal in strategies and professionals deal in logistics, and if ever we had any need to be confirmed in that thought, we found it over these last two days. Much preparation has gone into this meeting. If I were to name everybody who has made a contribution, you would be here all afternoon, but I would like simply to mention three people who played a key role in this. One is the person whom we had from our institute staff who worked in the Pentagon, Elizabeth Tencza, who worked on a daily basis with the Army staff before and after the tragic events of September 11. I would thank Polly Jordan, who has been my right-hand person, my left-hand person, dealing with all of the issues that we had to deal with in our Cambridge office, but doing so with the support of our staff in the Cambridge office and in Washington, D.C., but last, and not least, I want to pay special debt of gratitude and thanks to Omar Jones. Captain Omar Jones—(Applause) Hope Omar is here. Captain Jones has followed in the tradition that has been established by his immediate predecessors in these meetings. He has worked with me and I with him over these many months. We have gone through much together. And we have, of course, come through this, I hope, with flying colors, at least he has.

He has directed us to where we should be, and sometimes I have felt that I was misdirected, but not by him, only by my inability to recall where I was supposed to be at all times. He has even gotten a certain nickname here, which is unfortunate, I suppose, but nevertheless, I must tell you this. It is Mullah Omar, and I (Laughter) and that comes from the senior leadership, so he has established himself very clearly here with all of us. So he is—the other Mullah, of course, is in the worst of the tradition and, of course, our Mullah is in the very best of the tradition. So we look at it that way. So on that note I would express thanks again to everyone here, and I would wish you Godspeed, safe return home, and that we look forward to future meetings of this kind especially, of course, continuing this series. And we are already beginning to make plans for next year and to use this facility to discuss the issues that will be on our agenda at that time. So, again, many thanks and best wishes. The meeting is now adjourned. (Applause)

BIOGRAPHIES

Dr. Gordon M. Adams

Dr. Gordon Adams is Professor of the Practice of International Affairs and Director of the Security Policy Studies Program, the Eliot School of International Affairs, George Washington University. Previously, he was Deputy Director, the International Institute for Strategic Studies in London. Before moving to London, he served as the Associate Director for National Security and International Affairs at the Office of Management and Budget for the Executive Office of the President. Dr. Adams has also taught at Rutgers and Columbia Universities. He has held positions at the Council on Economic Priorities, the Council on Foreign Relations, and the Social Science Research Council. He was founder and director of the Defense Budget Project from 1983 to 1993. Widely published in the areas of security policy, defense policy, and the defense budget, Dr. Adams graduated *magna cum laude* in political science from Stanford University. He received his Ph.D. in political science from Columbia University.

Lieutenant General Edward Anderson III, USA

General Edward Anderson is Deputy Commander in Chief and Chief of Staff, United States Space Command and Vice Commander, U.S. Element, North American Aerospace Defense Command. In this capacity, General Anderson helps lead the unified command responsible for directing space control and support operations including missile defense and computer network defense and computer network attack. General Anderson has also served as Director for Strategic Plans and Policy, the Joint Staff. His awards and decorations include the Defense Distinguished Service Medal, the Army Distinguished Service Medal, the Legion of Merit with two Oak Leaf Clusters, the Bronze Star Medal, and Bronze Star Medal with V Device. He is a graduate of the United States Military Academy and holds an M.S. in Aeronautical Engineering from the Georgia Institute of Technology and an M.A. in National Security and Strategic Studies from the Naval War College. General Anderson is also a graduate of the British Higher Command and Staff Course.

The Honorable Avis T. Bohlen

Ms. Avis Bohlen was sworn in on November 24, 1999, as the Department of State's Assistant Secretary for the Bureau of Arms Control. She joined the

Foreign Service in 1977 and had several assignments in the Bureau of European Affairs. She served as U.S. Ambassador to Bulgaria (1996-1999); Deputy Chief of Mission at the U.S. Embassy in Paris (1991-1995), and Deputy Assistant Secretary of State for European and Canadian Affairs (1989-1991) with responsibility for European security issues. She has also served on the policy planning staff and as executive director on the U.S. Delegation for Nuclear and Space Talks in Geneva. Prior to joining the Foreign Service, Ms. Bohlen worked for the U.S. Arms Control and Disarmament Agency and was a member of the U.S. delegation to the Mutual and Balanced Force Reduction talks in Vienna. She has a BA from Radcliffe College and an MBA from Columbia University.

Ambassador L. Paul Bremer III

On October 11, 2001, Ambassador Bremer was named Chairman and Chief Executive Officer of Marsh Crisis Consulting Company, a subsidiary of the Marsh & McLennan Companies. Prior to his work there, he served as a managing director at Kissinger Associates. Ambassador Bremer joined the Diplomatic Service in 1966. He served as the Deputy Ambassador and Charge d'Affaires at the American Embassy in Oslo, Norway. In his Washington assignments, Ambassador Bremer served as Special Assistant or Executive Assistant to six secretaries of state. President Reagan named Ambassador Bremer as the United States Ambassador to the Netherlands in 1983. He was subsequently appointed Ambassador-at-Large for Counterterrorism, responsible for developing and implementing U.S.'s global policies to combat terrorism. In September 1999, Ambassador Bremer was appointed Chairman of the National Commission on Terrorism. He received his BA from Yale University, a CEP from the *Institut D'Etudes Politiques* at the University of Paris, and an MBA from Harvard University. Ambassador Bremer received the State Department Superior Honor Award, two Presidential Meritorious Service Awards, and the Distinguished Honor Award from the Secretary of State.

The Honorable Frank C. Carlucci

Mr. Frank Carlucci is chairman and a partner in The Carlyle Group, a Washington, D.C. based merchant bank. Prior to joining The Carlyle Group in 1989, he served as Secretary of Defense from 1987 to 1988 and as President Reagan's National Security Advisor in 1987. Before returning to government service, Mr. Carlucci was Chairman and CEO of Sears World Trade, a business he joined in 1983. His government service included positions as Deputy Secretary of Defense; Deputy Director of Central Intelligence; Ambassador to Portugal; Under Secretary of Health, Education, and Welfare; Deputy Director of the Office of Management and Budget; and Director of the Office of Economic Opportunity. Mr. Carlucci was a Foreign Service officer from 1956 to 1980. He currently serves on numerous corporate boards, including Ashland, Inc.; BDM International, Inc.; General Dynamics Corporation; Kaman Corporation; Neurogen Corporation; Northern Telecom Limited; Texas Biotechnology Corporation; Pharmacia & Upjohn, Inc.; Westinghouse Electric Corporation; and the Board of Trustees for the RAND Corporation. Among his awards and honors are the Herbert Roback Memorial Award, 1989; George C. Marshall Award, 1989; Honorary Doctor of Laws Degree, University of Scranton, 1989; Woodrow Wilson Award, 1988; James Forrestal Award, 1988; Presidential Citizens Award, 1983; National Intelligence Distinguished Service Medal, 1981; Defense Department Distinguished Civilian Service Award, 1977; Health, Education, and Welfare Distinguished Civilian Service Award, 1975; and the State Department Superior Service Award, 1971.

General Wesley K. Clark, USA (Ret.)

General Wesley Clark was the Supreme Allied Commander, Europe (SACEUR), from July 1997 through May 2000. He was also the Commander in Chief, U.S. European Command. In his position as SACEUR, General Clark was also the overall commander of the approximately 75,000 troops from 37 NATO and other nations participating in ongoing operations in Bosnia-Herzegovina and Kosovo. In 1999, General Clark commanded Operation Allied Force. He also served as: Commander in Chief, U.S. Southern Command, in Panama from June 1996 to July 1997; and Director, Strategic Plans and Policy, J5, the Joint Staff from April 1994 to June 1996. In addition, he led the military negotiations for the Bosnian Peace Accords at Dayton. General Clark is a 1966 graduate of the United States Military Academy at West Point, New York, and holds a master's degree in philosophy, politics, and economics from Oxford University, where he studied as a Rhodes Scholar.

Dr. Jacquelyn K. Davis

Dr. Jacquelyn Davis is executive vice president of the Institute for Foreign Policy Analysis and president of National Security Planning Associates. Dr. Davis is an authority on force planning and military technology trends, U.S.-allied security relations in NATO-Europe, the Persian Gulf, and the Asian-Pacific region; counterproliferation and deterrence issues, and regional security dynamics. Her other areas of expertise include defense problems related to the former Soviet Union and the CIS (Central Independent States) republics and the security policies and programs of key European countries, particularly the United Kingdom, France, and Germany. As a member of the Chief of Naval Operations' (CNO) Executive Committee, she has written and lectured extensively on issues of naval strategy and maritime power. Her recent publications include: *Strategic Paradigms 2025: U.S. Security Planning for a New Era* (co-author) and *CVX: A Smart Carrier for the New Era*. Dr. Davis served a four-year tenure (1992-96) on the Board of Advisers at the Naval Postgraduate School in Monterey, California. In addition, she was a member of the Defense Advisory Committee on Women in the Services (DACOWITS), serving as national chairperson from 1986-88. Dr. Davis is a member of the Council on Foreign Relations, the CNO Executive Panel, the Hart-Rudman Study Group, and the International Institute for Strategic Studies. Dr. Davis received her MA and PhD from the University of Pennsylvania.

The Honorable Douglas J. Feith

Mr. Douglas Feith is Under Secretary of Defense for Policy. His responsibilities include the formulation of defense planning guidance and forces policy, Department of Defense relations with foreign countries, and the department's role in U.S. government interagency policy making. Before President George W. Bush appointed him in July 2001, Mr. Feith was for fifteen years the managing attorney of the Washington, D.C., law firm of Feith & Zell, P.C. From March 1984 until September 1986, Mr. Feith served as Deputy Assistant Secretary of Defense for Negotiations Policy. Prior to assuming that position, he served as Special Counsel to the Assistant Secretary of Defense for International Security Policy. Mr. Feith worked from 1981 to 1982 as a Middle East specialist on the National Security Council staff. Mr. Feith's writings on international law and on foreign and defense policy have appeared in *the New York Times*, *the Washington Post*, the *Wall Street Journal*, the *New Republic*, and elsewhere. He has contributed to a number of books, including James W. Müller, ed., *Churchill as Peacemaker*; Douglas J. Feith, et al., *Israel's Legitimacy in Law and History*; and Uri Ra'anan, et al., eds., *Hydra of Carnage: International Linkages of Terrorism*. Mr. Feith holds a J.D. from Georgetown University Law Center and AB from Harvard College.

The Honorable Gary Hart

Senator Gary Hart currently serves as co-chair of the U.S. Commission on National Security/21st Century, a bipartisan commission chartered by the Department of Defense. Since 1988, Senator Hart has also practiced law as a strategic and legal adviser to American companies in the field of international business. He travels extensively to Russia, Europe, the Far East, and Latin America. He is a member of the Board of Directors of the U.S.-Russia Investment Fund, created by Congress in 1993, and of the Council on Foreign Relations. Most recently, Senator Hart has been a Visiting Fellow and McCallum Memorial Lecturer at Oxford University. He completed his ninth book, *The Minuteman*, in 1997. Gary Hart received his B.A. in 1958 from Southern Nazarene University; attended Divinity School in 1961 at Yale University; received his J.D. in 1964 from Yale Law School; and served as a U.S. Senator for Colorado from 1975 through 1987.

The Honorable James Inhofe (R-OK)

Senator James Inhofe was first elected to the Senate in 1994. He is a member of the Armed Services Committee, and serves on the Strategic Forces Subcommittee, the AirLand Subcommittee and is the ranking member of the Readiness and Management Support Subcommittee. He also serves on the Environment and Public Works Committee, the Intelligence Committee, and the Indian Affairs Committee. Senator Inhofe plays a leadership role on defense and national security issues and previously served four terms in the U.S. House of Representatives. He graduated from the University of Tulsa with a degree in economics. He served in the U.S. Army and has been a small businessman for over thirty years. He was elected to the Oklahoma State House of Representatives in 1966, served one term, and was then elected to the State Senate, where he served two terms and became minority leader. From 1978 to 1984, he was mayor of Tulsa.

General William F. Kernan, USA

As Commander in Chief, United States Joint Forces Command (JFCOM), and Supreme Allied Commander, Atlantic, General William Kernan is responsible to the President and the Secretary of Defense through the Chairman of the Joint Chiefs of Staff for JFCOM's mission of maximizing the nation's present and future military capabilities to ensure that U.S. forces continue to advance in a multiservice and multinational mission capacity. He also provides ready U.S.-based Army, Navy, Air Force, and Marine Corps forces to support the command's geographical area of responsibility, domestic requirements, and other unified combatant commands around the world. General Kernan entered Officer Candidate School as a staff sergeant, gaining his commission as an infantry officer in 1968. He has served several staff and command-level units, including stints as the commander of the 101st Airborne Division (Air Assault) and XVIII Airborne Corps, Fort Bragg, N.C. He completed combat tours in Vietnam, Grenada, and Panama. He is a native of Fort Sam Houston, Texas, and holds an MA in personnel administration.

Admiral James M. Loy, USCG

Admiral James Loy has been Commandant of the U.S. Coast Guard since May 1998, during which time he has focused on restoring the readiness and shaping the future of the Coast Guard. Previously, Admiral Loy served as the Coast Guard Chief of Staff from 1996-98. From 1994-96, he was Commander of the Coast Guard's Atlantic Area. His other flag assignments were as Chief of Personnel and Training and Commander of the Eighth Coast Guard District. A career seagoing officer, Admiral Loy has served tours aboard six Coast Guard cutters, including command of a patrol boat in combat during the

Vietnam War and command of major cutters in both the Atlantic and Pacific Oceans. Admiral Loy graduated from the U.S. Coast Guard Academy in 1964 and holds masters' degrees from Wesleyan University and the University of Rhode Island. He also attended the Industrial College of the Armed Forces and interned at the John F. Kennedy School of Government at Harvard University. He has received the Department of Transportation Distinguished Service Medal, four Coast Guard Distinguished Service Medals, the Defense Superior Service Medal, two Legion of Merit awards, the Bronze Star with Combat "V," the Meritorious Service Medal, five Coast Guard Commendation Medals, the Coast Guard Achievement Medal, the Combat Action Ribbon, and other unit and campaign awards.

General Barry R. McCaffrey, USA (Ret.)

General Barry McCaffrey is the Olin Distinguished Professor of National Security Studies at the United States Military Academy. He is also president of his own consulting firm in Alexandria, Virginia, and has been elected to the Board of Trustees of MitreTek Systems and to the Board of Directors of both the Phoenix House Foundation and the Atlantic Council of the United States. Previously, General McCaffrey was Director, White House Office of National Drug Control Policy, from February 1996 to January 2001, where he served as member of the President's cabinet and the National Security Council. During a distinguished military career, he served overseas for thirteen years, which included four combat tours. His last assignment was Commander in Chief, U.S. Southern Command, coordinating national security operations in Latin America. General McCaffrey twice received the Distinguished Service Cross and was awarded three Purple Heart medals for wounds sustained in combat. He is a graduate of the U.S. Military Academy and holds an M.A. in civil government from American University. He also attended Harvard University's National Security Program.

Mr. John McWethy

Mr. John McWethy is Chief National Security and Pentagon Correspondent, Washington Bureau, ABC News, a position he has held since 1984. Mr. McWethy's assignments have included coverage of the air war over Kosovo and its aftermath, tensions in the Persian Gulf and in North Korea, and the India-Pakistan conflict. For more than a decade, he was ABC News' primary correspondent covering Secretaries of State Warren Christopher, Lawrence Eagleburger, James Baker, and George Schultz. He has traveled to more than fifty countries and covered the collapse of the Soviet Union and the rise of the nations that replaced it. He joined ABC News in 1979 as chief Pentagon correspondent, covering the Iran hostage crisis and the Soviet invasion of Afghanistan. He has received three national Emmy Awards for his reporting on Ross Perot, the Persian Gulf War, and the Soviet military. He has also received an Alfred I. DuPont-Columbia Award and the Overseas Press Club Award. From 1973 to 1979, Mr. McWethy was a reporter for *U.S. News and World Report*, the last two years as chief White House correspondent. He began his career in journalism at the *Congressional Quarterly*. A graduate of DePauw University, he holds a master's degree from Columbia University's Pulitzer School of Journalism.

General Montgomery C. Meigs, USA

General Montgomery Meigs is Commanding General, U.S. Army, Europe, and Seventh Army in Heidelberg, Germany, a position he assumed in 1998. He also served as commander of the multinational Stabilization Force in Bosnia-Herzegovina beginning on October 1998. General Meigs has held a variety of positions during his career, including Commander, 1st Squadron, 1st Armored Cavalry Regiment; strategic planner on the Joint Staff in Washington, D.C.; command of the 2nd Brigade, 1st Armored Division; and Chief of Staff, V Corps, and Deputy Chief of Staff for Operations of the U.S. Army, Europe, and 7th Army. General Meigs commanded the 3rd Infantry Division from July 1995 until its reflagging as the 1st Infantry Division in February 1996. In October 1996, he deployed with the 1st Infantry Division to Bosnia, serving nine months as COMEAGLE (Commander, Task Force Eagle) in command of NATO's Multi-National Division (North) in Operations Joint Endeavor and Joint Guard. He is a graduate of the United States Military Academy and spent a year at the Army's Command and General Staff College. He received a Ph.D. in history from the University of Wisconsin in 1982. His awards include the Distinguished Service Medal, the Bronze Star Medal with V device, and the Purple Heart.

General Richard B. Myers, USAF

General Richard Myers is the fifteenth Chairman of the Joint Chiefs of Staff, the nation's highest ranking military officer. In this capacity, he serves as the principal military adviser to the President, the Secretary of Defense, and the National Security Council. His career includes operational command and leadership positions in a variety of Air Force and Joint assignments. General Myers is a command pilot with more than 4000 flying hours in the T-33, C-21, F-4, F-15 and F-16, including 600 combat hours in the F-4. From August 1998 to February 2000, General Myers was the Commander in Chief, North American Aerospace Defense Command and U.S. Space Command; Commander, Air Force Space Command; and Department of Defense manager, space transportation system contingency support at Peterson Air Force Base, Colorado. Prior to assuming that position, he was the Commander, Pacific Air Forces, Hickam Air Force Base, Hawaii, from July 1997 to July 1998. From July 1996 to July 1997 he served as the Assistant to the Chairman of the Joint Chiefs of Staff, and from November 1993 to June 1996 General Myers was the commander of U.S. Forces, Japan, and 5th Air Force at Yokota Air Base, Japan. General Myers is a 1965 graduate of Kansas State University and holds an MBA from Auburn University. He has also attended the Air Command and Staff College at Maxwell Air Force Base, Alabama; the U.S. Army War College at Carlisle Barracks, Pennsylvania; and the John F. Kennedy School of Government at Harvard University.

Mr. Sean O'Keefe

Mr. Sean O'Keefe is the Deputy Director of the Office of Management and Budget. As the first deputy cabinet officer appointed in the Bush Administration, Mr. O'Keefe oversees the preparation, management, and administration of the Federal budget and government-wide management initiatives across the Executive Branch. Prior to his current appointment, Mr. O'Keefe was the Louis A. Bantle Professor of Business and Government Policy at the Syracuse University Maxwell School of Citizenship and Public Affairs. He also served as the Director of National Security Studies, a partnership of Syracuse University and Johns Hopkins University for delivery of executive education programs for senior military and civilian Department of Defense managers. Mr. O'Keefe was appointed Secretary of the Navy in July 1992 and after serving as Comptroller and Chief Financial Officer of the Department of Defense since 1989. Mr. O'Keefe was also a staff member of the United States Senate Committee on Appropriations staff for eight years and served as Staff Director of the Defense Appropriations Subcommittee. He is the author of several journal articles, contributing author of *Keeping the Edge: Managing Defense for the Future*, and co-author of *The Defense Industry in the Post Cold War Era: Corporate Strategies and Public Policy Perspectives*. Mr. O'Keefe earned his B.A. in 1977 from Loyola University in New Orleans, Louisiana, and his M.P.A. in 1978 from the Maxwell School.

Rear Admiral Kathleen K. Paige, USN

Admiral Kathleen Paige is the Systems Technical Director of the Ballistic Missile Defense Organization. She is a 1970 graduate of the University of New Hampshire and was commissioned in 1971. Her tours of duty include Technical Director, AEGIS Program Office; Chief Engineer, Naval Surface Warfare Center; and Baseline Manager, Combat Systems Division, of the AEGIS Shipbuilding Program. Her first flag officer assignment was as Commander, Naval Surface Warfare Center, July 1996. In June 1998, she was assigned as Deputy Program Executive Officer for Theater Surface Combatants. In April 1999, she was assigned the duty of Chief Engineer to the Assistant Secretary of the Navy for Research, Development, and Acquisition. In September of that year, she was assigned as Director, Theater Air and Missile Defense and Systems Engineering

In May 2000, Admiral Page was frocked to rear admiral (upper half). She earned an MS from the Naval Post Graduate School in Monterey, California, and is a graduate of the Defense Systems Management College and the Cornell University Program for Executives. Her personal decorations include the Legion of Merit, the Meritorious Service Medal, and the Navy Achievement Medal.

Major General John S. Parker, USA

General John Parker is Commanding General of the United States Army Medical Research and Materiel Command and Fort Detrick, Maryland. He was commissioned from the ROTC (Reserve Officer Training Corps) in 1963, and has since served as Assistant Surgeon General for Force Projection/Chief of Medical Corps Affairs in the Office of the Surgeon General; as Commanding General, Fitzsimons Army Medical Center/Commander, Central Health Service Support Activity; as the Special Assistant to the Surgeon General, Health Services Division, and as Chief of the Medical Corps Branch, Health Services Division. He holds degrees from Washington Jefferson College and Georgetown University, and has attended the Industrial College of the Armed Forces and the Armed Forces Staff College. General Parker's personal decorations include the Distinguished Service Medal, the Defense Superior Service Medal, the Legion of Merit with two Oak Leaf Clusters, and the Meritorious Service Medal with four Oak Leaf Clusters.

Dr. Keith B. Payne

Dr. Keith Payne is President and Director of Research at the National Institute for Public Policy and an Adjunct Professor in the Security Studies Program at Georgetown University. He also serves as Editor-in-Chief of *Comparative Strategy* and is a member of the Department of State's Defense Trade Advisory Group. He has authored *The Fallacies of Cold War Deterrence and a New Direction*; *Post-Cold War Requirements for U.S. Nuclear Deterrence Policy*; *Deterrence in the Second Nuclear Age*; *Peacekeeping in the Nuclear Age* (co-author); *A Just Defense: The Use of Force, Nuclear Weapons and Our Consciences* (co-author); *Missile Defense in the Twenty-First Century: Protection Against Limited Threats*, *Countering Proliferation: New Criteria for European Security*; and *Proliferation und westliche Sicherheit*. Dr. Payne frequently testifies before congressional committees and has also testified before the British Parliament. He received his Ph.D. in international relations from the University of Southern California.

Dr. Robert L. Pfaltzgraff, Jr.

Dr. Robert Pfaltzgraff is the president of the Institute for Foreign Policy Analysis and Shelby Cullom Davis Professor of International Security Studies at the Fletcher School of Law and Diplomacy, Tufts University. He has held a visiting appointment as George C. Marshall Professor at the College of Europe, Bruges, Belgium, and as professor at the National Defense College, Tokyo, Japan. He has advised key Administration officials on military strategy, modernization, the future of the Atlantic Alliance, nuclear proliferation, and arms control policy. Dr. Pfaltzgraff has published extensively and lectured widely at government and industry forums in the United States and overseas, including the National Defense University and the NATO Defense College. Dr. Pfaltzgraff leads the Institute's research projects on future security environments, technology diffusion, and curricular development on issues associated with WMD. His work encompasses alliance relations, crisis management, missile defense, the development and conduct of gaming exercises, arms control issues, and strategic planning in the emerging security environment. He holds an M.A. in international relations, a Ph.D. in political science, and an M.B.A. in international business from the University of Pennsylvania.

Admiral Joseph W. Prueher, USN (Ret.)

Admiral Joseph Prueher was sworn in on December 2, 1999, as U.S. Ambassador to China, a position he held until earlier this year. On May 1, 1999, Ambassador Prueher completed a 35-year career in the Navy, during which time he flew over 3,300 hours in 52 types of aircraft with over 1,000 carrier landings. His last assignment was as Commander in Chief, U.S. Pacific Command. Immediately following his retirement, he was a consulting professor and senior adviser for the Stanford-Harvard Preventive Defense Project. Admiral Prueher received a M.S. in international relations from the George Washington University and a B.S. in naval science from the U.S. Naval Academy. He has published numerous articles on leadership, military readiness, and Pacific region security issues and has received multiple military awards for combat flying as well as for naval and joint service. Additionally, he has been decorated by the Governments of Singapore, Thailand, Japan, Korea, the Republic of the Philippines, and Indonesia and is an Honorary Officer in the Military Division of the Order of Australia.

The Honorable Tom Ridge

Governor Tom Ridge was appointed Director of the Office of Homeland Security in October 2001. Previously, he served as Governor of Pennsylvania where he focused his efforts on education, land conservation, and reconfiguration of the state's fiscal management. Prior to becoming Governor, Director Ridge served six terms as the first Vietnam veteran elected to the U.S. House of Representatives. He has also served as an assistant district attorney in Erie, Pennsylvania, and as an infantry staff sergeant in Vietnam, where he won the

Bronze Star for valor. Director Ridge graduated with honors from Harvard University, and earned his J.D. from the Dickinson School of Law.

Air Vice-Marshal John Thompson

Air Vice-Marshal John Thompson was educated in Palmerston North, New Zealand, and at the Royal Air Force College, Cranwell, where he was commissioned in 1968. After a tour flying the Hunter in Bahrain, he served as a qualified weapons instructor on a Harrier squadron in Germany. In 1975, he returned to the United Kingdom on posting to the Harrier Operational Conversion Unit before becoming a staff officer at Group Headquarters in 1982. The next three years were spent commanding Number 3 (Fighter) Squadron in Germany before returning to take up post as an Air Plans Staff Officer at the Ministry of Defence. In 1989 he assumed command of Royal Air Force Wittering, which was followed by attendance at the 1991 course, Royal College of Defence Studies. Subsequently, he completed the Higher Command and Staff Course at Camberly, prior to a tour as Senior Staff Officer at Headquarters 2 Group at Rheindalen, which included three months as the NATO Liaison Officer in Headquarters, UNPROFOR Zagreb. In 1996, Air Vice-Marshal Thompson spent 6 weeks on the staff at the Royal College of Defence Studies before moving for an 11-month detachment to Brussels and Sarajevo as the Military Advisor to Mr. Carl Bildt. In January 1997, he was appointed Air Officer Commanding and Commandant of the Royal Air Force College Cranwell. In July 1998 he was posted as the Air Officer Commanding Number 1 Group. He came to the U.S. in April 2000 as the Defence Attaché and Head of the British Defence Staff in Washington.

Dr. Loren B. Thompson, Jr.

Dr. Loren Thompson is the Chief Operating Officer of the Lexington Institute, a nonprofit, nonpartisan public-policy research organization headquartered in Arlington, Virginia. In that capacity he directs the Institute's national security program and participates in its research on a variety of domestic issues. Dr. Thompson is a long-time adviser to major defense and aerospace companies, the federal government, and various public-policy organizations on national security issues ranging from military logistics and industrial-base trends to nonlethal weapons and infrastructure management. For nearly 20 years, Dr. Thompson has taught graduate level seminars on strategy and military affairs in Georgetown University's National Security Studies Program and from 1988 to 1993 was Deputy Director of the program. He has also taught at Harvard University's Kennedy School of Government. Prior to assuming his current position, Dr. Thompson was Executive Director of the Alexis de Tocqueville Institution's national security program. A frequent author of articles and commentaries on national security, he holds a Ph.D. in Government from Georgetown University.

Ms. Michelle Van Cleave

Ms. Michelle Van Cleave is President of National Security Concepts, a Washington, D.C., firm specializing in strategic planning and senior-level policy analysis for government customers. In the 105th Congress, Ms. Van Cleave was Staff Director and Chief Counsel of the Senate Judiciary Subcommittee on Technology, Terrorism, and Government Information. From 1993 to 1997, Ms. Van Cleave was Counsel to the Washington law firm of Feith & Zell, P.C. During this time, she also worked as a consultant to several government agencies including Los Alamos National Laboratory and the Central Intelligence Agency. Ms. Van Cleave has also held the positions of General Counsel and Assistant Director for National Security Affairs in the White House Office of Science and Technology Policy. Ms. Van Cleave holds an MA and BA in International Relations from the University of Southern California (USC) and a J.D. from the USC School of Law.

The Honorable Curt Weldon (R-PA)

Congressman Curt Weldon was elected to represent the Seventh Congressional District of Pennsylvania for an eighth term in 2000. A member of the House of Representatives since 1987, he has taken leadership roles on a wide variety of issues ranging from national security to the environment. A senior member of the House Armed Services Committee, Mr. Weldon served six years as the Chairman of the Military Research and Development Subcommittee, overseeing the development and testing of key military systems, weapons programs, and technologies that fulfill military needs, followed by service as Chairman of the Readiness Subcommittee. The congressman now serves as the Chairman of the Armed Services Procurement Subcommittee. He has worked with Russian leaders on a variety of issues, including efforts to improve Russia's energy supply, correct environmental damage, and protect both nations from ballistic missile attack. In addition, Mr. Weldon is the founder of the Duma-Congress Study Group.

The Honorable Paul Wolfowitz

Dr. Paul Wolfowitz was sworn in on March 2, 2001 as Deputy Secretary of Defense. Before assuming these duties, Dr. Wolfowitz served for seven years as Dean and Professor of International Relations at the Paul H. Nitze School of Advanced International Studies, Johns Hopkins University. From 1989 to 1993, Dr. Wolfowitz served as Under Secretary of Defense for Policy. During this period, Secretary Wolfowitz and his staff had major responsibilities for the reshaping of strategy and force posture at the end of the Cold War. Under his leadership, the Policy Staff played a major role in reviewing war plans for the Gulf War. During the Reagan administration, Dr. Wolfowitz served for three years as U.S. Ambassador to Indonesia. Prior to that posting, he served as Assistant Secretary of State for East Asian and Pacific Affairs. In addition to contributing to substantial improvements in U.S. relations with Japan and China, Assistant Secretary Wolfowitz played a central role in coordinating the U.S. policy toward the Philippines that supported a peaceful transition from the dictatorship of Ferdinand Marcos to democracy.

General Anthony C. Zinni, USMC (Ret.)

General Anthony Zinni is currently a distinguished Senior Adviser at the Center for Strategic and International Studies. For the last three years of his career with the armed forces, General Zinni was Commander in Chief, U.S. Central Command. He joined the U.S. Central Command in September 1996 as Deputy Commander in Chief. Following Operation Desert Storm, he served as the Chief of Staff and Deputy Commanding General of combined task force Provide Comfort. During 1992-1993, General Zinni directed the Unified Task Force Somalia during Operation Continue Hope, and earlier he was Deputy Commanding General of the U.S. Marine Corps Combat Development Command at Quantico, Virginia. He served in Vietnam as a company commander in 1970. A graduate of Villanova University, General Zinni holds a B.A. in economics, a M.A. in international relations, and an M.A. in management and supervision. His decorations include the Defense Distinguished Service Medal, the Defense Superior Service Medal with two oak leaf clusters, the Bronze Star Medal with Combat "V" and gold star in lieu of a second award, and the Purple Heart.

www.ingramcontent.com/pod-product-compliance
Lightning Source LLC
Chambersburg PA
CBHW081205280526
45787CB00006B/2330